Preparing for Success
in Healthcare Information
and Management Systems
The CPHIMS Review Guide

Second Edition

HIMSS MISSION

To lead healthcare transformation through the effective use of health information technology.

ISBN: 978-1-938904-30-1

For more information about HIMSS, please visit www.himss.org.

For more information about the CPHIMS program, please visit www.cphims.org.

■ About the Authors

Chris Arricale, MS, PMP, CPHIMS, is a regional manager with ERP International, LLC, providing management consulting, IT support services and healthcare staffing support to clients throughout the United States. With more than 15 years' experience in information systems and project lifecycle management, Mr. Arricale has extensive knowledge in all aspects of managing medical information systems. He spent 25 years on active duty with the U.S. Air Force, where he led numerous projects implementing medical information systems at Air Force medical facilities worldwide and served as CIO at several Air Force clinics. Mr. Arricale has served as a member of the CPHIMS Technical Committee and was among the first group of candidates to earn the CPHIMS certification in 2002.

Melissa Barthold, MSN, RN-BC, CPHIMS, FHIMSS, is the Senior Clinical Solutions Strategist at the University of Mississippi Medical Center, in Jackson, MS. She has more than 25 years of nursing practice, with more than 15 years as a nursing informaticist. She obtained her Masters in Nursing Informatics in 1999 from Loyola University of Chicago's Niehoff School of Nursing. She has served on the HIMSS Nursing Informatics Taskforce and Committee, as the Chair of both the Annual Conference Education Committee (2010) and the Distance Education Committee (2011). Ms. Barthold has chaired the NI Taskforce's *Standard Practices Forum* for the last several years. She has served as adjunct faculty at Loyola University of Chicago and Barry University, Miami Shores, FL, and as a faculty facilitator at Excelsior College for the last eight years. She holds certifications from HIMSS (CPHIMS) and board certification from the American Nursing Credentialing Center, where she is serving her second term on the Content Expert Panel: Nursing Informatics. She is a doctoral student at Loyola, with completion planned for December 2013.

James W. Brady, PhD, M.Ed, CISM, CISSP, PMP, CPHIMS, FHIMSS, is the CISO/ Director of Technical Services at Hawaii Health Systems Corporation in Honolulu, HI, the state's fifth largest employer and the nation's fourth largest community hospital system with more than 1,270 beds, 4,000 employees, and 14 facilities. Before working in Hawaii, he played an integral role in healthcare IT at Cedar-Sinai Health System in Los Angeles. Dr. Brady has earned 19 technical and professional certifications, and has been featured in news articles and at industry and academic conferences. He is currently the Chair of the HIMSS Mobile Security Workgroup, Vice President of Programs for HIMSS Southern California Chapter, and a member of the Hawaii Health Information Exchange Technical Committee. Dr. Brady has previously held an adjunct professor role at the University of Redlands' School of Continuing Studies.

Vic Eilenfield, MS, MHA, FACHE, CPHIMS, is the President and CEO of HCAdvance, a health information technology consulting firm focusing principally on health information exchange among federal agencies. He previously served as the Deputy National Coordinator for Health IT at the Office of the National Coordinator (ONC), where he facilitated the establishment of ONC under the nation's first health IT czar, Dr. David Brailer, and provided oversight to the Nationwide Health Information Network programs. Prior to his work at ONC, then Colonel Eilenfield served as program manager of the Military Health System's Electronic Health Records (EHR) program, leading the implementation of the military EHR for health facilities across the United States and around the globe in support of over nine million beneficiaries.

Raymond A. Gensinger, Jr., MD, CPHIMS, FHIMSS, is the Chief Medical Information Officer for Fairview Health Services, an integrated delivery network in Minnesota. Dr. Gensinger is responsible for the clinical information technology strategy for the organization. He previously held a similar role at the Hennepin County Medical Center in Minneapolis. A general internist, Dr. Gensinger holds an appointment as an assistant professor in the Departments of Medicine, Nursing and Informatics at the University of Minnesota. Dr. Gensinger is an associate of the American College of Physicians, a past president of the HIMSS Minnesota Chapter, and a former member of the HIMSS Board of Directors. He has authored or presented on more than 50 different healthcare information systems-related topics.

Susan M. Houston, MBA, RN-BC, PMP, CPHIMS, is the Chief Portfolio Officer at the National Institutes of Health Clinical Center where she is responsible for the full lifecycle of the clinical and administrative applications. She has extensive clinical, informatics and project management experience with a variety of healthcare-related organizations. Ms. Houston has taught project management at the University of Maryland School of Nursing. She has presented at local and national conferences as well as co-authored a number of articles and the book *Project Management for Healthcare Informatics*. Ms. Houston has authored a number of courses in the HIMSS eLearning Academy, as well as the book, *The Project Manager's Guide to Health Information Technology Implementation*.

David H. Miller, CPHIMS, has over 30 years' experience in healthcare IT. He started by managing the implementation of patient accounting and general accounting applications as a hospital IT manager. He has since spent most of his career with a vendor, managing the development of a radiology information system and a physician billing application, served as a product manager for technology products, managed the installation of various applications for an integrated healthcare network, managed a project to upgrade 1,000 systems for Y2K, and is currently a system architect helping design high availability clinical systems. He has co-authored two books on programming related to healthcare. He is an active member of the HIMSS Delaware Valley chapter and is serving on the Enterprise Information Systems committee.

John B. Salmon, CPHIMS, is Senior Director, EMR Group at Penn Medicine in Philadelphia. Mr. Salmon is responsible for leading people and projects in support of both inpatient and outpatient electronic medical records across 4 hospitals and approximately 1,800 physicians in 250 practice locations. He has over 20 years' experience in information technology, more than 10 of which is in healthcare. Past areas of focus include deployment of systems and analytic tools in support of patient safety, patient flow, and transitions in care. Mr. Salmon has served as faculty for the Institute of Healthcare Improvement.

Brando C. Sumayao, MSCIS, CPHIMS, FHIMSS, serves as the Senior Healthcare Analyst for Navy Medicine West's regional headquarters, which oversees the management of Navy Medicine's healthcare system in the Western Pacific, providing healthcare to more than 675,000 beneficiaries at military treatment facilities and dental centers on the northern and southern west coast, Hawaii, Japan and Guam. As an Air Force Reservist, Major Sumayao functions as the Deputy Chief Information Officer for TRICARE Regional Office West, which oversees regional contractors and an integrated healthcare delivery system for the nation's western-based TRICARE region. Major Sumayao is also a Senior Adjunct Faculty Member and a Certified Advanced Facilitator for the University of Phoenix, and is currently finishing his Doctorate in Management with a focus in Information Management and Technology.

■ Acknowledgments

This book would not have been possible without the support of members of the CPHIMS Technical Committee who served as advisors to the chapter authors and reviewed the manuscript.

HIMSS wishes to express gratitude to:

Greer Lynda Barlow, RN, MSc, CPHIMS (International Advisor)

Joseph F. Brusatto, RN-BC, CPHIMS

Adam Chee, PhD, MSc, CPHIMS (International Advisor)

Daniel W. Clark, RN, MBA, CPHIMS, FHIMSS (Chair)

Michael S. Derhak, MHA, CPHIMS

Kris Elliott, MS, CPHIMS

Katherine A. Ervin, MBA, CPHIMS (International Advisor)

Ralph A. Franco, Ret. Col, MBA, MHA, CISSP, CPHIMS, FACHE, FHIMSS

Andrew C. Galbus, MBA, CPHIMS, FHIMSS

Neil Gardner, CPHIMS-CA (COACH Liaison)

Brian G. Gould, MSIT, CPHIMS, FHIMSS

Peggy J. LeVora, PMP, CPHIMS

Scott T. MacLean, CPHIMS, FHIMSS (HIMSS Board Liaison)

V. Sean Mitchell, RN, BC, MSN, CPHIMS

Stephen M. Stewart, MBA, CPHIMS, FACHE

Fred H. Strobel, CPHIMS, FACHE

Richard G. Verrill Jr., MPA, PMP, CPHIMS, FACHE

Carole 'Tina' Wilson, MBA, PMP, CPHIMS

Deepest gratitude is also due to the HIMSS Career Services team for guiding this project to completion.

■ Contents

Introduction ix

SECTION I: GENERAL

Chapter 1: The Healthcare Environment 3
Vic Eilenfield, MS, MHA, FACHE, CPHIMS

Chapter 2: TheTechnology Environment 25
Melissa Barthold, MSN, RN-BC, CPHIMS, FHIMSS

SECTION II: SYSTEMS

Chapter 3: Systems Analysis 47
Brando C. Sumayao, MSCIS, CPHIMS, FHIMSS

Chapter 4: Systems Design 77
David H. Miller, CPHIMS

Chapter 5: Systems Selection, Implementation, Support and Maintenance 95
Susan M. Houston, MBA, RN-BC, PMP, CPHIMS

Chapter 6: Systems Testing and Evaluation 115
Chris Arricale, MS, PMP, CPHIMS

Chapter 7: Systems Privacy and Security 123
John B. Salmon, CPHIMS

SECTION III: ADMINISTRATION

Chapter 8: Administration Leadership 133
Raymond A. Gensinger, Jr., MD, CPHIMS, FHIMSS

Chapter 9: Administration Management 159
James W. Brady, PhD, M.Ed, CISM, CISSP, PMP, CPHIMS, FHIMSS

Questions 181

Answer Key 203

Acronyms Used in This Book 217

Index 223

■ Introduction

Your purchase of this book is the first step in becoming a Certified Professional in Healthcare Information and Management Systems (CPHIMS) and being recognized for your specialized knowledge and skills. For more than a decade, CPHIMS certification has been the preeminent certification in healthcare information technology (IT) and is administered globally to healthcare IT professionals practicing in a variety of work settings.

The development and maintenance of the CPHIMS Exam is the responsibility of the CPHIMS Technical Committee within HIMSS. This committee is made up of experts from around the world who possess subject matter expertise in the areas tested on the Exam.

This Introduction provides an overview of the eligibility requirements, testing procedures and the content of the CPHIMS Exam itself. Specific questions can also be addressed to certification@himss.org at any time.

The benefits of CPHIMS certification are broad and far-reaching. Certification is a process that is embraced in many industries, including healthcare IT. CPHIMS is recognized as the "gold standard" in healthcare IT because it is developed by HIMSS; has a global focus; and is valued by clinicians and non-clinicians, management and staff positions, and technical and non-technical individuals.

Certification, and CPHIMS certification specifically, provides a means by which employers can evaluate potential new hires, analyze job performance, evaluate employees, market IT services, and motivate employees to enhance their skills and knowledge. Certification also provides employers with evidence that the certificate holders have demonstrated an established level of job-related knowledge, skills and abilities and are competent practitioners of healthcare IT.

ELIGIBILITY REQUIREMENTS

To be eligible for the CPHIMS Exam, candidates must fulfill one of the following requirements for education **and** work experience.

Baccalaureate degree, or global equivalent, **and** five (5) years of associated information and management systems experience*, three of those years in healthcare.

Graduate degree, or global equivalent, **and** three (3) years of associated information and management systems experience*, two of those years in healthcare.

---

* Associated information and management systems experience includes the following areas: information technology; clinical information systems; systems design; systems analysis; systems design; implementation, support and maintenance; systems testing and evaluation; systems privacy and security; administration leadership; administration management.

ADDITIONAL RESOURCES

The CPHIMS Technical Committee recommends that review for the CPHIMS Exam focus on resources and programs that cover the tasks in the CPHIMS Content Outline. **It should not be inferred that questions on the CPHIMS Exam are selected from any single resource or set of resources or that study from this or other resources listed guarantees a passing score on the CPHIMS Exam.**

- **CPHIMS Candidate Handbook** | A must for all CPHIMS Exam candidates, the candidate handbook provides information that is helpful when applying for and scheduling the CPHIMS Exam. The handbook includes the CPHIMS Content Outline, directions on how to apply for the Exam and schedule your Exam appointment, what to expect on the day of the Exam as well as following the Exam. It is recommended that all CPHIMS candidates download a copy of the handbook from www.CPHIMS.org.

- **CPHIMS Self-Assessment Exam (SAE)** | The SAE, or practice test, is available for purchase from Applied Measurement Professionals, Inc.'s LXRStore (http://store.lxr.com/). The SAE simulates the CPHIMS Exam in content, cognitive level, difficulty and format. After taking the SAE, you will receive valuable, practical feedback in detailed score reports.

- **HIMSS Dictionary of Healthcare IT Terms, Acronyms and Organizations** | This dictionary was developed and extensively reviewed by industry experts. The resource includes:

  - ☐ Definitions of terms for the IT and clinical, medical and nursing informatics fields.

  - ☐ Acronyms, with cross references to current definitions.

  - ☐ Academic and certification credentials commonly used in healthcare and IT.

  For more information and to order a copy, visit the HIMSS Store at www.himss.org/store.

- **HIMSS eLearning Academy (eLA) CPHIMS Review** | The eLA offers three options to assist candidates in preparing for the CPHIMS Exam.

  - ☐ Option 1: Online Course Only

  - ☐ Option 2: Virtual Instructor Led Training Only (four live webinars offered at various times throughout the year)

  - ☐ Option 3: Online Course & Virtual Instructor Led Training Combo (available at various times throughout the year)

  For more information and the upcoming schedule, visit www.himss.learn.com

- **CPHIMS Review Course (face-to-face)** | The CPHIMS Review Course is a full-day course designed to review the skills and knowledge candidates have gained through previous education and work experience. Interact with an authorized CPHIMS Review Course instructor to get answers to your questions. The Course features lecture, discussion, practice questions, and study materials available exclusively to CPHIMS Review Course participants. For more information on attending a course as a participant, or to schedule a course for employees at your facility, email certification@himss.org.

CPHIMS EXAM ADMINISTRATION

The CPHIMS Exam is delivered by computer at AMP Assessment Centers throughout the world. Candidates who meet the eligibility requirements for the CPHIMS Exam may submit an application and fee at any time by visiting www.goAMP.com. The CPHIMS Exam is administered by appointment only Monday through Saturday (except major holidays). As a candidate, you may test where you wish and when you feel you are prepared to take the CPHIMS Exam.

Special group administrations of the CPHIMS Exam may be scheduled with HIMSS Chapters, Corporate Members, Organizational Affiliate Members, Non-Profit Partners, Regional Extension Centers, or other groups through arrangement with HIMSS. For special group administration, mobile computer units (or paper/pencil, if desired) are sent to your facility, where the proctored CPHIMS Exam will occur. For more information on hosting an administration for your group, please contact certification@himss.org.

The CPHIMS Exam is usually administered at national and international HIMSS events such as the Annual HIMSS Conference and Exhibition, World of Health IT, HIMSS AsiaPac, Middle East Health IT Leadership Summit & Conference, Government Health IT Conference and Exhibition, COACH eHealthAchieve, and COACH eHealth Conference. Special application and scheduling procedures may be in place for these events, so check with the event website to find out how to apply and schedule in conjunction with these events.

Section I.
General

CHAPTER 1

The Healthcare Environment

Vic Eilenfield, MS, MHA, FACHE, CPHIMS

LEARNING OBJECTIVES

At the conclusion of this chapter, the reader will be able to:

☑ Articulate characteristics and services of different types of healthcare organizations (e.g., hospitals, clinics and ambulatory centers, community health organizations, research and academic centers, healthcare payers).

☑ Understand the characteristics of interrelations within and across healthcare organizations (e.g., health information exchange, public, private, continuity of care).

☑ Differentiate the roles and responsibilities of healthcare information and management systems professions within the organizational structures in which they work.

☑ Describe roles of government, regulatory, professional and accreditation agencies related to healthcare and their impact on clinical outcomes and financial performance.

■ Introduction

In order to best understand the context of healthcare information and management systems, it is necessary to first understand the concept of health. The World Health Organization (WHO) asserts that "Health is a state of complete physical, mental and social well-being and not merely the absence of disease or infirmity."[1] The WHO has not amended this definition since 1948.

Why is it important that we more fully understand this more holistic concept of health? If we do not present for care until we are in an advanced stage of disease or arrive with injuries from unsafe working or living practices, the cost of providing that care is likely to be high and the health outcomes often less than desired. The practice of healthcare, and thus the systems and management processes supporting it, is increasingly focused on those activities which have the greatest overall impact on the health of populations. A state of health is not best achieved by limiting our engagement to patients' visits to the doctor's office and admissions to hospitals, but is increasingly extending to wellness encounters with non-physician healthcare providers, virtual encounters through telehealth or mobile health technologies, and safety and preventative care outreach programs. The increasing strain of healthcare costs on national economies is forcing us to continually re-evaluate our healthcare delivery paradigm to optimize health outcomes at an affordable cost. This is the macroeconomic context in which health information managers and technologists will be performing their art.

The healthcare environment is an exceptionally complex one in which multiple players compete for placement on center stage. The four pillars of quality, access, cost and safety[2] require dynamic trade-offs in which healthcare managers are under constant pressure to deliver the highest quality of care to the greatest portion of their supported population within tight cost constraints while not experiencing adverse outcomes due to safety issues. Placed upon this already complex four-legged stool are demands from multiple stakeholders, including governments, consumer groups, professional associations, regulatory organizations, payers/insurers, suppliers and more.

The Organisation for Economic Co-operation and Development (OECD) provides a solid basis for comparing international approaches to organizing and resourcing national healthcare with several key indicators on health system performance across countries. Figure 1-1 illustrates the substantial variance in spending by country and the proportion of public to private contribution to overall national health expenditures.

These investments have seen great reductions in cardiovascular and infant mortality rates, but lifestyle and risk factors show that over 20% of adults continue to smoke, while one in five children are now considered overweight or obese. Specific quality outcomes

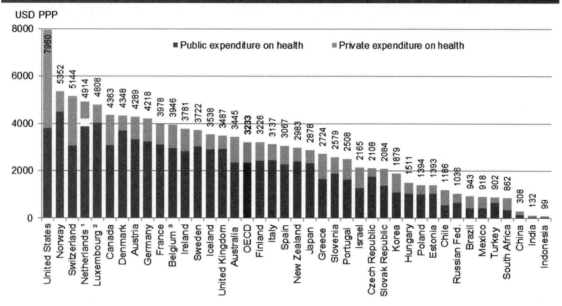

FIGURE 1-1. **Health Expenditure per Capita Varies Widely Across OECD Countries, 2009 (or latest year available)**[3] (From OECD. Health expenditure per capita. In: *Health at a Glance 2011: OECD Indicators.* OECD Publishing; 2011.)

1. In the Netherlands, it is not possible to clearly distinguish the public and private shares related to investments.
2. Health expenditure is for the insured population rather than the resident population.
3. Total expenditure excluding investments.

that nations are grappling with today are shown in Figures 1-2 and 1-3, with the examples of cervical cancer screening and survival rates, and readmission for asthma showing surprising variation across countries.

So it is not hard to develop a sense of the complexities of the healthcare environment in which we toil. The breadth of stakeholders, the balance of public versus private funding and the active engagement to improve the health of populations one individual at a time produce a daunting task. This is the arena the health information manager and technologist enter to ensure that the best possible information management and systems support are available to improve the quality of life for the greatest number of our world's citizens.

FIGURE 1-2. Screening and Survival Rates for Cervical Cancer Have Increased in Most Countries, But Survival Rates Remain Lower in Ireland and UK[4]
(From OECD. Screening, survival and mortality for cervical cancer. In: *Health at a Glance 2011: OECD Indicators*. OECD Publishing; 2011.)

Cervical cancer screening, percentage of women screened aged 20-69

Country	2009	2000
United States[2]	90.6	85.9
United Kingdom[1]	82.0	78.7
Norway[1]	78.9	78.5
Sweden[1]	78.2	78.4
New Zealand[1]	73.1	77.4
Canada[2]	77.2	75.3
Spain[2]		73.0
France[2]		72.4
Slovenia[1]		72.3
Finland[1]	70.3	69.8
Iceland[1]	74.0	69.0
Denmark[1]		66.3
Netherlands[1]	65.6	66.1
Chile[1]	64.5	65.6
Korea[2]		65.3
Belgium[1]	58.6	63.2
Ireland[1]		62.5
Australia[1]	61.3	61.2
OECD (17)	59.9	61.1
Estonia[1]		52.0
Luxembourg[1]	36.2	50.5
Czech Republic[1]	33.3	47.7
Italy[1]		49.0
Mexico[1]	38.9	
Turkey[1]	24.9	
Japan[2]	24.5	22.6
Hungary[1]	23.7	28.4
Slovak Republic[1]	22.9	23.2

% of women screened

Cervical cancer five-year relative survival rate

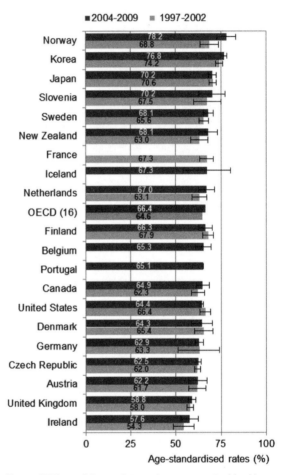

Country	2004-2009	1997-2002
Norway	78.2	68.8
Korea	76.8	74.2
Japan	70.2	70.6
Slovenia	70.2	67.5
Sweden	68.1	65.6
New Zealand	68.1	63.0
France		67.3
Iceland		67.3
Netherlands	67.0	63.1
OECD (16)	66.4	64.6
Finland	66.3	67.9
Belgium	65.3	
Portugal	65.1	
Canada	64.9	62.3
United States	64.4	66.4
Denmark	64.3	65.4
Germany	62.9	63.3
Czech Republic	62.5	62.0
Austria	62.2	61.7
United Kingdom	58.8	58.0
Ireland	57.6	54.3

Age-standardised rates (%)

1. Programme.   2. Survey.

Note: 95% confidence intervals represented by H.

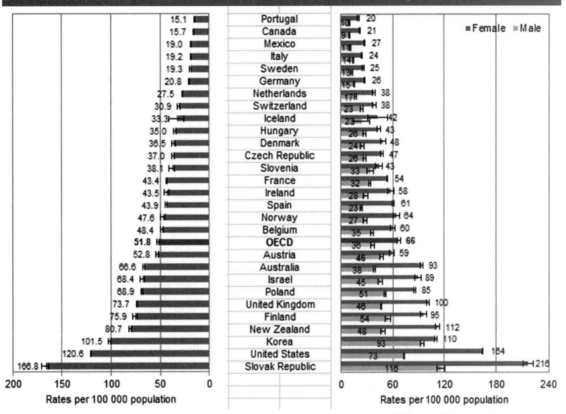

FIGURE 1-3. **Treatment for Chronic Diseases Is Not Optimal; Too Many Persons Are Admitted to Hospitals for Asthma. Asthma Admission Rates, Population Aged 15 and Over, 2009**[5] (From OECD. Avoidable admissions: respiratory diseases. In: *Health at a Glance 2011: OECD Indicators*. OECD Publishing; 2011.)

Note: Rates age-sex standardised to 2005 OECD population. 95% confidence intervals represented by H.

■ Healthcare Organizations

The number and types of organizations involved in the provision of care, supporting the provision of care and paying for the care provided is large, complex and constantly evolving. The simplest way to categorize these is through the eyes of the patient. When speaking of accessing care, often a patient will say, "I went to see my doctor at her office" or, "I was in the hospital last week to have my appendix out." So, in a broad sense, we have the constructs of hospital-based care—often referred to as inpatient care—and care from doctors' offices—referred to as outpatient or ambulatory care. Additionally, given the diverse types of diagnostic services and pharmaceuticals needed to support the healthcare process, providers of ancillary services are included as well. Lastly, regulators and payers of care are discussed. The interrelationships among these diverse players will be expanded upon in the next section. The following is an overview of many of these structures, which vary not only by country but often by geographic location within countries as well.

HOSPITALS

While hospitals may be categorized in any number of ways, a single hospital may also be classified in more than one way. For example, a hospital may be a private, not-for-profit and specialty hospital, thus falling into three categories. Notable systems for classifying hospitals include classification by the following:

1. **Ownership.** Public (government-managed) versus private hospitals.

   a. In public hospitals, governments (at the national, provincial, state or other level) own and are responsible for the operations. The healthcare providers in such hospitals are generally private practitioners, although in some countries the providers may be government employees as well (e.g., in the National Health Service [NHS] of the United Kingdom or the U.S. Veterans Health Administration hospitals).

   b. In private hospitals, staffing arrangements span a broad spectrum of private practitioners or groups of healthcare providers. Private hospitals in some countries are further classified as for profit versus non-profit.

      i. For-profit private hospitals, also referred to as investor-owned hospitals, often exist as part of a multi-hospital system with varying degrees of inter-relationship among the system's hospitals. Examples of large, investor-owned hospital systems include the Hospital Corporation of America (http://hcahealthcare.com/) and BMI Healthcare in the United Kingdom (http://www.bmihealthcare.co.uk/).

      ii. Non-profit private hospitals are not investor-owned, but rather exist under laws at national and state levels allowing them to organize as non-profit corporations, generally providing them the advantage of avoiding federal and property taxes. Canada's hospitals, although publicly financed, are almost exclusively private, non-profit organizations[6] albeit funded through the provincial/territorial governments. Just over half of the hospitals in the United States operate as private, non-profit organizations.[7]

2. **Types of Service Provided.** Hospitals are often classified by the types of service they provide. While the majority of hospitals will be general hospitals supporting the most common types of medical and surgical care requirements, hospitals specializing in more focused areas of care are becoming more prevalent. Such hospitals include psychiatric hospitals, which focus on mental healthcare; rehabilitation hospitals, which generally focus on restoring neurological and musculoskeletal functions following treatment in an acute-care facility; and children's hospitals, which focus on the care and treatment of children.

3. **Teaching Status.** In addition to providing inpatient clinical services, teaching hospitals train future physicians (and other healthcare providers). Often associated with academic institutions or universities, teaching hospitals may be further classified as

academic medical centers or university hospitals. Many such institutions also contribute substantially to medical research and publish much of the knowledge that advances the science of medicine.

4. **Geographic Location.** Hospitals may be further classified as urban hospitals when located in large cities or as rural hospitals when substantially distant from major urban areas with greater resources. While such classifications appear mundane, the challenges of operating in urban and rural environments are different enough to require programs of specialization. Meeting government standards for classification as urban or rural may provide such hospitals access to special government funding programs.

OUTPATIENT, OR AMBULATORY, CARE

When a patient's care does not require the intensive management of a hospital setting, that care is generally received in an outpatient, or ambulatory, care setting—most frequently in a doctor's office. Most primary care—the care practiced by primary care providers (PCPs) or general practitioners (GPs)—is provided in the outpatient setting. Similarly, most PCP/GP referrals to clinical specialists for evaluation are completed in the ambulatory setting as well. There are multiple modes of accessing outpatient care, including single independent provider offices, larger multi-provider group practices in which a broader range of specialists may be available, and—while not a preferred approach from an expense perspective—hospital emergency departments. In the last few years, many less complicated surgical procedures not requiring an overnight hospital stay have been moved to the outpatient setting as well. The facilities providing such day surgeries are frequently called ambulatory surgery centers or surgicenters.

COMMUNITY HEALTH ORGANIZATIONS

In the healthcare environment, a "community" generally refers to the specific geographic location in which healthcare is delivered. Thus, healthcare organizations serving the population of local areas tend to be broadly referred to as community health organizations. Community-centered hospitals and clinics in most nations provide most of the care available to their local populations. Some nations provide more formal designations of community healthcare organizations that impose both legally constrained definitions and operational characteristics on such organizations. In Canada, a community health centre (CHC) is a key provider of local health services and aspires to support access and comprehensive care, including health promotion and illness prevention, through a publicly administered process.[8] In the United States, community health centers are generally associated with medically underserved areas as defined by the Health Resources and Services Administration (HRSA). These health centers strive to provide "comprehensive, culturally competent, quality primary health care services to medically underserved communities and vulnerable populations."[9] Small community hospitals located in rural areas of the United States may apply for designation as critical access hospitals (CAH), allowing them to receive higher reimbursement rates.

DIAGNOSTIC AND PHARMACEUTICAL SERVICES

The most effective healthcare treatment quite frequently requires the aid of diagnostic services and pharmaceutical treatments. While larger hospitals will generally have these capabilities, smaller hospitals and outpatient care centers will usually rely upon external providers of such services to support comprehensive care to their patients. Key services provided in this area include laboratory and anatomic/anatomical pathology services, diagnostic imaging/radiology services and pharmacies. Close associations with these service providers are formed with provider offices and hospitals to ensure effective and comprehensive healthcare delivery.

HEALTHCARE PAYERS

From the perspective of the healthcare delivery organization, payments generally come from three types of entities: government-financed and managed programs, insurance programs administered by private entities, and personal funds.

Government-financed and managed programs are generally funded through countries' general taxes. These programs may pay for the healthcare system directly, as does the single-payer system of the National Health Service (NHS) of the United Kingdom, which finances hospitals and salaries of most NHS providers. Alternatively, government programs may provide funding for a national health insurance program, such as that in Canada, where the program is administered through provincial health plans. These plans fund hospitals through community trusts and pay providers through the government's insurance program. Multi-payer systems, such as that of the United States, are more complex to administer. The U.S. system includes the federally managed program Medicare, through which citizens 65 years of age and over have most of their healthcare needs provided for; the shared-cost federal/state program Medicaid, which supports care for low-income families; another federal/state program called the Children's Health Insurance Program, or CHIP, which provides care to children of uninsured families that do not qualify for Medicaid; and several others for smaller groups of special populations. These three programs provide coverage for roughly one third[10] of the U.S. population.

Insurance programs administered by private entities are generally funded by employers, citizens themselves or a combination of both. Germany mandates shared health insurance contributions from employers and employees, but these funds are administered by about 1,100 private, non-profit sickness funds that cover over 90% of the population by making payments to hospitals and providers. In the United States, roughly 55% of citizens have employer-based insurance, and an additional 10% purchase insurance directly.[11] Even in the many countries that have universal healthcare programs, people who can afford to purchase private health insurance are usually allowed to do so. The purchase of private health insurance generally allows the purchaser to receive services that may not be covered under a national benefit structure and may improve access to care. When healthcare organizations treat patients insured through a private entity, they bill the private health insurance entity rather than a government organization.

Healthcare services are often personally funded by individuals who have government or employer-supported health plans, as well as by the uninsured. While patient co-payments were not required by many universal coverage programs in years past, an increasing number of countries are contemplating adding this requirement to offset growing healthcare costs. In the United States, co-payments are required under most healthcare programs, whether government or privately managed. Persons with higher incomes may choose to avoid the constraints of insurance programs and, as they can tolerate the financial risk, are cash payers. Lastly, and perhaps most perversely, those who fail to qualify for government-supported programs such as Medicaid in the United States but still cannot afford to purchase health insurance find themselves at the mercy of a healthcare system that charges premium, non-negotiated rates to those least able to afford such costs. A 2009 study on bankruptcies in the United States found that 62.1% of all bankruptcies in 2007 were medical; 92% of these medical debtors had medical debts over $5000, or 10% of pretax family income. The rest met criteria for medical bankruptcy because they had lost significant income due to illness or mortgaged a home to pay medical bills. Most medical debtors were well educated, owned homes, and had middle-class occupations. Three quarters had health insurance.[12]

In summary, from the perspective of the healthcare delivery organization, three basic types of payers are at play: government-financed and managed programs, insurance programs administered by private entities, and patients who pay with personal funds. Add to that the number of potential insurance companies in the market and the differences in payers' health benefits coverage, and the management of accounts receivable can become an incredibly complex task requiring sophisticated administration and automation support.

■ Interrelations Within and Across Healthcare Organizations

The purposes of interrelationships among healthcare organizations are many. Some of the key requirements include enabling comprehensive care, assuring effective transfers of care, ensuring the general portability of information in support of care, reporting public and population health information, obtaining appropriate reimbursement for care, and supporting particular organizational models of care.

ENABLING ACCESS TO COMPREHENSIVE CARE SERVICES

As noted in the section above, healthcare organizations are reliant upon a number of partners within or outside of their organization to enable the delivery of comprehensive care. Providers in the outpatient setting often rely upon external laboratory and radiological services to ensure accurate diagnoses and upon the availability of pharmacies to provide prescribed medications to complete the provider's care plan for the patient. Absent effective communications—increasingly electronic today—the care process will break down and patient outcomes could suffer as a result.

ASSURING EFFECTIVE TRANSFERS OF CARE

When a provider determines that the scope of care required for a patient's treatment is outside of his or her capability, care is generally transferred to another provider or healthcare organization. Effectively communicating health information during the transfer of care is exceptionally important to the patient's welfare. When a complete set of information is transferred with the patient regarding the history of the present illness, along with subjective and objective findings that include the results of diagnostic tests performed, medications prescribed and administered, and the like, the receiving organization can advance the patient's treatment in a substantially more efficient and effective manner. When such information does not accompany a patient during transfer, precious time is often lost as that information is recreated through repetitive evaluations and re-administering diagnostic tests that are sometimes of an invasive nature. To facilitate the provision of essential health information during transfer of care between providers or facilities, an initiative in the United States encourages the use of Health Level Seven (HL7) International's Clinical Document Architecture (CDA), which is a standard for electronically transmitting continuity of care information.[13]

Both the loss of time in treating an acute patient and the need to repeat invasive tests can have adverse consequences for a patient. Not having a clear awareness of the pharmaceutical products a patient may be taking or has been administered in the present course of care can be life-threatening and has led to attempts in some countries to ensure that medication reconciliation has taken place. In the United States, medication reconciliation is defined as

> "…the process of identifying the most accurate list of all medications that the patient is taking, including name, dosage, frequency, and route, by comparing the medical record to an external list of medications obtained from a patient, hospital, or other provider."[14]

ENSURING THE GENERAL PORTABILITY OF CARE

Even when patients are enrolled to a specific clinical organization or provider for care, there are times when they will need care from other providers. This occurs not only under the two scenarios covered above, but also when patients travel away from their routine places of care. If a patient who is several hundred miles away from home becomes ill or is injured in an automobile accident, having the correct health information available can have a powerful influence on the patient's health outcomes from the clinical intervention. The most common example is that of the new provider who does not know a patient's medication allergies. To overcome these challenges, some nations are implementing national health information exchanges, or HIEs, that endeavor to provide virtual, real-time access to patients' health information. One such initiative is Canada's Health Infoway, a non-profit organization made up of the 14 federal, provincial and territorial deputy ministers of health. The Infoway Electronic Health Record Solution Blueprint states that their intent is to "provide a comprehensive framework for sharing health information across the Country."[15] In the United States, much work is under way to define standards to facilitate ease of sharing health information both through HIEs at the state level and nationally via the Nationwide Health Information Network (NwHIN). The United Kingdom has also invested heavily in its Connecting for Health initiative, which connects 27,000 healthcare organizations to facilitate the availability of clinical information that can be shared with NHS staff to support the continuity of care and safety of patients in the healthcare process.

REPORTING PUBLIC AND POPULATION HEALTH INFORMATION

Improving health status at the local or national level requires more than ensuring information availability at the point of care. It requires a sort of information use that is often referred to as the secondary use of health information because the information is used outside of the direct healthcare delivery process, which is viewed as the primary use of health information. The United Kingdom's Secondary Use Services (SUS) of its Connecting for Health program leverages the SUS in support of public health, research and management, among other activities. Similarly, the United States' Centers for Disease Control and Prevention has been receiving health information from across the country for many years to support not only such public health activities as actively responding to disease outbreaks, but also to work proactively through education on prevention and healthy lifestyles through its Division of Population Health.

OBTAINING APPROPRIATE REIMBURSEMENT FOR QUALITY CARE

In most publicly funded healthcare systems, the hospitals and clinicians delivering the care are private entities, so a substantial amount of communication must occur to ensure reimbursement for the care provided. Whether a healthcare organization is a one-provider office, a multi-specialty outpatient clinic, a hospital or other entity, it must submit claims to be reimbursed for care provided. The exception to this rule of course is in those countries, such as the United Kingdom, that have a national health system with both government facilities and a largely government-paid healthcare staff. Claims may be submitted to state Medicaid offices, the Centers for Medicare & Medicaid Services (CMS) for Medicare, or private insurance companies in the United States or to provincial offices in Canada, but no healthcare organization will exist for long absent an ability to efficiently process—and be reimbursed for—claims for care. In multi-payer systems, such as in the United States, this process can be exceptionally complex and require a surprising investment of administrative overhead and systems complexity. Both governments and major employers are increasingly concerned that improved health outcomes are associated with the cost of care. In the United States, the Physician Quality Reporting Initiative (PQRI), managed by CMS, will provide incentive payments to "eligible professionals who satisfactorily report quality-measures data for services furnished during a PQRS [Physician Quality Reporting System] reporting period."[16] Similarly, The Leapfrog Group supports healthcare purchasers and insurers by "mobilizing employer purchasing power to alert America's health industry that big leaps in health care safety, quality and customer value will be recognized and rewarded."[17]

SUPPORTING PARTICULAR ORGANIZATIONAL MODELS OF CARE

While the number of models of care is too great to discuss at length here, a key trend we see in the industry today is the need to share increasing volumes of information among partners in the healthcare system. Such partners in care are often referred to as an integrated delivery system, or IDS. Steven Shortell has defined the IDS as

> "...administrative entities that bring together a set of organizations that provide a coordinated continuum of services to a defined population and are willing to be held clinically and fiscally accountable for the outcomes and health status of the population served."[18]

While some IDSs are more integrated (from an ownership or a systems point of view) or more complete (providing a broader continuum of services) than others, the trend in the United States has been toward increasing integration. A type of IDS referred to as an accountable care organization, or ACO, has been around for a few years and was recently codified in law by the Patient Protection and Affordable Care Act—often referred to as simply the Affordable Care Act. In an ACO, inpatient and outpatient providers of care are administratively organized into a single organization, often including a health insurance company, to provide a full spectrum of healthcare services to large groups of Medicare patients. If the ACO is able to reduce costs to CMS for their enrolled population while improving the quality of care, the ACO gets to share in the cost savings. As might be imagined, proving improvements in quality concurrently with reduction in healthcare costs is an information-intensive process that requires close integration of the partners in an ACO. Many ACOs will likely be developed from existing IDSs, as the IDS model already has many of the components necessary to achieve the quality and cost objectives of CMS.

In summary, interrelations within and across healthcare organizations can be as simple as a general practitioner requesting an x-ray for a patient or reporting a patient disease observation to a public health entity. On the other end of the spectrum, the relationship could be as complex as assembling an integrated network of care providers under an ACO with sophisticated cost and quality-reporting requirements. Each of these constructs not only requires effective coordination but is also increasingly supported by sophisticated automation capabilities that reduce the labor involved while ensuring more reliable process support.

■ Roles and Responsibilities of Healthcare Information and Management Systems Professions

The number of position titles in the health information management (IM) and health information technology (IT) space is quite large. In a single-provider office, the person who performs the broad range of health IM/IT tasks may work less than full-time or double as the office manager. In a large academic medical center or integrated delivery system, the IT department could include over 100 personnel. The top IT position in healthcare organizations is usually referred to as the chief information officer, or CIO. The CIO is generally accountable for a broad range of IT activities, including many that are not directly related to healthcare. Among these would be such things as maintaining organizational computing rooms, individual desktop computers, telephone communications (including an increasing variety of portable computing platforms), secure Internet access, local and wide area networks, the organization's website, and much more.

In larger organizations, the complexity of IM and IT functions leads to specialization. The chief security officer, or CSO, endeavors to secure the healthcare organization's computing and communications assets from either intentional or unintentional security breaches from inside or outside the organization. Lead IT security personnel may carry the Certified Information Systems Security Professional (CISSP®) credential from the Information Systems Security Certification Consortium, Inc., (ISC²®).[19] Similarly, the privacy officer is responsible for ensuring that personally identifiable data, including personal health information, is accessed exclusively by those authorized to do so under a broad range of laws—in the United States, the Privacy Act and the Health Information Portability and Accountability Act (HIPAA), among others. A credential leveraged in supporting this role is the Certified in Healthcare Privacy and Security (CHPS) credential.[20]

The chief technology officer (CTO) is generally responsible for the technical architecture of the IT systems supporting the organization and often looks toward the developing market in IM and IT to try to keep the organization competitive from a technology perspective. This could range across the full spectrum of such things as mobile computing platforms, cloud-based computing and state-of-the-art clinical applications.

Health information managers have had roles in medical records departments for decades, but prior to the common availability of electronic health records (EHRs), there was not a strong relationship between health information management (HIM) departments and IT departments. As medical records functions have become increasingly automated over the past few years, culminating in EHRs of advanced capabilities, HIM departments are finding themselves at the center of the IT activities in healthcare organizations. In the HIM area, you will find professionals with the Registered Health Information Administrator (RHIA) or Registered Health Information Technologist (RHIT)[21] credential in the United States or with the Certification in Health Information Management (CHIM) credential in Canada.[22] Healthcare organizations may also rely on the Certified Professional in Healthcare Information and Management Systems (CPHIMS)[23] credential to ensure that staff members in the IT department have a broad base of knowledge and experience in healthcare information and management systems.

The role of clinical informatics professionals is also expanding as the practice of medicine is increasingly supported by EHRs and other health information systems. The Stanford School of Medicine defines clinical informatics as

> "…the scientific discipline that seeks to enhance human health by implementing novel information technology, computer science and knowledge management methodologies to prevent disease, deliver more efficient and safer patient care, increase the effectiveness of translational research, and improve biomedical knowledge access."[24]

The American Medical Informatics Association (AMIA) advocates advanced training for clinicians to develop a clinical informatics subspecialty in the practice of medicine.[25] A frequently used title for staff with such backgrounds in the health information space is that of chief medical information officer (CMIO). Popular variants are chief medical informatics officer and chief health information officer (CHIO), and in the area of nursing, chief nursing informatics officer (CNIO). With the increasing use of IT in healthcare processes, effective integration of clinical insights into systems solutions is of great importance.

While the great variety of organizational structures in IT departments is driven by such factors as organization size, geographical distribution and line of business, a sample organization structure a CIO may oversee could include:

- Accounts management

- Application development

- Application support

- Data center operations

- Database administration

- Desktop support

- Information security

- Network operations

Similarly, the specific roles an IT organization may expect to fill would vary based upon the functions the organization supports. These roles could be filled by staff, consultants or contractors. Examples of the more common types of positions one might expect to see includes:

- Desktop support technician

- Database administrator

- Programmer/application developer

- Web developer

- Network engineer/analyst

- Systems analyst/administrator

- Project manager

- Security analyst

In summary, there is great variation in the size and structure of IT departments within healthcare organizations, which drives the number and specialization of jobs within the IT organization.

■ The Roles of Government, Regulatory, Professional and Accreditation Agencies in Healthcare

Given the importance of healthcare in our lives—including our quality of life, our longevity and even our ability to continue living following life-threatening encounters with disease or accidents—and the incredible expense of delivering high-quality healthcare to very large populations, it is not surprising that a tremendous amount of government oversight and a great number of regulatory bodies are involved in healthcare processes. An overview of these organizations and their associated activities is provided below.

GOVERNMENT

The role of governments in healthcare is quite pronounced, as discussed in the section above on healthcare organizations. Because most countries continue to experience increases in the proportion of their gross domestic product (GDP) consumed by healthcare activities, they are concerned that these trends will weaken their national economies if not slowed—or even stopped and reversed. Stopping the growth in healthcare costs as a percentage of GDP requires exceptionally difficult decisions for governments in industrialized countries as citizens have grown accustomed to the existing health benefits programs. While OECD countries average just under 10% of their GDPs consumed by healthcare expenditures, the United States is currently at over 17% and Korea at just under 7%.[26] The growth in healthcare expenses annually has averaged 4%, while the growth in GDPs has averaged only 1.6%,[27] so it is easy to see that healthcare is consuming our national economies at an unsustainable rate, making governmental engagement in these factors essential.

To address healthcare cost growth, many nations' governments are considering changes to their health programs. Among these are enhancements to the primary-care delivery system to manage chronic diseases more effectively in Australia, experimentation with privatization in Canada, global budgeting and competition among sickness funds in Germany, requiring long-term care residents to pay for room and board in Japan, and consideration of pro-market reforms in the United Kingdom.[28] Similarly, the development of accountable care organizations in the United States is being encouraged with a goal of producing better health outcomes at lower cost. Such trends will continue as we collectively grapple with the best ways to balance quality, access, cost and safety for the greatest proportion of our populations.

HEALTHCARE REGULATORS

Healthcare regulatory agencies serve a broad range of functions in the healthcare environment, generally by implementing the provisions of a nation's health laws through a more explicit system of regulations. In the United Kingdom, the Health and Care Professions Council (HCPC) is the statutory regulator for over 300,000 health and care professionals in the country. The HCPC maintains standards of proficiency and conduct for the professions it regulates. In the United States, the dominating regulatory entity is the Centers for Medicare & Medicaid Services. CMS drafts the rules and finalizes the regulations for the management of multiple federally subsidized healthcare programs for the nation through a complex process of rule making involving public engagement. The Food and Drug Administration (FDA) in the United States evaluates and approves medical devices and new drugs used in the treatment of patients. Similarly, medical devices in Canada are regulated by Health Canada's Therapeutic Products Directorate.

While it may be a common belief that regulatory organizations are always government entities, it is not uncommon to find that private-sector organizations, commissions and associations may perform in a regulatory capacity as well. These are addressed in the following sections.

PROFESSIONAL ASSOCIATIONS

According to the *Merriam-Webster Dictionary*, a profession is "a calling requiring specialized knowledge and often long and intensive academic preparation."[29] Professional associations in the healthcare environment have proliferated greatly, many serving in a semi-regulatory role. Total Professions, of the United Kingdom, provides a good description of the roles and functions of professional bodies, stating that they may:

- Set and assess professional examinations;

- Provide support of continuing professional development through learning opportunities and tools for recording and planning;

- Publish professional journals or magazines;

- Provide networks for professionals to meet and discuss their field of expertise;

- Issue a code of conduct to guide professional behavior; and

- Deal with complaints against professionals and implement disciplinary procedures.[30]

Total Professions further distinguishes between professional and regulatory bodies by stating that "A regulatory body is like a professional body but it is not a membership organisation and its primary activity is to protect the public. Unlike professional bodies, it is established on the basis of legal mandate."[31]

Professional associations exist for nearly every medical specialty, nursing and allied health profession, health administration and IT profession. A sampling of professional associations related to healthcare and healthcare information technology in the United States is shown in Table 1-1.

TABLE 1-1. Professional Associations Related to Healthcare and Health Information Technology in the United States	
Clinical	**Administrative and IT**
American College of Surgeons	American College of Healthcare Executives
American Congress of Obstetricians and Gynecologists	American College of Physician Executives
American Gastroenterological Association	American Academy of Medical Administrators
American Academy of Physician Assistants	Information Systems Security Certification Consortium, Inc. (ISC2®)
American Academy of Family Physicians	Healthcare Information and Management Systems Society
American Academy of Pediatrics	American Health Information Management Association
American Nursing Association	Project Management Institute

ACCREDITATION ORGANIZATIONS

Accreditation organizations (AOs) have substantial interactions with healthcare organizations and generally play a semi-regulatory role in that they often serve on behalf of federal organizations to ensure that specific standards or Conditions of Participation (CoP) are met. The Joint Commission and Joint Commission International (JCI)[32] are perhaps the most recognized AOs utilized for certification of hospitals in the United States and internationally. JCI currently operates in more than 90 countries around the globe. In the United States, the AOs under CMS are very visible examples of accreditation agencies. CMS AOs determine compliance with Medicare CoP. When a healthcare organization is certified by a CMS AO for compliance with CMS requirements, the organization is deemed to have met the requirements and may then bill CMS for covered services. For participation in Medicare programs, a number of other organizations are authorized to act as AOs, as shown in the Table 1-2.

The interrelationships among government agencies, regulators, professional associations and accreditation organizations can be surprisingly complex, especially in the United States. The graphic in Figure 1-4 shows the many organizations that play a role in the life of a physician assistant moving through training and into medical practice.

FIGURE 1-4. Steps and Organizations Involved in Becoming a Practicing Physician Assistant[34]

- Attend institution accredited by the Accreditation Review Commission on Education for the Physician Assistant (**ARC-PA**)
- Graduate

| Accreditation Organization |

Take the Physician Assistant National Certifying Exam (PANCE) administered by the National Commission on Certification of Physician Assistants becoming certified as a Physician Assistant-Certified or PA-C

| Accreditation Organization serving A Regulatory role |

Maintain national certification by completing 100 hours of continuing medical education through the American Academy of Physician Assistants (AAPA) every two years and take a recertification exam every six years

| Professional Association |

- Obtain a state license to practice
- Obtain a National Provider Identifier (NPI) from CMS and become an enrolled provider to allow PA to bill patients covered by federal healthcare programs

| State & Federal Government Organizations |

Begin provision of care

* Adapted from http://www.aapa.org/your_pa_career/becoming_a_pa.aspx

TABLE 1-2. **CMS-Approved Accreditation Organizations**[33]	
Organization	**Program Type**
Accreditation Association for Ambulatory Health Care (AAAHC)	Ambulatory surgical centers (ASCs)
Accreditation Commission for Health Care, Inc. (ACHC)	Home health agencies (HHAs) Hospices
American Association for Accreditation of Ambulatory Surgery Facilities (AAAASF)	ASCs Outpatient physical therapy providers (OPTs) Rural health clinics (RHCs)
American Osteopathic Association/ Healthcare Facilities Accreditation Program (AOA/HFAP)	ASCs Critical access hospitals (CAHs) Hospitals
Community Health Accreditation Program (CHAP)	HHAs Hospice
DNV Healthcare (DNVHC)	Hospitals CAHs
The Joint Commission	ASCs CAHs HHAs Hospices Hospitals Psychiatric hospitals

■ Summary

At the beginning of our discussion, we determined that it was important to be able to:

■ Articulate characteristics and services of different types of healthcare organizations.

■ Understand characteristics of interrelations within and across healthcare organizations.

■ Differentiate the roles and responsibilities of healthcare information and management systems professions.

■ Describe roles of government, regulatory, professional and accreditation agencies related to healthcare.

We have covered the breadth of organizational structures in the public and private domains, defined the nature of their interactions, identified roles of healthcare information and management systems professionals, and described the great number of government, regulatory, professional and accreditation organizations affecting our healthcare delivery systems today. The complexity of the processes can be overwhelming. Fortunately, advances in automation, including inexpensive data storage, increasing network capacities and simplified software programming tools, will allow professionals in healthcare information and management systems to make life simpler for those who deliver care by transferring much of the information processing requirements to automated tools. This chapter provides a high-level framework for the environment in which you will employ these tools.

■ References

1. Preamble to the Constitution of the World Health Organization. Adopted by the International Health Conference, June 19-22, 1946; New York, NY.

2. Healthcare Information and Management Systems Society. The four pillars. http://www.himss.org/ASP/aboutHimssHome.asp. Accessed September 16, 2012.

3. OECD. Health expenditure per capita. In: *Health at a Glance 2011: OECD Indicators*. OECD Publishing; 2011. http://dx.doi.org/10.1787/health_glance-2011-60-en.

4. OECD. Screening, survival and mortality for cervical cancer. In: *Health at a Glance 2011: OECD Indicators*. OECD Publishing; 2011. http://dx.doi.org/10.1787/health_glance-2011-47-en.

5. OECD. Avoidable admissions: respiratory diseases. In: *Health at a Glance 2011: OECD Indicators*. OECD Publishing; 2011. http://dx.doi.org/10.1787/health_glance-2011-40-en.

6. Mapleleafweb. Canada's Health Care System: An Overview of Public and Private Participation. http://www.mapleleafweb.com/features/canada-s-health-care-system-overview-public-and-private-participation#public. Accessed August 30, 2012.

7. *Statistical Abstract of the United States*. Table 172. http://www.census.gov/prod/2011pubs/12statab/health.pdf. Accessed August 30, 2012.

8. Canadian Association of Community Health Centres. http://www.cachc.ca/?page_id=7. Accessed August 30, 2012.

9. United States Department of Health and Human Services, Health Resources and Services Administration. http://bphc.hrsa.gov/about/. Accessed August 30, 2012.

10. *Statistical Abstract of the United States.* Health and nutrition section. http://www.census.gov/prod/2011pubs/12statab/health.pdf. Accessed August 30, 2012.

11. United States Census Bureau, US Department of Commerce. Income, Poverty, and Health Insurance Coverage in the United States: 2010. September 2011; 29. http://www.census.gov/prod/2011pubs/p60-239.pdf. Accessed August 31, 2012.

12. Himmelstein DU, Thorne D, Warren E, Woolhandler, S. Medical bankruptcy in the United States, 2007: results of a national study. *Am J Med.* June 2009. http://www.pnhp.org/new_bankruptcy_study/Bankruptcy-2009.pdf. Accessed August 31, 2012.

13. Health Level Seven International. HL7/ASTM Implementation Guide for CDA Release 2 - Continuity of Care Document (CCD®) Release 1. http://www.hl7.org/implement/standards/product_brief.cfm?product_id=6. Accessed September 17, 2012.

14. Centers for Medicare & Medicaid Services. Eligible Hospital and Critical Access Hospital: Meaningful Use Menu Set Measures, Measure 6, Stage 1. http://www.cms.gov/Regulations-and-Guidance/Legislation/EHRIncentivePrograms/downloads/6_Medication_Reconciliation.pdf. November 7, 2010. Accessed September 2, 2012.

15. Canada Health Infoway. EHRS Blueprint: An Enterprise Architecture for Sharing Electronic Health Records. June 15, 2009. Accessed September 2, 2012.

16. Centers for Medicare & Medicaid Services. Physician Quality Reporting System: Analysis and Payment. http://www.cms.gov/Medicare/Quality-Initiatives-Patient-Assessment-Instruments/PQRS/AnalysisAndPayment.html. Accessed September 3, 2012.

17. The Leapfrog Group. http://www.leapfroggroup.org/about_leapfrog. Accessed September 3, 2012.

18. Shortell SM, Casalino LP, Fisher ES. Achieving the vision. In: Crosson FJ, Tollen LA, eds. *Partners in Health: How Physicians and Hospitals Can Be Accountable Together.* San Francisco: Jossey-Bass; 2010:53-54.

19. Information Systems Security Certification Consortium (ISC²®). https://www.isc2.org/cissp/default.aspx. Accessed September 9, 2012.

20. American Health Information Management Association. http://ahima.org/certif http://ahima.org/certification/chps.aspx. Accessed September 9, 2012.

21. American Health Information Management Association. http://ahima.org/certification/credentials.aspx. Accessed September 9, 2012.

22. Canadian Health Information Management Association. https://www.echima.ca/national-certification-exam. Accessed September 9, 2012.

23. Healthcare Information and Management Systems Society. http://www.himss.org/ASP/certification_cphims.asp. Accessed September 16, 2012.

24. Stanford School of Medicine. https://clinicalinformatics.stanford.edu/background.html. Accessed September 9, 2012.

25. American Medical Informatics Association. http://www.amia.org/request-preparatory-coursework. Accessed September 9, 2012.

26. OECD. Health expenditure in relation to GDP. In: *Health at a Glance 2011: OECD Indicators*. OECD Publishing; 2011. http://dx.doi.org/10.1787/health_glance-2011-61-en.

27. OECD. Annual average growth in real per capita expenditure on health and GDP. In: *Health at a Glance 2011: OECD Indicators*. OECD Publishing; 2011. http://dx.doi.org/10.1787/health_glance-2011-60-en.

28. Shi L, Singh DA. *Delivering Health Care in America: A Systems Approach*. 5th ed. Burlington, MA: Jones & Bartlett Learning; 2012:20-27.

29. Merriam-Webster. http://www.merriam-webster.com/dictionary/profession. Accessed September 14, 2012.

30. Total Professions. Role of Professional Bodies. http://www.totalprofessions.com/more-about-professions/role-of-professional-bodies. Accessed September 14, 2012.

31. Total Professions. Regulatory Bodies. http://www.totalprofessions.com/more-about-professions/regulatory-bodies. Accessed September 14, 2012.

32. Joint Commission International. http://www.jointcommissioninternational.org/About-JCI/. Accessed October 10, 2012.

33. Adapted from http://www.cms.gov/Medicare/Provider-Enrollment-and-Certification/SurveyCertificationGenInfo/Downloads/AOContactInformation.pdf. Accessed September 14, 2012.

34. Adapted from American Academy of Physician Assistants. Becoming a PA. http://www.aapa.org/your_pa_career/becoming_a_pa.aspx. Accessed September 14, 2012.

CHAPTER 2

The Technology Environment

Melissa Barthold, MSN, RN-BC, CPHIMS, FHIMSS

LEARNING OBJECTIVES

At the conclusion of this chapter, the reader will be able to:

☑ Articulate characteristics of applications commonly used in healthcare (e.g., clinical, administrative, financial, consumer and business intelligence).

☑ Describe the characteristics of technology infrastructure that support the healthcare environment (e.g., network, communications, data integration, privacy and security).

■ Introduction

The world now is steered by computers—from Twitter to the National Oceanic & Atmospheric Administration, everything we do and touch and that touches us has a computer in the process. Healthcare may have been a little bit slower than other parts of life to adopt information technology (IT), but now the electronic health record (EHR) is an essential part of every facility that provides care to patients—from home health to the intensive care unit. While it is not common for providers to use electronic records, patients are no longer surprised when the provider pulls out a computer instead of a pad and pen.

Most hospitals and outpatient sites provide wireless networks for staff to use in caring for patients and a different network for family and visitors to access. It is common to see patients updating their status on Facebook or Twitter from their hospital beds or outpatient center during their visits. Where hospitals used to have policies forbidding employees from accessing social networks during working hours, many institutions now have instructions on how to friend the hospital. Many patients have separate personal health records (PHRs) that they manage on an Internet site[36] as well as a PHR module in the facility's EHR. Healthcare IT is changing the way that healthcare does business, as well as the way that clinicians care for patients. An understanding of the attributes of healthcare IT, as well as knowledge of the applications and hardware required for their use, are essential in helping to improve the care and the safety of the care provided to patients.

There are three components of the technology environment:

1. **Hardware:** the actual servers (virtual and physical), network connections and devices used to access information;

2. **Applications:** the software used by administrative, clinical and support staff to process and store data, manage patients' records and provide information; and

3. **Networks:** the wired or wireless connections that link the infrastructure together and enable accessibility of the applications and patient data.

A healthcare facility requires these three components to function. While this may seem a very simplistic listing, these are essential to providing IT to a healthcare institution. And, while essential, with the rapid changes in technology and improvements in software, the sections of these components change frequently. A central processing unit (CPU) that was fast a year ago has been replaced by a new model—which is three times faster. A storage server of four gigabytes (GB) was large two years ago; now, that is a small hard drive. Mobile devices used to be large and cumbersome; now they fit in the palm of the hand. The decreased access time—and increased speed—for a hard drive enables the application to return data to the requesting clinician much more quickly. The technology changes are supporting—and changing—the applications and the functions of the applications. The illustrations here are not intended to be a complete listing but to provide an overview.

■ Hardware in Healthcare IT

TECHNOLOGY INFRASTRUCTURE

The basis of any technology has to be the hardware systems that store data, run applications and connect those applications and tools together. The physical routers, switches, and virtual and physical servers are some of the integral parts needed to connect clinicians, administrators, providers and patients to necessary clinical systems, information and support. Firewalls, both physical and software-based, protect the network from unauthorized access as well as maintain security of the information in the system.

The network, while still dependent on network cables, is increasingly connected using wireless points. Putting the information for clinicians at the point of care requires wireless access points, not hard wires. Clinicians want data at their fingertips and do not accept the model of going to the patient's room and then back to the nurses' station to log in to the clinical system and retrieve results. Providers now take the (electronic) chart with them to the patient's room, where they can review lab results, x-ray reports and other tests with the patient. Wireless access points can support this workflow, permitting clinicians to work with the information they need when and where they need it. This wireless and cabled access supports more than just documentation stations. Virtual private networks (VPNs), voice over Internet protocol (VoIP) using fiber optic cables and coaxial cables and supporting protocols govern the connection of routers and switches. Local area networks (LANs) (using Ethernet and token ring), wide area networks (WANs) (using multiprotocol label switching–MPLS) or asynchronous transfer mode (ATM) are all in use, supporting the hard-wired and wireless networks. VPN technology is a safer, more secure method of providing remote access to an organization's network and servers. VPNs, using tunneling protocols and encryption, require authentication to block out unauthorized users.

There are guidelines, rules from regulatory bodies and professional organizations, and professional standards that require documentation about patients and the care given to those patients, as well as documentation of procedures. One of the major requirements of an EHR is that it must be able to support the documentation, order entry and lab-results reporting required by regulations, professional standards and patient need. Ideally, that care is documented where it is provided, thereby reducing errors.[28]

There are many areas in an organization that have cabled access to the organization's intranet. Cabled access is more reliable and faster.[5] Many institutions already have cable that was installed before wireless was within the price range and speed requirements of most IT departments. Clinical departments as well as administrative and support services usually have hard-wired desktop computers. Some healthcare providers, especially in outpatient settings, have installed a desktop or fixed device in each patient room/exam room. Specific clinical areas, such as radiology examination rooms, need special hardware, such as larger, high-resolution monitors and high-speed graphic cards that will support detailed images. In addition, hardware devices in patient care areas have to be able to be cleaned with harsh cleansing agents. To make this possible, some hospitals have installed microstatic keyboards and mice, as well as silicone covers for monitors.[14,23,44]

Hardware needs to be designed to support clinical workflow, and increasingly that means portable devices and wireless connectivity. Healthcare institutions are using mobile wheeled carts with wireless access, as well as smaller handheld devices. Carts can be configured to meet end users' needs, from drawers for storage to holders for bar code medication scanners and locked drawers for security of medications. Carts that carry only some version of computer (carts can support thin and fat clients) can be designed for outpatient clinics and other clinical areas that have no need for drawers or scanners, and other carts can have medical devices mounted on them. It is important to remember that while standardization may be a goal, one documentation device will not meet every area's or end user's needs.

The popularity of smartphones, and their increased functionality, is prompting end users to ask for similar devices for use in the healthcare units. The iPad is one of the most popular handheld devices. Currently, few EHRs are designed to operate on iPads or other tablets, though many of the EHR vendors are working on applications for the handheld devices. Devices with touchscreens are being configured for healthcare, with attention to the concern about maintaining good infection-control practices while using equipment that is touched by gloved hands. Several devices, such as MRI scanners, employ touchscreens to program the examinations and review the images.

A major concern with any handheld device that connects to the institution's network is security, especially when end users actually bring their own devices to work. Prior to permitting staff's use of their personal devices in the clinical areas, it is important to establish a policy to ensure that personal healthcare information (PHI) is safe, that the institution can wipe a device if it is compromised, and that passwords are required to access the device. The decision to permit data storage on a personal device must be dependent on maintenance of the data's security.[47,66]

MEDICAL DEVICES

Many physiologic devices, such cardiac monitors, ventilators, some IV fluid pumps, medication pumps and vital sign monitors have the ability to send out the data they obtain, often in HL7 format. This integration with the EHR helps the staff by decreasing transcription errors as well as saving time. Depending on the EHR, this data could be directly sent to preconfigured fields, or a third-party device can be used to translate the data into EHR-acceptable format. It is important to require validation of the information by the clinician prior to permanently storing that data in the EHR.

Laboratory devices can conduct tests and export the information to the EHR. Typically, radiologic images are stored in a picture archiving and communication system (PACS) and viewed via a link from the EHR to the image in PACS. Both areas have specific regulatory agencies that supervise the use of those devices and regulate them. As an example, in the United States, the Food and Drug Administration (FDA) regulates medical devices. Since so many of those devices have incorporated advanced technology, IT must be aware of the laws and regulations from the FDA that apply to hardware and software that is IT supported. In addition to radiologic images, any display of physiologic data, such as heart rhythms, fetal monitor tracings, ventilator or heart waveforms, and any implantable device, such as an automatic cardiac defibrillator, is covered by the FDA. In addition, the FDA is looking at mobile medical apps. Examples of these are applications that display fetal heart tracings or cardiac waveforms on physicians' cell phones.[12,63] The institution's biomedical engineering department must work closely with IT to maintain these important systems.

In Europe, the Parliament and the Council of the European Union have developed directives for medical devices and in-vitro diagnostics. Canada has medical-device regulations, as does Japan.[42] In Russia, the Ministry of Public Health and Social Development of the Russian Federation controls medical devices.[58] The World Health Organization (WHO) has published a large amount of information about medical device requirements on their Web page.[62] According to the WHO, "65% of 145 countries have an authority responsible for implementing and enforcing medical device specific product information."[61] There is discussion that the European Commission's regulations for devices are not strong enough to really protect patients.[17]

■ Software in Health IT

SOFTWARE APPLICATIONS

Software provides the face of healthcare IT. Hardware is not visible to the end users, but the applications that sit on that hardware really are. Use of the various software applications, along with changes in workflow and processes, can benefit the organization. The software is what the end user works with, using a human-computer interface. There is a large number of applications, so we will discuss the major groups of applications and examine some of the newer ideas that are in the pipeline.

■ Clinical Applications

As with most specialties, healthcare IT has developed its own terminology and acronyms. Some of the terms seem interchangeable when, in fact, they do have different meanings. The electronic health record (EHR), the electronic medical record (EMR) and the personal health record (PHR) are examples of this. The EMR is the continuous, longitudinal electronic record in one specific setting—a provider's office, a hospital or a home healthcare service. The EHR is a longitudinal record covering multiple settings over time.[20,39,60] The PHR is a medical record often created, edited, maintained and controlled by the patient and possibly includes importation of clinical data from other sources. Often created on a website, it is accessible by providers when the patient invites providers to review information in the PHR using secure access.

Clinical applications support patient care wherever it is being delivered. The most apparent clinical application is the EHR. In some institutions, this is a one-vendor application; in others, it is a best of breed, with many different applications performing different functions. The EHR is used by clinicians to document patient care, from medication administration to order entry, as well as to retrieve patient data from the lab or from radiology. The provider's office EHR often can send electronic prescriptions to the patient's pharmacy as well as import data from an inpatient stay or outpatient testing.

The EHR interfaces with specialized systems in different departments. As an example, in the United States, radiology and pathology labs have specific requirements, with formatting and data display governed by different accrediting agencies, such as Clinical Laboratory Improvement Amendments (CLIA), the College of American Pathologists (CAP) and the American College of Radiology.[2,7] In Europe, the European Cooperation for Accreditation[59] covers laboratory certifications. Professional dietitians, case managers and social workers all have specific needs in software functionality, often dictated by professional or regulatory standards.

Some clinical areas, such as the perinatal areas (labor and delivery, nursery, neonatal intensive care and postpartum), the perioperative areas (preop unit, operating rooms and post-anesthesia care unit), the critical care units, the outpatient centers for primary care, and special functions like renal dialysis, all have specialized documentation and information needs. The PACS stores and displays images from ultrasound to CT scans and MRIs. These systems require fine-resolution monitors, large storage drives and large amounts of RAM for image display. Some of the major EHR vendors are able to support all the specialty areas; others do not and require the purchase and interface of a niche system specific to each specialty. The goal of all these systems is to communicate. Interoperability is one of the most important attributes of clinical systems, since data should not be entered into systems more than one time. It is essential that these systems communicate with each other. Table 2-1 presents examples of specialized systems and their related clinical areas and users.

TABLE 2-1. Sample Specialized Systems and Their Clinical Areas and Users

System	Clinical Area	Users
PACS	Radiology	Radiologists Nurses Technologists Physicians providing direct care
Fetal monitor archiving	Labor and delivery	Physicians Nurses
Perioperative system	Preoperative area Postoperative area Operating room	Physicians Nurses Schedulers Billers and coders
Intensive care	Intensive care units	Physicians Nurses

The availability of clinical data at the point of care has transformed how clinicians care for patients. They no longer need to go to the radiology department to look at MRIs or CT scans; those images are available in the record application, saving time for clinicians as well as money for the institution, since there are no films to create, store or retrieve. Perinatal systems archive the fetal monitor strips electronically, saving thousands of dollars in charges for storage of paper fetal strips.

■ Administrative Applications

Administrative applications provide support for clinicians as well as the administrative staff in an institution. These applications run the gamut from electronic time cards, payroll, staff competency record keeping, and educational applications, to scheduling both staff for work shifts and patients for procedures and office visits. Bed-management systems, which include staff from housekeeping and patient transportation as well as clinicians, are very helpful in getting patients into a room as soon as possible. Popular applications in the last few years include equipment-tracking applications that use radio frequency identification (RFID) technology, thus saving staff time spent in just hunting for needed equipment. Web-based applications that permit staff to bid for understaffed shifts are being implemented, reducing overtime labor costs and increasing staff satisfaction, as do systems that permit self-scheduling.

INTEROPERABILITY AND STANDARDS

An important facet of all healthcare IT applications is the use of standards. Interoperability is essential to smooth functioning of healthcare IT, and systems that support standards ensure that functionality. Health Level Seven (HL7) is an international standard interface language used in healthcare[7]; Digital Imaging and Communications in Medicine (DICOM) is used as a standard for images[54] and the SNOMED Clinical Terms (SNOMED CT) is the most comprehensive multilingual clinical healthcare terminology in the world,[45] while the International Statistical Classification of Diseases and Related Health Problems (ICD) provides diagnosis codes for most disease conditions.[6,24,53] In the United States, these codes, along with current procedural terminology (CPT) codes, classify patients' diagnoses and the procedures they have had, and provide a link between each procedure and the diagnosis that required it.[57] In France, the International Society for Pharmacoeconomics and Outcomes Research (ISPOR) has developed charge codes for providers that include the correct prices that can be charged for a specific procedure.[35] These codes can be entered into the system by clerical staff as well as providers, and in most cases, these codes have a large part in determining if an institution or provider will receive the maximum amount of reimbursement for performing a procedure or the minimum amount.

Interoperability is "the extent to which systems and devices can exchange data and interpret that shared data,"[25] and "Uniform movement of healthcare data from one system to another such that the clinical or operational purpose and meaning of the data is preserved and unaltered.[20] With the current movement to exchanging patient data, regardless of the physical location of the patient and the patient's home data, those standards, especially for data formats and programming languages, have become increasingly important.

Without standards, interoperability is impossible; without standards, healthcare IT would most resemble the Tower of Babel, with no system or device speaking the same language and resulting in duplicative effort and work from clinical and administrative staff. In the United States, governing standards are included in the Final Rule, published by CMS in August 2012, as well as the Advisory Board for Health Standards in Europe.[55]

Included in the discussion of standards are nursing and other disciplines' terminologies. These terms can be used by nurses as well as other providers, including physicians, to document patient care. The need to standardize terms affects all parts of healthcare and especially impacts quality reporting. The use of standard words for documentation improves research—it is always oranges and oranges that are being discussed, since it is clear what the standardized terms mean.

There are challenges to EHR implementation throughout the world. The integration effort currently in place in Europe is improving the chances of implementation. This integration needs to move quickly, as the number of specialty systems is increasing. The speciality systems are often intended for use by only one discipline, moving away from an integrated EHR.[29]

◼ Financial Applications

Financial applications in healthcare IT cover all the features of any organization's financial needs, but possibly with more variables than most businesses have to entertain. From the solo provider's office to the multi-hospital, multi-provider health system, there is a need for financial systems. Multiple regulations govern how billing can be done, how bills are submitted, the details that have to be included with a bill, including diagnosis codes, providers' numbers—the list is incredibly long. Systems have to handle charge posting via both orders and manual charge entry, payment posting, and billing based on the providers. Insurance, coinsurance and deductibles have to be part of the calculations, as do revenue codes, and supply items, tests and medications that require a provider's order and cannot be billed to patients without an order must be distinguished from items that do not require an order and can be billed to patients. Statements need to be provided to patients and insurance companies. A general ledger must accurately track charges, bills and payments. Payroll systems need to accept data from the electronic time-card system and convert it to salary costs, correctly matching hours worked, both regular and overtime, and calculating overtime bonuses, holiday bonuses, shift differentials and additional wages earned from professional certifications. It also has to track earning for paid time off, usually based on the number of hours worked by the employee. The accounts payable portion of the software must also be in sync with all the other systems; financial systems have to communicate in real time. The supply chain mission and support has to include all methods of supply purchasing, as well as invoice payment, and ensure that they are linked correctly.

◼ Consumers and Healthcare IT

Consumers are more and more involved in electronic records. Not infrequently, patients request electronic versions of their charts from providers. The importance of the consumer's relationship to the record and the information in that record is more apparent. While there used to be discussions about who owned the medical record, that seems to have been decided in the patient's favor. Some EMRs have a patient portal that permits the patient to view test results (after provider review and release to the patient), ask for prescription refills, and send the provider or the office staff an e-mail as well as schedule an appointment. Some portals permit the patient to add comments to the EMR.[32,67]

Some PHRs are stand-alone and are not connected with an institution's EMR. These applications may be web-based, such as HealthVault from Microsoft[22] or an application installed on the user's computer. In the United States, CMS encourages the use of PHRs[40,41] and provides a link to MyPHR, a website that assists the user in determining what type of PHR—web-based or software, free or fee required—is best. The website is sponsored by the American Health Information Management Association

(AHIMA) and also provides information on the value of a PHR for seniors, parents and caregivers.[56] The National Committee on Vital and Health Statistics also provides detailed information on the advantages of a PHR.[52] AHIMA provides a questionnaire for consumers interested in setting up a PHR. Convenient guides such as this one are helpful to patients around the world.[3] Web-based PHRs give the patient full control of the record's contents, and often offer the opportunity to import prescription medication history from national drugstore chains or results from laboratories. According to Gherardi, Kensing and Osterlund,[18] PHRs are becoming very popular in Europe, the United Kingdom and Scandinavia. The publication *IT and People* issued a call for articles on PHRs for their August 2012 edition to encourage discussion of the implementation, design, forms, security and use of PHRs by patients and care providers.[18] There are vendors that are increasing presentation about the PHR across Europe, the United Kingdom and China.[31]

Some healthcare organizations have partnered with web-based PHR vendors and upload records into patients' PHR applications from those healthcare institutions. Some healthcare insurers also provide the ability to create a PHR from their websites.[4] In the United States, a national survey conducted by the California HealthCare Foundation (CHCF) provides evidence that PHRs actually support patients in improving their own health.[38] In the survey, caregivers did note that PHRs were almost a necessity in maintaining knowledge and continuity of care for family members with multiple chronic conditions.

The numbers of patients using PHRs is growing rapidly, with the CHCF survey reporting that most patients want to use PHRs that their doctor, nurse practitioner or insurer provides. The survey also identified security as the major stumbling block to PHR adoption, with patients looking for evidence that any information they enter into the PHR is completely secure. Most websites clearly provide information on how security and privacy of the patients' records is maintained. Most allow the patients to decide who can view their information, often by providing a secure URL or separate login/password for the healthcare provider. Patients have found that after establishing a PHR through their insurance company or other third-party vendor, information could not be easily transferred to a different PHR, resulting in the patients' having to re-enter the data in their new systems. PHR use may increase with the medical home and accountable care platforms, as they provide incentives for keeping patients healthy.[30] In the United Kingdom, the National Health Service's Summary Care Record project is under way. The Summary Care Record also includes HealthSpace, a personal health record.[26] Patients are encouraged to participate in HealthSpace by adding in medications that they take or appointments with providers that they have scheduled.

Patients are very interested in communicating electronically with their providers. According to the *Wall Street Journal*,[48] doctors are far behind the rest of the world in using electronic communications, and either patient portals or secure messaging applications can provide security for this increasingly popular communication. Most patient issues can actually be addressed in e-mail by office staff, leaving only a few e-mails that the physician or nurse practitioner needs to address. Patients want the convenience of electronic communication with their providers, but at the same time, both sides of the communication have to be secure. While providers may not have the skill to set up secure communications, there are web-based and application-driven tools that will provide that security and convenience.[19]

The requirement to be able to provide "human-readable" medical records in electronic format is something very new to healthcare. In the past, patients had to go to the health information management department, complete paper work to request their own records and often pay a per-page fee for a copy of the paper record. As an example, in the United States, Stage 1 of Meaningful Use requires that a copy of the medical record be available to the patient within 24 hours of the request.[11] While it is not always easy to retrieve data from EHR systems, this requirement has to be fulfilled. Ensuring that the EHR can provide this information, whether on a portable drive, DVD or CD, is essential. And regardless of the regulations, the smarter patients that we now have want copies of their records. Patients want to see their records, as determined by a group of researchers in the United States and Canada.[65]

■ Business Intelligence

According to the HIMSS Clinical Business Intelligence Committee, business intelligence (BI) consists of "technologies, applications and practices for the collection, integration, analysis, and presentation of clinical information, for the purpose of better clinical decision-making. In recent times, quality in healthcare is being shaped by evidence-based medicine and the proper utilization of data."[8] Tools of business intelligence can provide support to clinicians to improve patient safety and patient care, as well as analyzing operating room use and staff overtime patterns. Collecting—and reporting in a meaningful way—supports not only direct patient care, but all aspects of healthcare. Hospitals want to show that they are providing high-quality, low-cost care for their patients; providers want to show that they are doing the same. Data and data analysis are the only keys to providing that information. More and more organizations around the world are collecting business intelligence, whether by using specific applications or by constructing data warehouses, to document the care they provide, as well as to show trends in patients' conditions and document improvements in patients' status based on the care that they were given.

TELEHEALTH

One of the fastest growing healthcare fields that requires IT support is telehealth. According to the American Telemedicine Association (ATA), there were 38,000 telehealth visits for Medicare patients in 2009.[33] Telehealth can be simply two professionals communicating or a consultation from an academic medical center to a rural hospital with a severely injured trauma victim.

This type of telehealth consult requires broadband accessibility for both sides of the telehealth visit; video cameras with detailed resolution capabilities; audio/mic equipment; equipment that will directly transmit data through the computer, such as blood pressure cuff and pulse oximeter; as well as the ability to send radiologic images, lab results and any other reports needed for the visit to the physician being consulted.

Telehealth can provide specialized care to those living in underserved areas. Patients like telehealth as they can often see a specialist faster than in a face-to-face appointment; their physician is included and they do not have to drive to the visit. The Veterans Administration did a large study that demonstrated the effectiveness of home health monitoring for patients with chronic diseases—both cost-effectiveness and patient outcomes—which showed decreased readmission of these patients within 30 days of discharge.[10] School children, working with the school nurse, can have a telehealth consultation and get appropriate medication and treatment while their parents stay at work and the children stay at school.[46] Academic medical centers offer emergent consults for emergency department patients and new babies with medical issues, as well as interpretation of cardiac rhythms, reading of radiologic studies and scheduled telehealth office visits. Equipment selection and configuration, transmission of data and image files, as well as real-time video/audio during a consultation all must be supported by the IT department to make telehealth as easy and seamless as a face-to-face office visit.[50]

According to the HIMSS Asia-Pacific Newsletter, there are more than 200 million mobile health (mHealth) applications in use. Mobile health is a growing aspect of healthcare IT, with countries as large as India using mHealth to support safe sex and family planning.[1] The World Health Organization has a large mHealth project for tobacco control in progress.[37] There are mHealth programs in place or being developed to support maternal health; assist with the global health survey of communicable and infectious diseases, and diabetes/obesity; and develop an mHealth global strategy.[61] Mobile health, with more than one-half of the population of rural areas having a cellular phone, is going to become increasingly important in worldwide healthcare, education and provision.

■ Health Information Exchanges

Health information exchanges (HIEs) and regional health information organizations (RHIOs) are essential to supporting a longitudinal health record for Americans. The primary stone in building an RHIO is ensuring that the HIE accurately links each patient's data across the different venues, from an inpatient visit to office visits to an emergency department in a different state, and transmits that data. Ensuring this transmission of data to connect varying types of information from various systems is a work in progress,[13,43] and is essential to the creation of the any countrywide—or hopefully, worldwide—health information network. In Europe, the eHealth organization is sponsoring the Digital Agenda for Europe, which includes proposing broadband connections for healthcare.[9] The European Commission provides the Health-EU portal, a website that presents eHealth work in progress, from projects to reduce air pollution to the EuroNeoStat II, a neonatal European information system.[16] At completion, in the United States, RHIOs will connect inpatient records, records from providers' offices, home health services and patients' PHRs, and will be a true electronic medical record. Privacy and security standards are strict to ensure privacy and confidentiality of every patient's information. The vision is that the HIEs will connect around the world, supporting patient care wherever the patient is.

DATA INTEGRATION

Data integration and the use of interface engines are essential in healthcare IT. Interface engines permit systems to be connected correctly. It is not enough to simply send data from one application to another—there are many rules that must be followed. If data does not go to the right patient's chart, errors in the patient's care, bill and final report could result. Interface engines in a healthcare IT environment really drive the systems, matching data and patients correctly. Without data integration and interface engines, a national health information network in either the United States or the rest of the world will never exist.

COMMUNICATIONS

There are many different types of phones in healthcare IT today, from the standard landline with conferencing and video capabilities to various devices that use VoIP. Some of the devices look like the same cell phones that are used outside the hospital, while some are clip-on, hands-free phones worn by staff members. As with other devices in use in the clinical areas, infection control is a major concern. Materials for these devices need to be antibacterial and cleanable. While some of these devices can send and receive text messages, there are questions about the legality and safety of using text messages for patient orders.[27,51]

DATA STORAGE

Most healthcare IT departments have used magnetic tape storage, optical disc storage, even hard drive storage for patient information, bills, financial accounts—all the thousands of data elements generated by each patient's care. There are, depending on the type of patient, regulations on how long patient data must be maintained. For example, in the U.S. information about a baby's birth must be maintained for 23 years, or 2 years after the baby reaches majority. Many healthcare organizations are simply resigned to keeping charts forever.

With paper records, that translates to a large amount of money to store stacks of paper that will probably never be looked at again. Health information management departments have looked for a less expensive and more reliable storage method. Most organizations store patient charts off-site and have to order them when or if they are needed, thus adding transportation costs to and from the storage area to the record-keeping costs. Some health systems have a practice of scanning paper charts, then discarding the paper, while others are saving electronic records.

Current practice, where data is stored, backed up and archived, is changing—often to the cloud. The cloud can provide room for storage, even when those storage needs may double every few years.

SERVERS

While the vision that many people have of IT is a room full of servers, that is no longer completely accurate. Most healthcare IT departments have virtual as well as physical servers. What application is installed on which type of server is determined by the vendors' recommendations. Virtual servers can serve as test servers as well as production servers. The servers are part of the most expensive equipment in a healthcare IT shop and must be managed well and appropriately.

DATA WAREHOUSES

Data warehouses are being developed and used much more frequently in today's healthcare. The value of being able to store data from multiple sources, such as the EHR, the EMR and ancillary systems, is clearly recognized. Storing data in one place—the warehouse—from multiple sources allows it to be queried at the same time. Healthcare institutions have multiple requirements for submission of their data to different organizations, from the Bureau of Vital Statistics to the American Heart Association in the United States or the European Society of Cardiology. Often, these organizations require submission of the same quality improvement data elements but just want it in a different format. The warehouse can support this type of quality reporting as well as clinical research. Data mining can be used to identify populations at risk, search for patterns of illness, and identify potential study candidates or those patient populations that are doing well.[64] Defining a data model, deciding if a data mart would be more helpful than a warehouse, and determining how to search the warehouse are all decisions that should be made by an experienced database manager.

PRIVACY AND SECURITY

Maintaining patients' information, ensuring that it is kept private and secure, is the first charge for EHR administration. As an example, while patients' data has to be shared through HIEs and RHIOs, it must remain confidential. Increasingly, data regulations are including strong language about privacy and security, emphasizing that the EHR can and must be developed without compromising a patient's privacy. Systems, as part of their design, have to be able to provide the patient an accounting of disclosures. The system must be able to maintain levels of confidentiality. For example, a nurse or physician must be able to see the patient's laboratory results, but a nurse's aide using that same EHR should not be able to see that information.

While disclosures of information can be made to appropriate agencies, such as the patient's insurance provider, those agencies cannot be given complete access to the patient's record but must be given the minimum amount of information necessary.

Ethically, healthcare providers have an obligation to keep any patient's information private and confidential. The healthcare professions have codes of ethics that clearly detail the nurse's and physician's obligation to protect the patient's information.[15]

■ Conclusion

These three sections of healthcare IT combine to create, support and maintain healthcare information technology. Knowledge of these areas is the basis of building healthcare IT and supporting healthcare providers in their work of caring for patients in a safe, accurate and timely manner.

■ References

1. 200 million mHealth applications in use; 2011. http://www.himssasiapac.org/ newsletter/2011/dec/200m-mhealth.html.

2. *ACR-AAPM-SIM technical standard for electronic practice of medical imaging* [Resolution ACR-Resolution 35]; 2012. Website of the American College of Radiology: http://www.acr.org/~/media/AF1480B0F95842E7B163F09F1CE00977. pdf.

3. AHIMA Personal Health Record Practice Council. Helping consumers select PHRs: Questions and considerations for navigating an emerging market; 2006. http://library.ahima.org/xpedio/groups/public/documents/ahima/bok1_032260. hcsp?dDocName=bok1_032260.

4. Aetna's personal health record; 2008. http://www.aetna.com/showcase/phr/.

5. Bjorn. 5 benefits of wired vs. wireless networks [blog post]. July 25, 2010. http://www.icantinternet.org/2010/07/benefits-of-wired-vs-wireless-networks/.

6. CDC Classification of diseases, functioning, and disability website; 2009. http://www.cdc.gov/nchs/icd/icd9.htm.

7. Certifications, licenses and accreditations. http://wwwn.cdc.gov/clia/.

8. Clinical business intelligence committee; 2012. http://www.himss.org/asp/topics_clinicalbusiness.asp.

9. Commission proposes over 9 billion for broadband; 2011. http://ec.europa.eu/information_society/newsroom/cf/item-detail-dae.cfm?item_id=7430&language=default.

10. Darkins A, Ryan P, Kobb R, Foster L, Edmonson E, Wakefield B, Lancaster AE. Care coordination/home telehealth: The systematic implementation of health information, home telehealth and disease management to support the care of veteran patients with chronic conditions. *TELEMEDICINE and e-Health*. 2008; 14(10):1118-1126. http://dx.doi.org/10.1089/tmj.2008.0021.

11. Department of Health and Human Services. *Health information technology: Initial set of standards, implementation specifications, and certification criteria for Electronic Health Record Technology; Final Rule* (45 CFR Part 170); 2010. Washington, DC: Government Printing Office.

12. Draft guidance for industry and Food and Drug Administration staff - mobile medical apps; 2011. http://www.fda.gov/MedicalDevices/DeviceRegulationandGuidance/GuidanceDocuments/ucm263280.htm#5.

13. E-HIM Work Group on Patient Identification in RHIOs. Surveying the RHIO landscape: A description of current RHIO models, with a focus on patient identification; 2006. http://library.ahima.org/xpedio/groups/public/documents/ahima/bok1_028980.hcsp?dDocName=bok1_028980.

14. Eisen J. Oh no - computer mice have more "germs" than toilet seats [blog post]; April 6, 2012. http://www.microbe.net/2012/04/06/oh-no-computer-mice-have-more-germs-than-toilet-seats-germophobia/.

15. Erickson JI, Millar S. Caring for patients while respecting their privacy: Renewing our commitment. *Online Journal of Issues in Nursing*. 2005; 10(2). http://nursingworld.org/MainMenuCategories/ANAMarketplace/ANAPeriodicals/OJIN/TableofContents/Volume102005/No2May05/tpc27_116017.html.

16. European Commission Health-EU. Your gateway to trustworthy information on public health; 2012. http://ec.europa.eu/health-eu/index_en.htm.

17. Fiore K. New device rules criticized at EASD meeting; 2012. http://www.medpagetoday.com/MeetingCoverage/EASD/35119?utm_content=&utm_medium=email&utm_campaign=DailyHeadlines&utm_source=WC&xid=NL_DHE_2012-10-04&eun=g440157d0r&userid=440157&email=mbarthold@umc.edu&mu_id=5537079.

18. Gherardi S, Kensing F, Osterlund C. Personal health records: Empowering patients through information systems? 2012. http://www.itandpeople.org/personalhealthrecords.pdf.

19. HIMSS. Secure messaging in healthcare; 2011. http://www.himss.org/asp/topics_FocusDynamic.asp?faid=658.

20. HIMSS. *HIMSS Dictionary of Healthcare Information Technology Terms, Acronyms and Organizations*. 2nd ed. Chicago: HIMSS, 2010.

21. Health Level Seven International website; 2012. http://www.hl7.org/.

22. HealthVault; 2012. http://www.microsoft.com/en-us/healthvault/.

23. Hedge A, James T, Pavlovic-Veselinovic S. Ergonomics concerns and the impact of healthcare information technology. *International Journal of Industrial Ergonomics.* 2011; 41:345-351.

24. HIMSS. ICD-10 Playbook; 2012. http://himss.org/ASP/topics_icd10playbook.asp.

25. HIMSS. Interoperability & standards; 2012. http://www.himss.org/asp/topics_interoperability.asp.

26. Introduction to summary care records; 2012. http://www.nhs.uk/NHSEngland/thenhs/records/healthrecords/Pages/servicedescription.aspx.

27. Joint Commission. Text messaging should not be used in patient orders; 2011. http://www.ihealthbeat.org/articles/2011/11/21/joint-commission-text-messages-should-not-be-used-in-patient-orders.aspx.

28. Kohle-Ersher A, Chatterjee P, Osmangeyoglu HU, Hochheiser H, Bartos C. Evaluating the barriers to point-of-care documentation for nursing staff. *CIN: Computers, Informatics, Nursing.* 2012; 30(3):126-133.

29. Lakovidis I. Towards personal health record: current situation, obstacles and trends in implementation of electronic healthcare record in Europe. *International Journal of Medical Informatics.* 1998; 52(1-3):105-115. http://dx.doi.org/http://dx.doi.org/10.1016/S1386-5056(98)00129-4.

30. Lewis N. Consumers slow to adopt electronic personal health records. *Information Week.* April 8, 2011. http://www.informationweek.com/healthcare/electronic-medical-records/consumers-slow-to-adopt-electronic-perso/229401249#.

31. MMRGlobal moving into Europe with MMRPro and MyMedicalRecords; 2012. http://phx.corporate-ir.net/phoenix.zhtml?c=178404&p=irol-newsArticle&ID=1704074&highlight=.

32. Mayo Clinic Staff. Personal health record: A tool for managing your health; 2011. http://www.mayoclinic.com/health/personal-health-record/my00665

33. Medicare - Telehealth coverage. In Medicare - ATA Wiki. http://wiki. americantelemed.org/index.php?title=Medicare. Accessed September 15, 2012.

34. Medicare & Medicaid EHR incentive program Meaningful Use stage 1 requirements overview [PowerPoint slides]. Website of Centers for Medicare & Medicaid Services; 2010. https://www.cms.gov/Regulations-and-Guidance/ Legislation/EHRIncentivePrograms/downloads/MU_Stage1_ReqOverview.pdf.

35. Meyer F, Denis C. France - Medicial Devicies; 2011. http://www.ispor.org/ htaroadmaps/francemd.asp.

36. Microsoft Healthvault; 2012. http://www.microsoft.com/en-us/healthvault/.

37. Mobile health (mHealth for tobacco control); 2012. http://www.who.int/tobacco/ mhealth/en/.

38. California HealthCare Foundation. New national survey finds personal health records motivate consumers to improve their health; 2010. http://www.chcf.org/ media/press-releases/2010/new-national-survey-finds-personal-health-records-motivate-consumers-to-improve-their-health.

39. Office of the National Coordinator, Department of Health and Human Services; 2012. *Benefits of EHRs* [Issue brief]. http://www.healthit.gov/providers-professionals/electronic-medical-records-emr.

40. Personal Health Records; 2012. http://www.cms.gov/Medicare/E-Health/ PerHealthRecords/index.html.

41. Personal health records (PHR); 2011. http://www.medicare.gov/manage-your-health/personal-health-records/personal-health-records.html.

42. Process Quality Associates; 2006. http://www.pqa.net/ProdServices/ISO/ ISO13485.html.

43. Regional health information network; 2010. Retrieved from http://searchhealthit. techtarget.com/definition/Regional-Health-Information-Organization-RHIO.

44. Requirements for a medical grade keyboard; 2012. http://www.man-machine. com/applications/medical-grade/7-Requirements-for-a-medical-grade-keyboard. htm.

45. SNOMED CT website. http://www.ihtsdo.org/snomed-ct/.

46. *School-based telehealth: An innovative approach to meet the health care needs of California's children* [Issue brief Digital Opportunity for Youth Issue Brief Number 6]; 2009. California Primary Care Association. http://www.cpca.org/cpca/index. cfm/data-reports/.

47. Seymour D. Mobile security toolkit considerations for employee-owned mobile computing devices; 2012. http://www.himss.org/content/files/PrivacySecurity/MS03_MS_Toolkit_Consumerization.pdf.

48. Should physicians use email to communicate with patients? 2012. http://online.wsj.com/article/SB10001424052970204124204577152860059245028.html.

49. Stephenson C. Inside the mind: What leaders in high-performing organizations know; 2012. http://www.studergroup.com/newsletter/Vol1_Issue2/newsletter.htm.

50. Telehealth; 2012. http://www.himss.org/asp/topics_focusdynamic.asp?faid=721.

51. *Text messaging in health care - a clinical perspective.* [Video file]; June 12, 2012. http://webinars.medtechmedia.com/registration/webinar/text-messaging-healthcare-%E2%80%93-clinical-perspective?partnerref=website.

52. The National Committee on Vital and Health Statistics. *Personal health records and personal health record systems: a report and recommendations from the National Committee on Vital and Health Statistics* [Report]; 2006. National Committee on Vital and Health Statistics. http://www.ncvhs.hhs.gov/.

53. Website of CDC's classification of diseases, functioning and disability; 2011. http://www.cdc.gov/nchs/icd/icd10.htm.

54. Website of DICOM. http://medical.nema.org/.

55. Website of the CEN-CENELEC Advisory Board for Healthcare Standards; 2009. http://www.cen.eu/cen/Sectors/Sectors/Healthcare/Forum/Pages/currentissues.aspx

56. Website of the American Health Information Management Association; 2012. http://www.myphr.com/Default.aspx.

57. Website of the American Medical Association; 2012. http://www.ama-assn.org/ama/pub/physician-resources/solutions-managing-your-practice/coding-billing-insurance/cpt.page.

58. Website of the Emergo Group; 2012. http://www.emergogroup.com/resources/articles/russia-medical-device-approval-process.

59. Website of the Euorpean Cooperation for Accreditation; 2012. http://www.european-accreditation.org/content/ea/EuropNetwork.htm.

60. Website of the European Commission/Information Society; 2012. http://ec.europa.eu/information_society/activities/health/index_en.htm.

61. Website of the World Health Organization; 2012. http://www.who.int/en/.

62. Website of the World Health Organization; 2012. http://www.who.int/medical_devices/en/.

63. What are bio-medical devices? http://www.engr.sjsu.edu/bioengineering/ BiomedicalDevices/WhatAreBiomedicalDevices.html.

64. Wickramasinghe N, Calman RA, Schaffer JL. *Defining the landscape: Data warehouse and mining: Intelligence continuum* [HIMSS white paper]; 2007. http://www.himss.org/content/files/Intel_Continuum06052007.pdf.

65. Wiljer D, Urowitz S, Apatu E, DeLenardo C, Eysenbach G, Harth T, Leonard KJ. Patient accessible electronic health records: Exploring recommendations for successful implementation strategies. *Journal of Medical Internet Research*. 2008; 10(4). http://dx.doi.org/10.2196/jmir.1061.

66. Wireless, smartphones and applications; 2012. http://blogs.csoonline.com/1812/ useful_settings_alert_how_to_secure_iphones_ipads?source=CSONLE_nlt_ salted_hash_2011-11-15.

67. HIMSS. eConnecting with consumers; 2012. http://www.himss.org/ASP/topics_ connectingConsumers.asp.

Section II.

Systems

CHAPTER 3

Systems Analysis

Brando C. Sumayao, MSCIS, CPHIMS, FHIMSS

LEARNING OBJECTIVES

At the conclusion of this chapter, the reader will be able to:

☑ Describe the purpose and list the major components of the systems analysis with regard to IT implementation in healthcare.

☑ Articulate the problems that can be resolved through proper policies based on IT.

☑ Explain the current and developing trends in IT systems analysis.

☑ Describe how to perform a cost-benefit analysis of a proposed initiative.

☑ Describe the project management stages which are most important to the systems analysis phase.

■ Introduction

Over the last two decades, different industries have adopted the use of information technology (IT) in their various operations in order to enhance growth, conform to emerging standards, attract new customers, maximize profitability and acquire business intelligence. Different sectors, however, have adopted IT use in different capacities. The health sector, like all others, is striving to enhance the acceptance of better and easier techniques available through an IT implementation. However, the average use of IT in healthcare has lagged behind other industry sectors for the better part of the last decade. Healthcare has many potential benefits from IT implementation in both managerial operations and patient-related operations. This chapter will focus on systems analysis with regard to IT implementation in healthcare facilities, and it will identify problems that could be solved through proper policies based on IT and link those problems with possible opportunities presented by current and developing IT trends. In addition, this chapter will present an example of a working proposal to aid in the implementation of profitable IT practices, as well as in performing a cost-benefit analysis of a sample proposed initiative.

■ Healthcare Problems and Opportunities for IT Implementation

The healthcare situation in the global platform is experiencing dynamic changes in several ways. The major avenues of the change involve the following:

CLINICAL FUNCTIONS

A significant percentage of modern care facilities is using healthcare IT systems in clinical operations. However, the majority of units are still dependent on traditionally used systems such as physical patients' document keeping, lab reports, drug-administration history and other functions. They lack computerized order information and histories for drugs and other substances, medical supplies catalogues and lab test results. In addition, they lack electronic health records, image and film archiving and associated communications systems, the result-analysis mechanism for ordinary patient processes such as lab tests and drug prescriptions, decision-support facilities in clinical systems, prescription error-alert systems, as well as electronic monitoring of high-care patients, especially in intensive care units (ICUs).

APPLICATION

Electronic health records (EHRs) involve standardizing the way in which patients' records are entered, stored and retrieved, not just within an organization but across different hospitals, caregivers, government-controled organizations and other interested parties. The biggest challenge regarding EHRs has been the establishment of an industry standard to use so that an efficient workflow can be realized that would allow for seamless retrieval and use of records for patients, even when patients are moved to units other than where they were initially treated.

This kind of data pool would imply a dedicated system with necessary checks and balances to prevent unauthorized access to and manipulation of patient records, while at the same time enabling data entry by different care units when patients make additional visits to any facility. This concept is delicate in view of the possibility of malicious addition or manipulation of patient data by different staff in different facilities. Moreover, proper coding and categorization of prescriptions and procedures has hindered the implementation of a universal EHR system in the last two decades. This problem can now be sufficiently handled by high-end software applications that are being developed by individual and corporate research entities.[1]

One such authority, the Health Information Technology for Economic and Clinical Health Act (HITECH Act), is a U.S. government initiative to enable EHR availability in a secure and safe manner that allows EHR use across the healthcare spectrum. Presently, other systems that are being pursued include computerized practitioner order entry (CPOE), which may replace conventional order cataloging and fulfillment in a manner that will enhance tracking, logistic synchronization and cost effectiveness, and the clinical decision support system (CDSS), which, in its basic form, will give informative guidelines to practitioners regarding medication and procedures, including warning systems relating to high-risk medications and processes.

In addition, the picture archiving and communications system (PACS) will integrate inputs from multiple radiological and diagnostic tools to allow easy, consistent and accurate treatment of different conditions, while radio frequency identification (RFID) may help to track patients within a medical unit without the need to restrict them to a particular location or allocate a nurse to them. The vital signs collectable from this system may include pulse rate, temperature level, blood pressure, and other metabolic/respiratory signals. Benefits of such a system, if properly collected, stored and secured, when integrated with other dedicated software applications, may shorten treatment time, allow more freedom and lead to cost efficiency and better resource utilization within a hospital or other healthcare facility. Automated dispensing machines (ADMs) may aid in drug dispensing, while electronic materials management (EMM) systems will operate like the resource planning systems used in other sectors to manage information processing regarding pharmaceuticals, new drug development and coding, among other functions. Such a system would reduce medication errors, which as of the year 2000, were responsible for over 98,000 deaths in the United States alone.[13]

ADMINISTRATIVE AND FINANCIAL SERVICES

Functions that could be enhanced through investment in IT in the administrative category include general ledger operations, including cash flows, expenses, purchases and other day-to-day transactions. Other functions are billing, cost accounting systems, payroll, personnel management and other integrated human resource functions, patient registration and booking, and electronic management of materials, among others.

Applications for Administration and Finance

Information technology may find many basic as well as advanced applications in administrative and financial services. Human resource management has experienced radical changes in form and operational methods as a result of IT implementation. Systems for employee management, role definition, reward and recognition support as well as performance development have been successfully automated thanks to dedicated software such as enterprise relational database management systems (RDBMS). Such systems allow easy, timely and accurate workflow management in human resource mobilization and development, saving time and costs that would otherwise be allocated for additional staff. Other functions, such as payroll, budgeting, budget implementation and internal audit, have also been made easier, more precise and tailor-made for specific analytical objectives without incurring additional monthly or yearly charges due to the use of IT systems. Patient registration and tracking can become more enhanced and efficient, and access to the online statistics of every facility within an area may be useful in referrals and in discharge notification, enabling time saving and better emergency handling.

INFRASTRUCTURE

Infrastructure is a broad category that incorporates various equipment with diverse applications, both general and specific. Current security standards have shifted toward biometric sensors for movement and access control in most major private and public buildings and premises. These security standards enhance accountability in system access and support user logging, which enhances safety and responsibility among authorized personnel. The healthcare sector could, perhaps, benefit the most from such systems, given the delicate nature of confidentiality requirements involved in patient records access and dissemination. Biometric sensors typically used include fingerprint scanners, voice recognition systems and eye scanners, among others. Such systems have become so common that they are available in modestly priced private homes. Other more dedicated systems include bar coding systems for medication grouping, ordering, cataloguing and stock control. Security infrastructure may also include closed-circuit TV cameras and night infrared cameras.

Security-Related Applications

Since information technology relates to healthcare security, it may find many uses, some of which may not be achieved in other ways. Patient information access logging is important in ensuring confidentiality and professionalism in the way patients are treated. It increases patients' confidence in their practitioners and boosts their trust levels. In addition, the use of biometric systems will eliminate to a large extent ambiguity in accountability in delicate cases due to their high precision levels and extremely low chances of identity theft or manipulation, unlike conventional securitization protocols when any person with forced access to pass codes may steal information. In addition, healthcare research facilities may hold expensive machinery that, if it falls into wrong hands, may be used in ways detrimental to society. For instance, ultra-modern DNA synthesis machines, if used by experts, may find applications in the terrorist underworld. Other chemicals and drugs in healthcare facilities may also be abused or sold to unsuspecting people as legitimate prescriptions and lead to catastrophic consequences. Such security measures cannot be overlooked, and government control is restricting the use of certain machinery and equipment to high-security facilities, limiting the range of services that healthcare units with lower security may offer.

Another broad category of infrastructure has to do with network development and all associated controls. Medicare processes huge amounts of information internally, not to mention external linkage requirements associated with referrals and national accountability reports that must be processed and sent to government control and data collection agencies and other industry regulatory bodies. The baseline network infrastructure includes servers, end-user computer stations, switches, network access points, all associated cabling and external access infrastructure. While very elaborate high-level applications have been incorporated into network infrastructures in a significant number of healthcare facilities, the majority of care units are using their network support equipment for only slightly more than baseline uses, such as record keeping and document sharing.

■ Needs Analysis in Healthcare Facilities

In order to develop a proper proposal for sustainable IT supplementation in the core processes of the healthcare sector, it is important to identify the main challenges in the sector and specifically those needs that can be sufficiently met by the implementation of sustainable, secure and cost-efficient IT practices. This section will give a detailed needs analysis to lay the foundation for the chapter. The analysis focuses on requirements that may be categorized as operational, administrative or industry-related.

OPERATIONAL NEEDS

Healthcare facilities need to streamline their core administrative and financial operations with the current global standards in order to foster interoperability in record keeping and analysis with other stakeholders, investors and business partners. Currently, healthcare as an industry is behind average industry standards in IT acceptance. Such processes as payment processing, e-bill systems, human resource systems, stock taking, auditing and other similar functions can be sufficiently integrated with the use of developing software.[2] In order for a system to be sustainable and standard, it is necessary to select a universally accepted platform for data storage and analysis in which organizations may pool data relating to logistics and facilities. Financial as well as private human resource information does not need to be pooled in a central storage facility, but adopting software dedicated to easing these functions on a private level is necessary in order to reduce costs, enhance operational efficiency and increase profitability. Operational needs may be broken down into several areas.

STAFF PRODUCTIVITY AND SATISFACTION

The use of information technology may reduce time wasted by operational staff performing administrative work and enhance patient attendance time, which is the key need for patients. It will also reduce unnecessary routines in patient care and reduce work of clinical staff due to rigorous, non-work-related duties. It will also improve employee satisfaction and reduce fatigue due to extensive overtime schedules. Better productivity will invariably lead to increased patient volumes.

REVENUE INCREASES AND COST OPTIMIZATION

Increased visitor capacity per unit may boost revenues for a care unit due to a larger number of admissions and discharges per month following shortened lengths of stay, reduced unit costs owing to bulk purchases by healthcare facilities and improved capability to meet overhead expenses. Cost optimization needs to be realized through bulk purchases, efficient stock control and reduced cost per day for each patient. In this regard, IT practices will save costs for the unit as well as daily treatment and accommodation charges on the customer.

PATIENT SAFETY

A significant number of deaths and serious medical malpractice cases are reported each year due to errors in treatment, procedures or prescriptions. The major cases involve adverse drug effects (ADEs) due to wrong prescriptions that affect patients negatively, admissions following adverse drug effects (AADEs), errors in surgical procedures and blood transfusions, as well as malpractice expenses such as corrective procedures, court litigations and compensations. There is an urgent need to reduce such occurrences, many of which can be satisfactorily handled by the application of proper IT processes.

QUALITY OF CARE

Patient quality of care deals with the satisfaction that patients get from care providers' efforts to resolve their problems. It may involve turn of delay, time of treatment, appropriateness of procedures used and drugs administered, and the levels of professionalism, confidentiality and courtesy of the staff. Moreover, it may involve specific professional services, such as recognition of accreditations, complication management, physician or nurse time with patients, as well as reduced length of stay.[2]

PATIENT ACCESS TO SERVICES

Apart from the length of stay, patients are concerned with delay time for such processes as lab reports, billing, online services such as viewing and scheduling, preventive care management, and outpatient care appointment bookings. There is a need to upgrade systems that can be automated to handle most of the routine work not requiring case-specific diagnosis, such as remote patient appointment bookings and all associated alerts on scheduling, integrated lab linkage with other hospital systems that eliminates the need for extended physical queues at facilities, and electronic procedures for alternative bill settlement by customers. If proper systems are established to meet the outlined objectives, other needs relating to healthcare that cannot be quantified but lie at the core of healthcare provision will also be realized. This will lead to nonmonetary benefits such as good patient-physician relationships and improved community health.[2]

NEEDS SUMMARY

The foregoing discussion highlights the need for all-around IT supplementation to help healthcare catch up with other sectors in terms of modernization and integration. In essence, what is required is a project plan to implement safe, sustainable and cost-effective IT practices to help healthcare in (1) administrative, (2) operational, (3) patient-related and (4) industry-related functions. There is a need for a seamless backbone IT platform that integrates these four needs as well as sustainable controls for the IT implementation to ensure it remains secure, serves the maximum purpose possible and is practical for universal adaptability in order to satisfy the core concern within various healthcare institutions, which is the integration of policy implementation.

■ Need Prioritization

While all the needs listed above are urgent and important, there are certain ones that must be prioritized in order for IT acceptance in healthcare to stand. These processes are the backbone of healthcare, and all other requirements are built on them. For instance, patient security and safety are core driving factors for any practitioner, and they surpass the need for good bookkeeping or profit optimization. Without proper observance of fundamental safety concerns, healthcare units are likely to face legal implications that could cause them to lose their license, rendering futile any advancement they may have in their other operations. This section will therefore seek to address the need for prioritization of IT acceptance in healthcare facilities based on the hierarchy of the needs model. The primary priority from an individual facility's perspective is patient safety,

FIGURE 3-1. **Differing Priorities of Individual Facilities and the Healthcare Industry**

followed by profitability, then ease of processes, and, lastly, industry standardization. From the healthcare industry's perspective, the priorities are likely to be patient safety and security, professionalism, standardization, profitability and ease of processes. Obviously, the ease of processes is in most cases tied with profitability.[3] The project must therefore address IT implementation issues from both perspectives and attempt to strike a balance. Figure 3-1 illustrates the differing priorities of individual facilities and the healthcare industry.

■ Work Plan Development

A work plan is aimed at establishing a step-by-step implementation setup for a project, including materials and equipment layout, intended workflow processes, managing the time, analyzing processes and evaluating outcomes. In the healthcare IT implementation plan, a proper work plan involves putting in place procedures to realize the needs for IT acceptance by healthcare facilities, starting with the primary priorities and proceeding to other priorities.[4] Sample elements of a work plan are presented below.

EXECUTIVE SUMMARY

This project is aimed at analyzing the efficiency of the current systems in healthcare and assessing the situation with the purpose of providing a working alternative that is

IT-enhanced and will lead to the realization of target objectives of the sector. The plan will provide the project implementation phases as well as define specific operations to be carried out during each phase.

INTRODUCTION AND BACKGROUND

The implementation of IT policies in healthcare has been faced with many challenges, rendering the process complex and non-standardized.[5] Establishing a comprehensive industry standardization process has been impossible due to various individual interests among care providers, drug and device manufacturers, pharmaceutical companies, as well as regulating bodies. Thus, there has been a diverse range of new drugs and other medication practices localized in small market segments without proper administration and regulation. In addition, a wide network of healthcare facilities operating in different geographical, economic, technological and cultural settings has made it difficult for the various stakeholders to come together and develop an enhanced global EHR system that will ensure standardization of procedures, leading to a net lag in technology acceptance in the healthcare sector. The IT sector, however, has advanced and infiltrated all major sectors on the global platform, forcing all industries to confirm or become outdated. This is the case in the healthcare sector as well, prompting stakeholders to start seeking urgent and sustainable methods of integrating the sector in preparation for standardization and alignment with emerging trends on the global IT platform. For instance, most sectors currently accept online payments through credit and debit cards; therefore, a significant volume of business may be lost due to nonalignment among healthcare sector players. Thus, it is important that a strategic work plan should be implemented to align the healthcare sector with current IT trends.

GOALS AND OBJECTIVES

The goal of this work is to find a structure for IT integration in the healthcare sector's main processes, which includes cost-effectiveness, patient safety and care, ease of processes, as well as industry standardization. To this end, specific objectives must be laid out that include the following:

- Evaluation of the current operational situation in an average healthcare facility. This step will include analysis of current clinical processes such as process mapping. It will also document the current trends that can be found in healthcare procedures, including administrative and operational trends and integration of workflows in an average facility.

- Identification of the major problems in these processes with respect to the optimization of the information technology use. This stage will involve comparing the efficiency of the current processes with the efficiency typically achievable in a similar setting with IT implementation.

- Identification of alternative solutions to these problems through the implementation of IT policies. This process will involve providing alternative solutions to the current processes and will include software and hardware recommendations as well as a proposal for a working interface with existing resources.

- Carrying out a comparative analysis of the alternative processes and the original routines. Flow charts, tables, process flows and other analytic tools will show relationships and deviations between the systems, thereby guiding the policy implementation decisions.

- Evaluation of alternative solutions' alignment with the specific objectives set out in the plan. This stage will involve rethinking the project intentions and comparing them with realized outcomes to assess efficiency.

- Evaluation of the ethical, legal, social and economic implications of the alternatives through a comprehensive cost-benefit analysis.

- Developing a proposal for implementing recommendations and following up the project to enable quality improvement.

RESOURCES AND CONSTRAINTS

The plan will involve the purchase of additional materials as well as the hiring of support staff. The major resources will be assigned as follows:

- Personnel—the category will involve all people contracted in the roll-out process, including software support teams, simulation teams, project evaluation teams, engineers in various capacities, technical teams and other necessary personnel.

- Partners—these may be governments, government-sponsored partners, nongovernment organizations and private investment agencies, among others.

- Equipment—includes facilities and computers, software, and related purchases.

- Legal and regulatory infrastructure intended for the implementation of information technology.

CONSTRAINTS

The project expects barriers to the legalization framework for integration of IT in healthcare standards. This opposition is expected mainly from medical practitioners' unions, software developers and others whose interests may be affected by this implementation. In addition, initial installation costs that pertain to individual healthcare institutions may be met with opposition from the concerned units, especially upcoming low-capital care units or those already using alternative IT services different from those suggested by this plan. In addition, the long period of time required for this project implementation may be challenged by the rapidly changing IT platform.[5]

STRATEGIES AND ACTIONS

The formation of a research group to develop stable and exhaustively adaptable software support for the global interoperability platform will facilitate the linking of all software systems and the analysis of multiple inputs. The research group's responsibilities could include:

- Convening a task force to explore the state of health IT implementation.

- Gathering and organizing data regarding the current operational statistics in the average care facility.

- Establishing an operational platform that member organizations will adapt in order to access global healthcare IT services, including legal documentation and an associated regulatory framework.

- Evaluation of the framework's success and pilot simulating to test its operability.

- Overseeing implementation of the new IT platform.

WORK PLAN ACCOUNTABILITY

The resources available for the implementation of a proposal will be regulated and governed by a project management committee that will be responsible for budgetary allocations, expenditure monitoring and accounts reconciliation. In addition, time management will be essential in order to complete the four phases of the project implementation within the specified time frame of three years.

■ Current Clinical Processes

Operations and processes in the healthcare sector can be analyzed in four broad categories, that is, administrative and financial, operational, process flow, and standardization. Generally, the hospital industry scores below average in terms of IT adoption. According to research conducted by the Lewin Group in North America in 2007, only about 2.5% of revenues were spent on IT in the hospitals sector. In addition, physicians invested even less in IT (1.5%).[6] In the year 2012, however, most healthcare institutions reported the implementation of some form of IT. According to a study done by the Healthcare Tech Review website, most respondent institutions will concentrate on developing their already existing IT infrastructure rather than implementing an additional one. In addition, staff training in IT implementation is a significant focus for a number of facilities. According to the survey, only 28% of respondent institutions allocated more than 10% of their revenues to IT implementation, despite the high cross-industry focus on IT implementation.

The majority of units reported increased investment in data storage equipment, but very few are willing to purchase high-cost imaging systems and tablets. The Healthcare Tech Review survey found that there was a variation in the EHR implementation related to unit size, with 85% of mid-to-large hospitals and other nonprofit care facilities with more than 400 beds reporting the implementation of some form of health record storage and retrieval system. Smaller nonprofit institutions had a higher EHR adoption rate of 87% and reported document management systems (DMSs) as their first priority and EHR as their second. Mid-to-large institutions still reported EHR system implementation as their major focus. Tablets, which are a new, more convenient technology for network access and document portability on the move, have become an important technology option for most industries. However, healthcare units have accepted this technology in varying degrees, and generally to a lesser extent than other industry sectors. Also, 40% of the respondents have used tablets in their operations. Mid-to-large care units reported 27% tablet use. Profit-making, independent healthcare providers were the least interested in the use of tablets. Respondents said they were using tablets in the following ways: accessing EHR records (72%), clinical decision support (39%), use of medical applications (28%), accessing network e-mail (59%), digital imaging (36%), electronically supported drug prescription (23%), laboratory work (18%), and medical bill and other financial service access and preparation (18%). The respondents were required to list their top priorities for the period 2012 to 2013 with respect to IT implementation, and the most important priorities were:

- Development of EHR systems and their maintenance;

- Staff training and development to meet IT implementation standards;

- Updating equipment to enable imaging functions, including replacement of analog systems;

- Adjusting to comply with HIPAA regulations and standards; and

- Installing increased of storage capacities, including data servers and cloud computing space.

The respondents also listed the following as mid-level priorities in the year 2012:

- Installing telehealth facilities to aid in remote diagnosis, prescription and patient follow-up;

- Implementing document management systems as well as practice management systems; and

- Implementing administrative and billing systems, including revenue cycle management systems.

The priorities that were generally given low ratings were as follows:

- Installing of newer wireless technology;

FIGURE 3-2. **Process 1: Laboratory Results Patient Information Process**

- Hiring IT implementation staff; and

- Acquiring new tablet devices.

With regard to their intended budgeting changes from 2012 to 2013, 36% expected their budgetary allocations to remain the same, while 28% expected their IT-related expenses to rise by 10% or more. Also, 25% stated that their IT budgets were expected to rise as much as 10%, 6% expected reductions in IT budgets of more than 10%, and 2% expected reductions of less than 10%. In this survey, 61% of respondents were medium-to-large hospitals and healthcare units; 29% were medium nonprofit-making institutions; 15% were profit-making private units; and 12% were profit-making independent care providers.

Figures 3-2 and 3-3 present typical process-flow diagrams that aid in identifying areas of two healthcare processes that are manageable using IT.[7]

Figure 3-2 shows the process flow for a typical client briefing about lab reports. A nurse will usually try to reach a patient more than four times in stated durations, usually from a few hours to a day. This process takes up time, delays other functions and, consequently, leads to fewer patients served per day. The proper IT implementation, even on the internal level, may allow convenient patient briefing and follow-up using trusted e-mail services, among other channels. Patients can usually be given the option to choose their preferred channel of communication before leaving the hospital or other care facility.

A typical referral process involves even more delay. The referral-patient booking process is diagrammed in Figure 3-3.[8] The figure clearly demonstrates delays introduced in

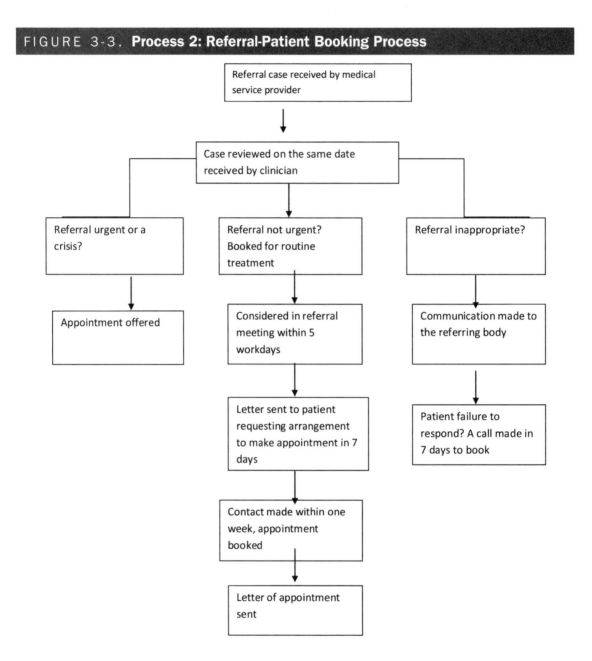

FIGURE 3-3. **Process 2: Referral-Patient Booking Process**

current healthcare systems due to lack of integration between the communication and decision-making systems involving care providers, referral centers and patients. In the flow diagram, it may be noted that a referral patient may wait up to two weeks between the date of referral and the date of appointment booking solely due to communication and work arrangement delays. Referrals may not appear urgent on the reported data sheet, but patients' situations may become aggravated during the waiting period when they are unable to obtain help. As a result, patient services are greatly compromised due to the systems' inefficiency. In addition, the lengthy waiting period can be greatly reduced if proper IT policies that incorporate remote meetings, such as video and audio conferencing, are implemented. The time spent between contacting a patient and receiving a response constitutes service degradation for the patient and revenue loss for the care provider.

A reduced number of patients get attended per day; therefore customer satisfaction levels decline. While authentication issues may be cited as the reason for insistence on the use of official letters by care providers, the bulk of the processes requiring care provider–client correspondence involve non-vital documents, such as requests for bookings. A possible method of bypassing this hindrance through the IT-based communication implementation is to develop a web-based communication and client-support system that would allow secure communication between the customer and the care provider. In this platform, customers would be able to receive e-mails and respond to booking notifications.

In addition, digital signing is a standard that is progressively being adopted by many industry sectors and is a concept that may be beneficial to health providers when they send documents requiring authorization or authentication. As an alternative, the use of registered mailing services may greatly reduce the feedback duration for sensitive medical cases. Apart from the operational perspective, billing systems and other workflow routines in most facilities are also very inefficient. The entire process, which includes a medical history review, booking to be attended by the physician, physician duration, prescription, queuing at the pharmacy and bill settlement, involves avoidable delays. These work stages can be sufficiently improved by computer-aided work management and decision making.

■ Current Healthcare IT Integration Status

The Healthcare Information Technology Standards Panel (HITSP) is the body in charge of seeking a way forward in healthcare IT standards integration. It enlists organizations, research facilities, vendors and healthcare providers to become actively involved in sponsoring and establishing a common standard for IT in healthcare. The organization was created in 2005 by the Office of the National Coordinator for Health Information Technology (ONC) and has standardized various protocols for EHRs and other clinical processes. One of its main priorities has been empowering consumers by allowing them access to their clinical information, such as medication history and lab results. It also seeks to integrate EHRs with laboratory systems and to streamline biosurveillance by defining standards for the exchange of information among healthcare providers and public health authorities.

In 2007, its main case uses included consumer access to information such as personal records transfer and access permissions grant. It also included emergency response services, medication management, and care facilities quality survey. In its last major release on January 20, 2010, HITSP laid out an interoperability program for North American healthcare institutions.[9] This record features a joint collaboration involving 498 system architects who tested more than 150 software applications for healthcare IT formulated by 104 HITSP members and partners.[10] In this forum, hundreds of system architects put a variety of administrative, operational, EHR and other software applications through rigorous tests with the goal of enabling standards-based interoperability. The results, however, were not documented, and as yet, no universally accepted healthcare IT backbone structure is in place. Best put, HITSP succeeded in formulating integrated healthcare IT protocols that are used regionally, typically in North America but not universally.

■ Deficiencies in Current IT Healthcare Practices

From the discussion provided above regarding process flows in the healthcare sector's IT policies and practices, it can be seen that there are major obstacles to customer satisfaction, healthcare business profitability and industry integration. These obstacles, which are restricting the sector's potential growth, will be analyzed in this section based on the industry's key performance indicators (KPIs). Client satisfaction through good services and support, business growth through revenue generation, efficient service process arrangement, and proper implementation integration can be attained through the corporate initiative.

PATIENT SUPPORT AND SATISFACTION

Unnecessarily high numbers of patients leave healthcare units without treatment due to long waits for service. Physicians see fewer patients per day when lengthy delays are caused by lack of proper equipment. Such slow systems also lead to extra work for the available personnel, which causes degradation in service quality. Proper patient support and safety also have a correlation with employee retention. When healthcare workers are overwhelmed, they tend to perform more poorly and have higher exit rates than workers in places where IT supports workflow management.

REDUCTION IN REVENUE GENERATION

Many healthcare systems are not efficient in revenue generation, and there is a possibility for improvement through IT innovation. Delays in customer service lead to low numbers of attended patients per day, which results in revenue losses. In addition, many patients leave unattended, which leads to business loss. On top of this, healthcare facilities lose potential clients who might have been referred by existing customers if they had not been annoyed by long wait times. In addition to losing business, healthcare units incur extra expenses due to overtime work by doctors and nurses when workloads are heavy. These increased operational expenses and reduced business revenue contribute to overall reduction in business profitability. Inefficient facilities also require a significantly higher number of workers to cope with the physical workflow and lack of integration, which results in extra costs.[11]

PRESCRIPTION ERRORS

The current healthcare system does not fully utilize software-supported decision making for drug prescriptions, even though it would greatly enhance the checking of prescriptions to ensure proper diagnosis support, drug type and dosage. This has resulted in numerous prescription errors, which may lead to adverse patient reactions and deaths. Improper prescriptions have also led to an increase in drug-related claims, legal penalties, license withdrawals and other challenges that could be avoided by proper IT support.

INDUSTRY STANDARDIZATION

HITSP did not manage to achieve a global platform for the standardization of healthcare IT policies and procedures. This has led to the loss of tremendous opportunities to improve interoperability, client support, data sharing and long-distance referrals. In addition, it has led to losses due to the time and resources wasted on attempted integration. This situation could be significantly changed if sustainable policy frameworks could be laid down by IT experts and enforced by government to expand the implementation of IT for the integration of Medicare.

■ Alternative Approaches to Current Healthcare Processes

To increase revenue, provide a seamless link between facilities and regions, and improve the patient experience in healthcare workflows, certain IT-based procedures can be implemented. The following section explores these alternatives according to the deficiency area.

INDUSTRY STANDARDIZATION ALTERNATIVES

HITSP made a lot of positive achievements in IT integration in the last decade. However, it did not attain a globally acceptable mandate that would standardize IT in healthcare. While there are numerous challenges in such an attempt, the organization could still work toward this accomplishment through different avenues.[12] The 2010 forum it held did not come up with proper directions for integration, partly, due to the fact that instead of working from a common platform, individual members congregated to test their individual software options in a joint way. A worthwhile suggestion in this regard is for the HITSP organization to bring together all industry players in a bid to develop a joint platform from scratch, as opposed to testing different existing software which may meet many operational and legal challenges if adopted. During the 2010 meeting, for instance, the forum convened nearly 500 software engineers from individual development initiatives. It would be better if the organization commissioned these software engineers to work out and develop a new integrated system that would meet a cross section of market needs. This platform software would be such as to link with all major existing software and hardware configurations in the market, such as EHRs, DMSs, and imaging programs, among others.

ALTERNATIVE WAYS TO REDUCE PRESCRIPTION ERRORS

Unlike the global integration challenge, prescription errors can be handled from a local perspective while awaiting the market standards integration. Many software applications are dedicated to prescription information and decision-support systems. Avoidance of adverse drug effects is one major KPI that can be addressed by IT implementation in the healthcare sector. One such software category is called the clinical decision-support system, which provides updated information regarding recommendations for prescriptions to nurses, physicians and other qualified healthcare workers. This system can be integrated with the EHR and CPOE systems in order to perform a proper scenario analysis with appropriate patient backup before a provider writes a prescription. Many commercially available software options offer this functionality.

ALTERNATIVE PROCESSES FOR REVENUE GENERATION

Financial processes are, perhaps, the easiest to simulate in IT process integration due to their general nature and resemblance to other industries' financial processes. Revenue generation draws primarily from workflow optimization, which mainly seeks to reduce query time and thus queue time, reduce waiting time through the implementation of fast patient data retrieval and diagnostic support, and reduce laboratory scheduling and patient briefing time by enhancing fast decision-relay procedures and online client information alternatives. Online support may be an easy way for patients to obtain their lab results electronically signed by their care providers without having to wait in queue. Such a system is not out of reach and may be developed by most modern web applications. In addition to saving time and encouraging more customers, an IT-based process would lead to higher levels of perceived efficiency, better customer experiences and satisfaction and, therefore, more referrals.

This chain of flow would, in turn, generate more revenue and lead to higher growth rates. Many software applications have support for flow management, and most of them do not require very high initial investments in comparison to the average capital requirements of a modern healthcare facility. In a 2008 study of healthcare IT implementation effects conducted at Banner Health, a Phoenix-based healthcare establishment with 20 branches and a value of $3.3 billion, an integrated software model called the Intel HIT Value Model was applied in ordinary hospital processes to see the changes that the use of IT would bring to the operational and administrative processes. The Intel HIT Value Model led to an 84% decrease in admissions for adverse drug reactions, 21.9% fewer medical claims, a 15% reduction in nurse turnover, a 5.3% reduction in overtime claims, a 96% reduction in document storage costs per 1,000 records, and a 17.8% reduction in pharmacy costs (Digital Health Group, 2008).

■ Comparative Analysis of Alternatives

This section will summarize the current versus expected status of various aspects of a healthcare IT implementation.

Intended achievements attributable to the new system implementation are presented in Table 3-1 and supported by various research into IT-related healthcare practices. While the extent to which key industry players may benefit from the implementation of these new IT practices may vary, it is likely that the net results will be beneficial.[5] In addition, the capital implications of implementing IT-based healthcare-support systems are within investment range, with the possible exception of the industry standardization by HITSP, which may necessitate costly software and support hardware in the future. Such investment costs may be expected to be levied on any registering healthcare facility that wishes to be admitted in the HITSP online facilities catalog. However, in the long term those expenditures should be recoverable from the benefits obtained from global healthcare interoperability.

■ Proposal Evaluation

This section reviews the proposed solutions to the healthcare IT integration problem. The organizational business plan for most healthcare facilities has four major objectives: patient satisfaction, revenue generation, efficient processes that cut costs and increase profits, and conformity to industry standards. The proposed solution model meets all those requirements. First, customer satisfaction is achieved through efficient processes that reduce delay time, enhance the customer experience and offer good follow-up on patient issues. Second, revenue generation is enhanced through shortened staff time spent per patient, which leads to increased daily patient attendance figures. Third, efficiency in the process flows reduces work duplication and improves service quality, both of which increase revenue generation through cost cutting. Fourth, the proposal expressly seeks to establish a platform for global standardization of healthcare

TABLE 3-1. Comparative Analysis of Core Processes in Healthcare		
Variables	**Current Status**	**IT-Enhanced Status**
Patient Service	Lengthy queue times, typically 20 minutes	Queue times reduced by up to 5 times
	Long durations for record retrieval	Instant record retrieval
	Long waits for lab reports, prescriptions and correspondence	Shortened lab report delays, instant prescription information and instant messaging
Service Processes	Manually coordinated	Computer simulated and optimized
	Delays and inefficiency in processes	Very efficient monitoring
	Duplicated work and delayed completion	Proper process scheduling
	Lack of feedback, rigid decision making	Decisions based on feedback with continuous dynamic optimization
Erroneous Prescriptions	Prevalent errors, with numerous legal and financial implications	Greatly reduced number of prescription errors and minimal revenue loss
	High admission rates for adverse drug effects	Greatly reduced admissions due to adverse drug effects
	Capacity limited by number of prescription-related admissions	More capacity for new cases due to reduction of adverse drug effects
Industry Standardization	Highly localized	Universally available
	Business losses due to lack of interoperability	Enhanced business due to interoperability
	Limited data access	Optimized data access

IT processes. In summary, the proposed solutions enhance the general business requirements and objectives for the average healthcare provider.

PROPOSAL'S IMPACT ON HEALTHCARE SYSTEMS

This proposal will have several effects on existing and future healthcare systems. Even though the envisioned long-term effects are calculated to be positive, the proposal may lead to certain negative effects. First, integration of a global healthcare IT system is expected to destabilize local systems already in place in various market segments. For instance, the North American Medicare fraternity has already developed foundational strategies in healthcare IT through the mandate of HITSP. This scenario may not be replicated in world markets, where healthcare may be provided using different IT standards and regulations. The introduction of a unitary system may lead to investment losses for investors using noncompatible systems. The second effect is that the healthcare sector may experience growth in sales and revenues resulting from integrated process flows and efficient service delivery.

Similarly, annual profits are expected to rise due to the increase in revenue and a reduction in operational expenses. Integration in global healthcare IT procedures is likely to improve access to documents and records by various medical service providers during patient care. Easy retrieval of medical records will lead to improved quality of care and more precise diagnoses. A possible negative effect, however, is the greater vulnerability of patient records and the increased possibility of privacy and safety violations when records can be accessed in a number of places by various medical personnel. Table 3-2 provides a cost-benefit analysis for the enhanced IT project.

■ Cost-Benefit Analysis

The stakeholders who stand to gain or lose due to this policy implementation are healthcare facilities, patients, medical practitioners' representative bodies, drug and medical equipment manufacturers, governments, HITSP and related authorities, as well as computer equipment and software manufacturers and vendors. The expected cost/benefit elements include finance, service quality, control and time, among others. The important variables to be considered in the analysis are the time of implementation, cost of implementation, alternatives to the proposal, impact on stakeholders, impact on external parties, sustainability versus running costs per year, and value of time to be used in the implementation.

The anticipated outcome of the cost/benefit analysis predicts a continuous reduction in investment costs and a net increment in revenue generation for manufacturers of products that support or can be adapted to the new standard, healthcare facilities, and

TABLE 3-2. **Cost-Benefit Analysis of Proposed Healthcare IT Implementation**		
Variables	**Costs**	**Benefits**
Financial implications	• Internal equipment and software upgrade	• Increased revenues of up to 50% per year
	• Licensing fees • Loss of investment for users of non-standard applications	• Access to the global interoperability platform
Customers	• Possible compromise of privacy and safety due to malicious information access and manipulation	• Improved services, care and access to records • Reduction of prescription errors and resources wasted due to adverse drug effects
Healthcare practitioners' unions and associated regulatory authorities	• Deregulation and possible structural realignment, with financial and investment losses	• Increased long-term gains per member • Strengthened union due to merger of healthcare practitioners after global standardization
Drug and medical equipment manufacturers and related bodies	• Possible losses in equipment standardization, but generally minimal negative effects	• Better policy implementation due to globalization of standards • Less counterfeiting and associated losses • Possibility of forming stronger representative bodies
Governments	• Reduced control of medical and healthcare practices for member states	• Increased diplomatic ties • Better availability of globally competitive healthcare standards for citizens
HITSP	• Reduced control and possible realignment of the structure to include international representation • Possible disbandment	• Achievement of core objective of international standardization of healthcare IT procedures

TABLE 3-2. *Continued*		
Variables	**Costs**	**Benefits**
Hardware and software developers and manufacturers	• Possible loss of existing contracts • Loss of business for companies whose products fail to support the new standards	• Numerous opportunities for new developments and increase in sales

drug and medical equipment manufacturers. Similarly, the net long-term outcome for the patient is better service and greater satisfaction.

PROPOSAL SENSITIVITY ANALYSIS

The proposed IT implementation may exhibit various levels of sensitivity to different stakeholders at different times and also to all stakeholders over the course of time. The key element in the project implementation is the changing technology standards. The success of the implementation depends on the availability of standard operational processes in the external environment, such as credit transfer systems for bill settlement and global Internet and network communication protocols such as IPv4 or IPv6, among other backbone infrastructure. These standards may change, affecting the operational capability of the proposal. The project's sensitivity to these challenges or changes in the external environment will rely on the establishment of a support team to ensure conformity of the project's various elements to changing standards. The cost of the project's maintenance will be incorporated into the proposed annual subscription funds obtainable from each member.

OTHER EXTERNAL FACTORS

Other external factors that may challenge the new system's operability include government regulation and the global economy. These challenges are not expected to pose serious threats to the project, since standardized healthcare IT is an international initiative with strong backing, and therefore it is unlikely to be affected by individual member decisions. On the contrary, proper legislation will be formulated to ensure that interests of members are protected in accordance with international law in cases of disbandment, member pull-out and external legal suits, among other unforeseen occurrences. With regard to the project's sensitivity to the global economy, it may be assumed that the long-term capital implications of standardization will be spread among the various stakeholders, making it unlikely that individual members would be greatly affected by a global economic downturn.

■ Summary

Analysis indicates that the proposed implementation of a globally integrated healthcare IT infrastructure is a viable project with no equal or better alternatives. The project shows net gains in the long term for all stakeholders and is sufficiently positively sensitive to major environmental challenges. It should therefore be implemented.

PROJECT PROPOSAL FOR GLOBAL INTEGRATION OF HEALTHCARE IT PROCEDURES

Project Title: Global Integration of Healthcare IT Procedures

Project Manager: HITSP or any other appointee of the international community of healthcare procedures

Project Period: Total project period—3 years

Beneficiaries: The world healthcare fraternity, patients and other customers, global society

PROJECT SUMMARY

This project proposal is aimed at integrating healthcare IT practices to allow for interconnectivity between various localized care providers in terms of enabling secure information sharing, seamless connectivity between various equipment and software applications, enhancement of efficiency in the process flow, and improvement of client service quality through good and timely service delivery. The project features internal and external elements. The internal elements involve internal process flow enhancement and the responsibility of all member facilities to meet the required international standards, while the external elements involve global integration of IT standards and a joint venture between all aspiring members to be implemented through a trustee body, such as HITSP or any other delegated committee.

BACKGROUND

The healthcare fraternity has been facing numerous challenges in its effort to expand the acceptance of IT to increase efficiency and service delivery. The challenges are brought by variations in software vendor types, geographical localization of policies and lack of a global regulatory body. As a result, revenue is lost, customer service is poor, erroneous prescriptions are prevalent and decision support is lacking in the sector.

PROJECT OBJECTIVES

The project seeks to upgrade or replace existing localized service practices in the healthcare sector through the incorporation of IT-supported streamlining incentives to improve service quality. It also seeks to work out a platform for the formation of a task force that will oversee the formation of a body to implement standardization of healthcare practices, notably patient services, records storage and retrieval, and clinical decision-support systems, among others.[13] The project also seeks to implement a global consortium for medical practices with a view to enabling information sharing, pooling research and development articles, facilitating exchange programs and cataloguing healthcare facilities.

PROJECT EXPECTATIONS

The project expects to have an operational global standard for healthcare IT practices in three years. It expects to have an operational, secure and trustworthy patient record platform for all participating members in three years. In addition, the project expects to have an online medical practitioners' consortium with information regarding research, prescription data and technology application, among other topics.

TARGET POPULATION

The general target population is the global community. In addition, some specific target groups include healthcare institutions, patients, equipment manufacturers, sources of financing, medical practice regulatory bodies and governments.

PROJECT ACTIVITIES

- The formation of a research group to develop stable and exhaustively adaptable software support for the global interoperability platform that will be able to link all software systems and analyze multiple inputs.

- Convening a task force to explore the state of health IT implementation.

- Gathering and organizing data regarding the current operational statistics in the average care facility.

- Establishing an operational platform that member organizations will adapt in order to access global healthcare IT services, including legal documentation and the associated regulatory framework.

- Evaluation of framework success and pilot simulation to test operability.

- Implementation.

Table 3-3 indicates the activity timeline for the proposed project. Shaded regions would indicate the start and end times for each phase. Some activities will run concurrently.

PROJECT MANAGEMENT

Table 3-4 shows the initial budget proposal. Adjustments may be made during any stage in response to variations in operating costs, legalization, tax adjustments or any other contingencies.

TABLE 3-3. Implementation Plan for IT Integration Project							
Activity	**Duration**	**Time Frame**					
		6 months	**1 year**	**1.5 years**	**2 years**	**2.5 years**	**3 years**
Backbone infrastructure development	1.5 years						
Task force industry survey	2 years						
Laying out operational platform	1.5 years						
Evaluation of operational success	6 months						

TABLE 3-4. Project Budget			
Item	**Cost**	**Urgency**	**Comments**
Software development and associated support systems	$15 million	Initial phase 1.5 years	
Staff costs	$1 million	Continuous	
Industry survey	$1.5 million	Initial phase 1.5 years	
Implementation	$150 million	Mid stage 2.5–3 years	
Support and maintenance	$2 million	Continuous	

OTHER RESOURCE REQUIREMENTS

Personnel

The project will contract 500 software developers and protocol engineers, 200 industry survey and analysis personnel, 150 permanent support staff and 150 support services staff. Total personnel requirement is initially estimated at 1,000.

Equipment

Initial equipment estimates for the project include 2,000 personal computers, 10 main servers, associated network infrastructure such as cabling, switches and access points, as well as transport for an average of 1,000 workers daily.

Space

The project operation requires 330,000 cubic feet of space with associated office furniture.

PROJECT MANAGEMENT

The project will be overseen by three mid-level supervisors, one each from the software development division, the market survey division and the implementation division. The three supervisors will report to the chief project coordinator, who will be the project spokesperson in external matters and will oversee the project's development and implementation. The project expects to contract with various suppliers to provide and install building- and office-partitioning materials and computer equipment, and to manage logistics. These contracted companies will work independently but report to the chief project coordinator, who may delegate tasks for quality assurance, logistics control, public relations and other functions, if necessary.

PROJECT RISK ASSESSMENT

The identified risk factors for the project include global economic fluctuations, government policies and technological changes. In terms of impact and exposure, technological changes pose the most significant risk, especially changes in current international standards for such areas as communication, networking and online client support. The currently applicable transmission control protocol and Internet protocol (TCP/IP) are IPv4 and IPv6, which may change with time. Global economic fluctuation is the second greatest risk, and the effects of government policies are the third. To cope with changes in technology, the project will retain support teams of software and standards specialists who will continually monitor and upgrade the project platform to conform to industry standards. The likelihood that a significant economic downturn would affect the project is low, because the project's economic risk is widely spread and its capital range is moderate. Furthermore, the fact that the project is internationally founded shields it from government challenges.

BUSINESS VALUE ANALYSIS

The project has both quantifiable and nonquantifiable values. The quantifiable value involves the revenue gains to the healthcare, IT and associated sectors. In addition, patients will benefit from improved service, and quality of service will benefit the wider global community as it spreads across many countries.

QUALITY IMPROVEMENT

Quality improvement in the healthcare sector utilizes the same customer-inspired method that is used in the service sector. This approach targets customers' perceptions and is geared toward customer satisfaction.[14] The project will also continually take advantage of available process-optimization tools, such as business intelligence, to enhance process efficiencies and tap developing technologies. Given that healthcare is a customer-focused industry, monitoring customer trends will provide the necessary data to improve the business model.

Change management during project implementation will focus on changes in hardware, software specifications, communication equipment and project documentation. These changes will be handled through a change advisory board consisting of representative members of the three divisions, as well as the project coordinator and necessary external advisors. The board may perform such functions as reviewing requests for change, reporting necessary changes and managing any changes that may arise.[14]

■ References

1. Morrissey J. Capital crunch eats away at IT. *Modern Healthcare*. February 23, 2004; 34(8):32-62.

2. Armoni A. *Effective Healthcare Information Systems*. Hershey, PA: IRM Press; 2002.

3. Spekowius G, Wendler T. *Advances in Healthcare Technology Shaping the Future of Medical Care*. Dordrecht, the Netherlands: Springer, 2006.

4. HandsOn Network. *Developing a Work Plan*. Atlanta. Accessed November 25, 2012.

5. Tyrrell S. *Using Information and Communication Technology in Healthcare*. Abingdon, Oxon, UK: Radcliffe Medical, 2002.

6. Shoniregun C, Dube K, Mtenzi F. *Electronic Healthcare Information Security*. New York: Springer, 2010.

7. National Council of State Boards of Nursing, Inc. *New Nurse Toolkit*. Accessed November 25, 2012.

8. Hertfordshire Partnership NHS Foundation Trust. Schedule 4—Patient Booking. Accessed November 25, 2012.

9. HIMSS. Engaged in Interoperability at IHE 2010 North America Connectathon. January 20, 2010. http://www.himss.org/asp/contentredirector. asp?contentid=73001. Accessed November 25, 2012.

10. IHE. IHE Connectathons: A Unique Testing Opportunity. http://www.ihe.net/ connectathon/. Accessed November 25, 2012.

11. Duplaga M, Zielinski K, Ingram D. *Transformation of Healthcare with Information Technologies*. Amsterdam: IOS Press, 2004.

12. Bates D, Gawande A. Improving safety with information technology. *New England Journal of Medicine*. 2003;348(25):2526-2534.

13. Institute of Medicine. *Preventing Medication Errors*. Washington, DC: National Academies Press, 2006.

14. Moyers H, Shaw J, New W. Choosing a Quality/Performance Improvement Methodology. Accessed November 25, 2012.

■ Bibliography

Armoni A. *Effective Healthcare Information Systems*. Hershey, PA: IRM Press, 2002.

Bates D, Gawande A. Improving safety with information technology. *New England Journal of Medicine*. 2003;348(25):2526-2534.

Duplaga M, Zielinski K, Ingram D. *Transformation of Healthcare with Information Technologies*. Amsterdam: IOS Press, 2004.

HandsOn Network. Developing a Work Plan. Accessed November 25, 2012.

Hertfordshire Partnership NHS Foundation Trust. Schedule 4—Patient Booking. http://www.hertspartsft.nhs.uk/_uploads/documents/the-trust/trust-papers/ foundation-trust-contract/patient-booking.pdf. Accessed November 25, 2012.

HIMSS. Engaged in Interoperability at IHE 2010 North America Connectathon. http://www.himss.org/ASP/ContentRedirector. asp?ContentId=73001&type=HIMSSNewsItem. Accessed November 25, 2012.

IHE. IHE Connectathons: A Unique Testing Opportunity. http://www.ihe.net/ Connectathon/index.cfm. Accessed November 25, 2012.

Institute of Medicine. *Preventing Medication Errors*. Washington, DC: National Academies Press; 2006.

Morrissey J. Capital crunch eats away at IT. *Modern Healthcare.* February 23, 2004; 34(8):32-62.

Moyers H, Shaw J, New W. Choosing a Quality/Performance Improvement Methodology. http://www.shawresources.com/ artchoosingqualityimprovementmethod.html. Accessed November 25, 2012.

National Council of State Boards of Nursing. New Nurse Toolkit. http://transitiontopractice.org/files/module4/QI%20-%20Flow%20Chart.pdf. Accessed November 25, 2012.

Shoniregun CA, Dube K, Mtenzi F. *Electronic Healthcare Information Security.* New York: Springer, 2010.

Spekowius G, Wendler T. *Advances in Healthcare Technology Shaping the Future of Medical Care.* Dordrecht, the Netherlands: Springer, 2006.

Tyrrell S. *Using Information and Communication Technology in Healthcare.* Abingdon, Oxon, UK: Radcliffe Medical, 2002.

CHAPTER 4

Systems Design

David H. Miller, CPHIMS

LEARNING OBJECTIVES

At the conclusion of this chapter, the reader will be able to:

☑ Describe the key elements of creating a business case.

☑ Define and describe the differences between the request for information (RFI) and request for proposal (RFP).

☑ Describe what factors to consider in making a buy-versus-build decision.

☑ Describe the processes, techniques and deliverables when a system is developed in-house.

☑ Describe what factors to consider in making a best-of-breed versus tightly integrated system purchasing decision.

■ Introduction

The *Dictionary of Computing* defines *system design* as "the activity of proceeding from an identified set of requirements for a system to a design that meets those requirements."[1] System design depends upon the definition of *system*, which, according to the *Oxford English Dictionary*, means "a set or assemblage of things connected, associated, or interdependent, so as to form a complex unity."[2] Healthcare IT systems today take that complexity to a new level in function and interoperability. These systems must support advanced clinical functionality, patient accounting, and financial accounting and have been doing this for years. But now, the systems must support newer functions demanded by new healthcare regulations, medical devices, mergers, and acquisitions, as well as address changes and advances in the information technology industry. One author suggests that the complexity of an IT system, with thousands or millions of lines of code, coupled with the personalities of the people using it, the organizational dynamics, and the processes involved conspire to make system design extremely difficult.[3] A key relationship exists between people, processes, and the organization.

Every organization conducts its business in different ways, depending upon its vision, mission, history, government regulations, corporate culture and other factors. An organization's way of doing business becomes its business process, which may be well defined or more loosely defined. New methods of defining and improving business processes, such as Lean and Six Sigma, appeared and have gained adoption over the past 10 to 20 years. Business process management represents a method to understand an organization's processes and then apply this understanding to the design of a system.

The system design team drives the deliverables, and the team members required will be discussed in this chapter. The design team takes the system requirements from systems analysis and translates them into detailed technical specifications for the system. Some design teams benefit greatly by focusing on usability. The emergence of business process reengineering (BPR) or business process management (BPM) in healthcare offers a new approach to system design.

The system being designed may be internally developed or purchased from a vendor, and the process for system design varies with these two options. Dealing with a vendor requires more formal processes, including requests for information (RFIs) and requests for proposals (RFPs). The RFI assists the design team in deciding whether to solicit an RFP for a commercial off-the-shelf (COTS) solution or develop the system internally, known as a buy-versus-build decision. When selecting a COTS solution, the decision will often include discussions of selecting a best-of-breed system that requires more integration between vendors or a single-vendor, more tightly integrated solution. The RFP represents the key deliverable of the system design team once a buy decision has been made.

■ Business Process Management

In order to design successful systems, organizations must define their business objectives, create a business case, then use workflow analysis and mapping to align their business processes to support those objectives. In defining its business objectives, an organization must follow three rules. The objectives[4]

1. Must be measurable and quantifiable;

2. Must have a time frame; and

3. Must be attainable.

For a hospital, an example could be that they would like to improve their admission time from two hours to one hour within the next year to improve patient satisfaction.

Creating a business case to support the objective involves defining a comprehensive view of the project as well as the financial justification and return on investment (ROI). The key elements of the business case include[5]

■ Executive summary

■ Situational analysis and problem statement

■ Project description

■ Solution overview

■ Solution detail

■ Solution alternatives

■ Costs

■ Benefits

■ Implementation timeline

■ Critical assumptions and risk assessment

■ SWOT (strengths, weaknesses, opportunities, threats) analysis

■ Conclusions and recommendations

One solution alternative is to utilize workflow mapping and analysis. Workflow mapping involves diagramming a current process from start to finish in the correct order, including all inputs and outputs to the process. This is typically known as the "as-is process." At this point, the workflow may be analyzed to look for improvements that can be made to meet the ROI.

■ Compatibility of System Components

Any healthcare enterprise today owns and continually purchases a plethora of hardware, software, network components and medical devices. The hardware may include laptop computers, servers and tablets, each running its own operating system that is not necessarily compatible with other operating systems. The application software that runs on these devices serves a variety of purposes, from patient accounting to payroll, laboratory, pharmacy, radiology, dietetics, and the list goes on and on. Network components include routers (wired and wireless), firewalls, and Internet connectivity. Networks today must support connectivity of devices within the enterprise, but patients and visitors also demand wi-fi access. Medical devices such as ultrasounds, MRIs, critical care devices, and even blood pressure cuffs all provide information digitally and must connect to the network as well.

Organizations should define a process by which purchases of any of these components should be reviewed by the IT department for compatibility. Remember that compatibility does not mean that devices or software will work out of the box. There may be system integration involved to incorporate the device onto the network. For example, a new radiology information system may connect to the existing network from a physical standpoint but may need to have a Health Level 7 (HL7) interface customized in order to talk to the existing electronic health record system. This process dictates close cooperation between the IT department and procurement/purchasing so that IT reviews purchases to avoid such hidden costs of integration.

■ Standards Compliance

Healthcare providers face a huge number of external standards from government and industry in addition to their own internal standards. Some of these affect the entire organization and others affect just one department. Some countries even dictate which vendor's IT system the organization must purchase. ASTM International, HL7, Digital Imaging and Communications in Medicine (DICOM), and other international organizations publish many standards related to healthcare IT. The Institute of Electrical and Electronics Engineers (IEEE) publishes standards for wired and wireless networking used by most countries in the world. Just as an enterprise must have a process to address compatibility of system components, it must also develop a process to address standards compliance. Given the huge number of standards, this is not a simple effort. There must be an overlap between business process and compliance management. System design should attempt to address standards by the clear definition of technical specifications.

■ Process to Address Industry Trends

With the extensive changes occurring in healthcare and technology, a process must exist or be created to evaluate and incorporate industry, technology, infrastructure, legal, and regulatory trends. This process must address areas that in the past were governed by departments other than IT. The digitization of telephone systems means that these systems generally share the same networks as IT and have become a part of the IT organization. Medical devices such as electrocardiographs, ultrasound and magnetic resonance imaging devices now generate millions of bytes of medically relevant data and must be integrated into the electronic patient record. The purchase of such devices must include IT participation to ensure that they can be integrated without an additional large purchase of professional services.

■ Structure of the System Design Team

The members of the system design team may vary based upon the complexity of the project. A project sponsor, one of the team's key members, should kick off the project with the team and help determine the business goals and how those goals should be measured. Once the team has been established and the goals are clearly defined, the sponsor may not need to be involved in more detail-oriented design meetings. Below is a comprehensive list of members, some of whom may be excluded:

- Project sponsor

- Project manager/leader

- Business analyst(s)

- Data/process modeler

- Technical lead/architect

- Biomedical engineers

- Application developers

- Quality assurance analysts

- Information security officer

- Stakeholders/users

- Legal counsel

- Procurement expert

■ Detailed Technical Specifications

The design team must create comprehensive, detailed technical specifications that not only cover the function of the system or applications, but also address non-functional issues such as information infrastructure. Some of the key areas of technical specifications that should be addressed are:

■ **System and network architecture**—Does the system have to fit into the organization's existing architectures or may it vary?

■ **Security and data encryption**—Does the system integrate into the organization's security standards?

■ **Disaster recovery**—What is the recovery time objective (RTO), or the time it will take to recover the system in a disaster? What is the recovery point objective (RPO), or to what point in time must the system be restored?

■ **Data conversion**—What are the data conversion options if converting from one system to another with different data models?

■ **Response times**—What are the expected response times and how will they be measured?

■ **System backups**—What are the backup options? How long will backups run?

■ **System monitoring**—How will the system be monitored? Will it fit into the organization's existing monitoring infrastructure?

■ **Change management**—How does the vendor of a newly purchased system handle changes? Is there a regular schedule, or is it done at customer convenience?

■ **Availability**—What are the availability requirements? What is the downtime associated with system upgrades?

■ **Time zone and daylight savings time support**—Does the system support multiple time zones, especially if the organization has facilities in different time zones? Are system outages required for spring or fall clock changing?

■ **Standards**—Does the system support integration standards such as HL7, ICD10, or DICOM?

■ **Government regulations**—Does the system meet current government regulations? What is the vendor commitment for turnaround of new regulations?

■ **System integration**—Will the system automatically integrate with the other healthcare systems and medical devices in the enterprise, or will it cost more to integrate it?

- **Usability**—Much focus is being placed on usability today, and that topic will be discussed in more detail below. Usability should include accessibility for persons with disabilities as well as the use of mobile devices.

- **Workflow definitions**—The definition of desired workflows is another key area of the design that will be discussed in more detail later in the chapter.

- **Data management**—Does the system fit the organization's data management policies and procedures for such functions as backup, recovery and archiving? Data management will also be discussed in more detail shortly.

USABILITY

Within the past 20 years, interest in usability has grown to the extent that the Usability Professionals' Association has 50 chapters around the world to promote usability concepts and techniques.[6] The HIMSS EHR Usability Task Force created the Health Usability Maturity Model.[7] It examines three non-healthcare usability models and uses common themes from those models to create a healthcare model with five phases:

- Phase 1: Unrecognized—Lack of awareness of usability;

- Phase 2: Preliminary—Sporadic inclusion of usability;

- Phase 3: Implemented—Recognized value of usability and small teams using it;

- Phase 4: Integrated—Benchmarks implemented and have dedicated user experience team; and

- Phase 5: Strategic—Business benefit well understood, mandated, budgeted and results used strategically in the organization.

The report documents how an organization can take itself from one phase to another and recommends the following tactics to expand usability within the organization:

- Include usability in contracts;

- Create feedback loops from users to vendors;

- Talk about tasks and workflows;

- Educate about ROI related to usability;

- Engage organizational leaders in usability;

- Include usability metrics on one project;

- Interview users to determine key usability issues;

- Compile evidence from usability assessments;

- Look for and document usability wake-up calls; and

- Find a business/organization driver supporting need for usability.

BUSINESS PROCESS REENGINEERING

Reengineering is the fundamental rethinking and radical redesign of business processes to achieve dramatic improvements in critical, contemporary measures of performance such as cost, quality, service and speed.[8] Many organizations today employ Lean or Six Sigma to reengineer their processes. Lean focuses on creating more value for customers with fewer resources.[9] Lean emphasizes the transformation of the entire organization by looking at the business issues of purpose, process, and people. Denver Health generated more than $135 million in financial benefit over a six-year period through the use of Lean processes and has even started its own Lean training program marketed to parties outside the organization.[10] Six Sigma strives to eliminate defects in processes to a level of 3.4 defects per million opportunities.[11] Six Sigma utilizes an acronym to improve processes known as DMAIC: define, measure, analyze, improve, control. Valley Baptist Health System in Harlingen, Texas, won numerous awards for its use of Six Sigma and lists almost 100 quality initiatives in progress on its website (http://www.valleybaptist.net/qualityInitiatives/harlingenInitiatives.htm).

Many vendors offer BPR tools today and some of the process modeling tools are available for free downloading. BPR has matured to the extent that there are industry standards for process modeling called Business Process Model Notation (BPMN) and even for transferring models from one vendor to another called XML Process Definition Language (XPDL). Some healthcare IT systems today include BPR software that can allow organizations to design their own processes. In 2010, the Chester County Hospital in West Chester, Pennsylvania, received a CMIO IT Innovators Award for a workflow that decreased catheter-associated urinary tract infections by 50%.[12]

INFORMATION INFRASTRUCTURE

The information infrastructure must be able to support today's business requirements and anticipate emerging or future business requirements. A current trend, known as BYOD (bring your own device) is one example of an emerging requirement prompted by doctors, nurses and other employees who want to use their own notebook computers, tablets or smartphones on the enterprise network. Most healthcare organizations today probably do not have the proper security and network infrastructure in place to support a BYOD strategy. A good example of a future business requirement is Internet Protocol version 6 (IPv6). Most healthcare organizations today utilize Internet Protocol 4 (IPv4). While most of today's applications do not support IPv6 yet, new infrastructure purchases, including new operating systems and network hardware, now support both, and organizations that make sure their new purchases have that capability will be well positioned for the future. Overall, an organization should have a process in place to examine or evaluate emerging trends and technologies. This evaluation should be done on a regular basis as new technologies emerge or existing technologies begin to be adopted. As part of the process, the organization should decide where it wants to be on the technology adoption curve (see Figure 4-1).

FIGURE 4-1. **Technology Adoption Curve** (From Moore GA. *Crossing the Chasm: Marketing and Selling High-tech Products to Mainstream Customers*. New York: Harper Collins Publishers, 2002.)

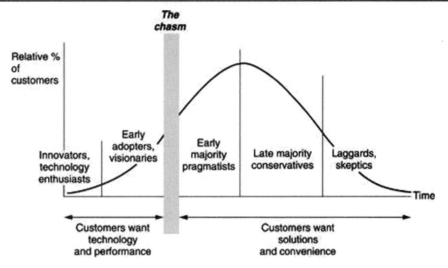

As more and more healthcare records are electronic, business continuity emerges as a key part of the IT infrastructure. Organizations must plan for various types of disasters, whether natural or man-made. Off-site storage of data becomes a minimal requirement. Many sites negotiate contracts with disaster recovery vendors to retain not only copies of data but also the capability to restore entire systems. Larger organizations may own multiple data centers in which they may mirror their data. Networks must be in place to access these remote sites. The business continuity plan must not only ensure that the remote sites are in place but also test the plan at frequent intervals to make certain that it can be executed.

DATA MANAGEMENT

Healthcare organizations must address a wide variety of issues related to their data. Data Management International (DAMA®) created a framework for data governance[13] that defines ten data management functions within the organization:

- Data governance—Planning, supervision and control over data management and use;

- Data architecture management—As an integral part of the enterprise architecture;

- Data development—Analysis, design, building, testing, deployment and maintenance;

- Database operations management—Support for structured physical data assets;

- Data security management—Ensuring privacy, confidentiality and appropriate access;

- Reference and master data management—Managing golden versions and replicas;

- Data warehousing and business intelligence management—Enabling access to decision support data for reporting and analysis;

- Document and content management—Storing, protecting, indexing and enabling access to data found in unstructured sources (electronic files and physical records);

- Metadata management—Integrating, controlling and delivering metadata; and

- Data quality management—Defining, monitoring and improving data quality.

The organization must define a process for addressing those data management functions. Then the system design team must ensure that the system fits into that process.

Now that the technical specifications have been completed, the system design team can proceed to the buy-versus-build decision. If the team is unsure whether or not a commercial product exists to meet the specifications, the next step should be to produce an RFI.

■ Creating a Request for Information

An RFI solicits background information on companies and their capabilities. It may be used to help decide whether vendors offer a solution to the healthcare IT need being addressed versus developing the solution in-house. A typical RFI includes the following sections, which were abstracted from an actual RFI released by the Veterans Health Administration[14]:

I. Introduction

- This section notes that the RFI is for information and planning purposes only and that no contracts will be offered.

II. Background

- This section describes the current environment.

III. Requirements

- This section clearly describes what the responding vendor must address. The specific RFI used in this example included requirements in the areas of:

  ☐ Project management support

  ☐ Reporting

  ☐ Development, integration, implementation, maintenance

  ☐ Training and education

  ☐ Adoption reporting

  ☐ User acceptance and field testing support

IV. Submittal Information

- Length of response requirements, such as maximum number of pages, font size and paragraph spacing (single vs. double)

- Responding company name, experience and qualifications

- Where, when and how to submit the proposal

■ Making a Buy-Versus-Build Decision

The design team should now have the information it needs to make the decision whether to build the system internally or proceed to the creation of an RFP for a buy decision.

The factors that influence the buy-versus-build decision include[15]:

- IT strategy—What is the overall strategy for IT? Are most systems internally developed or purchased?

- Core versus non-core systems—Is the system key to the success of the organization or ancillary?

- Commodity versus competitive advantage—Is the system a commodity, such as payroll or word processing, or specific to a healthcare line of business, such as a surgicenter?

- Maturity—Is the internal IT department mature enough for internal development? Is the market mature enough to have a wide choice?

- Requirements fit—Does the product meet the critical requirements?

- Cost and value—Does a product meet the cost requirements including implementation, support, maintenance, and upgrades? What are the ongoing maintenance costs of internally built solutions including retaining the knowledge of the developers?

- Time and timing—How long will it take to develop versus acquire? How long will it take to implement? How long will it take to get updates from the vendor versus in-house changes?

- Political factors—Does a particular vendor influence the decision? Does the project sponsor have a bias?

- Regulatory support—What is the track record of the vendor in providing regulatory support versus the experience meeting those requirements in-house?

- Platform—Does the vendor support the organization's preferred platforms, including hardware, network, security and infrastructure?

- Integration—How well will the vendor product integrate with other products in the organization's portfolio?

- Lifecycle cost estimate—What are the overall costs over five to ten years to deploy, implement and support the system?

After studying the above factors carefully, the design team can make the decision to build or buy.

PROCESS FOR A BUILD DECISION

Once a decision has been made to build the system, there must be changes to the membership of the design team to include more technical members, such as data modelers, technical architects and application developers. The State of New York Office of Information Technology Resources developed a guidebook that provides a good outline of the system design processes, techniques and deliverables when the system is developed in-house (Table 4-1).[16]

BUY DECISION: BEST-OF-BREED VERSUS TIGHTLY INTEGRATED SOLUTIONS

For decades, design teams lingered over the tough decision of selecting best-of-breed or single-vendor, tightly integrated solutions. Generally, smaller niche vendors develop best-of-breed systems because they can focus their resources on a small set of requirements for a specialized system to be used in, for example, a lab, radiology or emergency department. Larger vendors usually market tightly integrated systems since they have more resources to develop enterprise solutions that can meet a wide range of requirements, if not all. Among decision makers, preferences seem to have moved back and forth across the decades. Single-vendor decisions ruled the 1980s, while the pendulum swung back toward best-of-breed applications in the 1990s. Even though standards such as HL7 and DICOM had matured during the 1990s to assist in integrating best-of-breeds, individual vendors had their own interpretations of those standards that did not necessarily align. Healthcare IT departments had to hire integration analysts and purchase integration engines to enable such systems to talk to each other. Industry organizations such as Integrating the Healthcare Enterprise (IHE) evolved to promote integration between vendors, and IHE demonstrations at HIMSS national meetings still draw a crowd. Today, patient safety seems to have pushed the industry back toward single-vendor solutions that tightly integrate computerized practitioner order entry (CPOE), pharmacy and electronic medication administration records (eMAR).[17] The final decision should come from the RFP process.

TABLE 4-1: System Design Processes, Techniques and Deliverables When a System Is Developed In-house (Adapted from *New York State Project Management Guidebook.* New York State Office of Technology. http://www.cio.ny.gov/pmmp/guidebook2/index.htm. 2003.)		
Processes	**Techniques**	**Process Deliverables (Outcomes)**
Prepare for system design	Interviews Site walk-throughs	Established team and environment for system design
Define technical architecture	Interviews Document gathering and reviews Role/authorization analysis	Technical architecture
Define system standards	Interviews Brainstorming Policy and standards reviews	System standards
Create physical database	Formal walk-throughs Standard data definition languages Data administration techniques (data normalization, de-normalization)	Databases and system files
Prototype system components	Iterative prototypes/reviews Presentations Graphical user interface (GUI)/ report development tools	Prototype and proof of concept results
Produce technical specifications	Function decomposition Expressing logic: pseudo code, structured English, object-oriented logic Operational requirements assessment	Technical specifications

CREATING A REQUEST FOR PROPOSAL

If the decision is made to buy, then an RFP should be created to find an appropriate system on the market to meet the specified requirements. Here is an outline of a sample RFP that can be found on the HIMSS website[18]:

1. Request for proposal

    1.1 General contact information—Who should get the response?

    1.2 Background—What is the purpose of this RFP?

    1.3 Services requested—What is the application and services being requested?

    1.4 Technical questions—What is the hardware platform, operating system, etc.?

    1.5 Pre-bid conference call—For interested vendors, what are the date, time and details for a pre-bid conference call?

    1.6 Evaluation criteria—What are the criteria by which the proposal will be judged, such as proposer experience, reputation, financial stability, quality of submission, references, etc.?

    1.7 Selection process—What are the process and dates for reviewing proposals and responding to proposers?

    1.8 Addendums—Any other information that will be provided.

    1.9 Notable dates—What are dates for pre-bid call, close of questions, RFP submission and notice of award?

    1.10 Submission process—How can the proposal be submitted, including by e-mail, in person or by carrier, and who should receive it?

    1.11 Federal contractor—Insert this section if the requestor is a federal contractor.

2. Requested services/functions

    2.1 Detail of desired features

3. Deployment and development schedule

    3.1 What are the dates required to meet the requester's requirements?

4. Training/warranty

    4.1 What training and support are offered during the warranty period?

    4.2 What are the details of the warranty?

5. Professional services fees

    5.1 What are the fees for professional services during implementation?

    5.2 What are the fees after implementation?

6. References

    6.1 What references are available to contact who have done similar projects with the proposer?

The technical requirements represent the most important part of the RFP. The Mars Climate Orbital Mission spacecraft crashed because its software used metric units while the Mission Control software used English units. In the face of unclear requirements, some vendors may submit high bids to mitigate risks or to cause other vendors not to bid at all. When requirements are unclear, vendors make their own assumptions about what is being asked and submit vastly different bids based on those assumptions. Once a contract is signed, the differing assumptions of the vendor and the customer may lead to project delays, inability of the vendor to deliver or even litigation. When a contract gets to the point of litigation, unclear requirements make it much harder to plead a case.[19]

◼ Summary

Successful system design centers on the design team, which must include the proper members. The design team must create clear, documented technical specifications. Two ways in which the design team can produce such requirements are by examining usability and focusing on business processes. From the technical specifications, the team may generate an RFI to solicit industry input. This input can facilitate the buy-versus-build decision. If a build decision is made, the RFI can also assist the team to decide upon a best-of-breed versus a tightly integrated product. The team then focuses on the creation of the RFP, which will in turn lead to system selection as discussed in the next chapter.

◼ References

1. Daintith J. System design. A Dictionary of Computing. Encyclopedia.com. 2004. http://www.encyclopedia.com/doc/1O11-systemdesign.html. Accessed September 1, 2012.

2. System, n. OED Online. Oxford University Press; June 2012. http://www.oed.com/. Accessed August 11, 2012.

3. Berg M. Implementing information systems in health care organizations: myths and challenges. *Int J Med Inform*. December 2001. http://www.ijmijournal.com/article/S1386-5056(01)00200-3/fulltext. Accessed August 11, 2012.

4. How to set business goals and objectives 101: best practices for your business. Cojent Marketing and Communications. April 24, 2010. http://cojent7.wordpress.com/2010/04/24/how-to-set-business-goals-and-objectives-101-best-practices-for-your-small-business/. Accessed October 15, 2012.

5. Business case. BPR Online Learning Center. Prosci. http://www.prosci.com/business-case.htm. Accessed October 15, 2012.

6. About UXPA. User Experience Professionals Organization. http://www.usabilityprofessionals.org/uxpa/about/. Accessed September 23, 2012.

7. HIMSS Usability Task Force. Promoting usability in health organizations: initial steps and progress toward a healthcare usability maturity model. Healthcare Information and Management Systems Society. 2011. http://www.himss.org/content/files/HIMSS_Promoting_Usability_in_Health_Org.pdf. Accessed September 23, 2012.

8. Hammer M, Champy J. *Reengineering the Corporation: A Manifesto for Business Revolution.* New York: Harper, 1993.

9. What Is Lean? Lean Enterprise Institute. http://www.lean.org/WhatsLean/. Accessed September 24, 2012.

10. Denver Health Lean Academy. Denver Health. http://www.denverhealth.org/LEANAcademy/AboutLEANAcademy/CaseStudies.aspx. Accessed September 24, 2012.

11. What Is Six Sigma? iSix Sigma. http://www.isixsigma.com/new-to-six-sigma/getting-started/what-six-sigma/. Accessed September 24, 2012.

12. Stevens M. Health IT Innovation Awards: 5 health IT projects that improved care. *CMIO Magazine.* August 30, 2010. http://www.cmio.net/index.php?option=com_articles&view=article&id=23893:health-it-innovation-awards-5-health-it-projects-that-improved-care. Accessed August 18, 2012.

13. DAMA-DMBOK Functional Framework. Data Management International. September 10, 2008. http://www.dama.org/files/public/DAMA-DMBOK_Functional_Framework_v3_02_20080910.pdf. Accessed September 23, 2012.

14. My Recovery Plan, MyHealtheVet Office of Informatics and Analytics Sources Sought Notice. August 3, 2012. https://www.fbo.gov/?s=opportunity&mode=form&id=e7e03227fd31bf8d61a296a560f7cc6a&tab=core&_cview=0. Accessed August 11, 2012.

15. Low G. Factors affecting the buy vs build decision in large Australian organizations. *Journal of Information Technology.* 2008; 23(3):118-131. http://www.palgrave-journals.com/jit/journal/v23/n2/full/2000098a.html. Accessed August 18, 2012.

16. *New York State Project Management Guidebook.* New York State Office of Technology; 2003. http://www.cio.ny.gov/pmmp/guidebook2/index.htm. Accessed August 12, 2012.

17. Hoehn BJ. What is the best clinical information strategy? *J Healthc Inf Manag.* 2010; 24(4):10-12. http://www.himss.org/content/files/Code%2093_What%20 is%20the%20best%20clinical%20information%20system.pdf. Accessed August 18, 2012.

18. mHIMSS Website RFP Template. Healthcare Information and Management Systems Society. January 14, 2010. http://www.himss.org/content/output/ 88CE17A4CBA54E0F8D402040386EFACD.pdf. Accessed September 22, 2012.

19. Perkins B. RFPs: the costs of being unclear. *Computerworld.* June 11, 2007. http://www.computerworld.com/s/article/293860/RFPs_The_Costs_of_Being_ Unclear. Accessed August 11, 2012.

Systems Selection, Implementation, Support and Maintenance

Susan M. Houston, MBA, RN-BC, PMP, CPHIMS

LEARNING OBJECTIVES

At the conclusion of this chapter, the reader will be able to:

☑ Understand the solution selection criteria.

☑ Identify the solution selection activities.

☑ Describe the implementation process.

☑ Define the methods to manage the healthcare information system.

■ Introduction

The selection process begins with the identification of a need. The successful implementation and adoption of a new application is dependent on an organized system selection process followed by a well-planned and executed implementation strategy. Once a need has been identified within an organization, an effective governance committee evaluates it against the organizational mission, goals, objectives, technology IT strategic plan and available resources.

Once the decision is made to move forward, objectives, goals and measures of success should be clearly defined. Once the high-level strategy is defined, the team is assembled to analyze and further define the requirements. It is important to have the appropriate team members to ensure the analysis includes all parts of the organization affected by the new solution. Through this analysis, opportunities for process improvement and workflow efficiencies are identified.

The next key step is selecting a vendor, which includes a request for information (RFI) and/or a request for proposal (RFP).

An RFI:

■ Is an informal request for information that does not require commitment from either party.

■ Is a collection of documents designed to collect information regarding prospective vendors and their ability to meet the defined need or high-level requirements.

■ May or may not include budget or costing information.

An RFP:

■ Is a formal request that leads to a contract between the organization and the selected vendor(s).

■ Is a collection of documents that outline the detailed requirements and how each responding vendor will be compared for a final decision.

■ Always includes timelines and budget or costing information.

Evaluating the vendors that respond to the RFP includes on-site visits, reference checks and even demonstrations. After the list of possible vendors is narrowed down to a few, contract negotiations allow the organization to get the best possible deal based on price, payment plan, support levels and ongoing support. It is important to include a step to verify any federal, state and local government regulations as part of any standard selection practice.

After the application and vendor have been selected, it is time to begin implementation. Understanding the different implementation strategies will help the organization choose the one that best fits its culture, objectives and available resources. Proper planning and a defined methodology will help decrease project risk and lead to a successful activation. For a smooth transition to support, the implementation project should include planning for post-live activities such as configuration management, user communication, user support and new-employee training, along with operations and maintenance, to ensure continuous performance of the system.

◼ Solution-Selection Criteria

As mentioned earlier, system selection begins with a defined need based on the organization's strategic objectives or a solution to a problem that blocks achievement of an organizational or departmental objective. The selection and implementation processes are built around fulfilling the need and realizing the solution that will meet the organization's expected outcomes. The process defined below should be used as a template and modified as needed to fit the specific situation and satisfy the current regulatory requirements.

The need and justification for a project are often described in a formal business case or a needs assessment. This document outlines the goal and objectives of the request along with the high-level resources required to meet them. The needed resources may be financial, human, software, hardware or capital. Most organizations request a business case prior to approving the proposed system-selection process. If the organization does not require a business case, it is imperative that the IT governance committee request one. The challenge comes from defining the required resources this early in the process. Most often they are defined through scientific guesses. If time allows, market research can provide more accurate estimates. Market research starts with high-level requirements, not the detailed ones identified later in the process, and may be conducted formally or informally. Formal market research is completed through a process similar to the RFI process. With market research, however, it is clearly stated that the RFI is for research only, with no intent to purchase at this time. The informal process is completed through vendor exhibitions, Internet searches and contact with other similar organizations.

The business case should present the need and requirements, not the solution. The different options to meet the needs, with associated resources, should be defined. This document should avoid the identification of a single solution. The governance committee reviews the business case and decides whether to move forward based on the system's fit within the organization's strategic plan or operational goals and the availability of resources to complete.

Once approval to move forward is received, the selection criteria are built on the defined need and high-level requirements that the business case identified as necessary for the solution. Whether the need is to improve office scheduling processes through automation or to create a paperless environment in an acute care setting, the requirements go beyond end-user functionality to include non-functional necessities also.

A list of requirements could include the following:

Functional Requirements

- Application with organization-specific functionality
- Security and privacy requirements
- Regulatory requirements
- Reporting capability, including standard and custom reporting
- Integration with other applications or devices
- Access from multiple locations (acute care, long-term care, clinics, etc.)
- Access from mobile devices
- Redesigned workflow
- Decision support functionality

Non-functional Requirements

- Facility IT infrastructure space, cooling and power
- Hardware for production, development, testing and/or training environments
- Hardware for disaster recovery or high availability
- Hardware for reporting
- Backup and recovery plans and procedures
- Workstation and printer requirements and/or hardware
- Wired and wireless network
- System installation, configuration and maintenance documentation
- Supplemental staffing for implementation, training and post-live support
- Independent verification and validation to reduce risk by providing impartial reviews of business and technical aspects of the project
- Processes for issue resolution and requests for enhancement
- Maintenance and support process and procedures
- Expected procurement and implementation timeline along with any constraints that would affect the timeline
- Expected availability, reliability and scalability

A gap analysis might be the first step in defining these requirements. What is the status of your current application(s)? Are you planning to replace or enhance those systems? What manual processes can and must be improved through automation? Throughout this process, it is important to focus the analysis on the identified need. Requirement creep can occur very quickly if the team is not focused. The governance committee and executive sponsors are there to help with ensuring the requirements fit within the defined goals and objectives.

Once the requirements are defined, they should be ranked to show which are required, preferred or optional. It is rare for vendors to be able to meet every requirement, so clarity about which are absolutely necessary helps during the evaluation of responses. The rankings should be agreed upon by all committee members and used consistently for all vendors. The requirements and rankings feed into the RFI or RFP documentation as defined earlier in this chapter.

Through this process a decision to build versus buy should be made. There are many factors that influence this decision. Does the organization have the skill set to build and support the new solution? Is there room in the budget to buy? What is the expected timeline? Which option fits with the organizational IT strategy? Is there a vendor who can meet the need and defined requirements? Based on these factors, the decision to build or buy may occur early in the process, after reviewing the RFI/RFP responses, or anytime in between.

Having the appropriate people involved in the selection process is key to being successful. The governance committee and executive sponsors have already been introduced. A facilitator should be identified early on to ensure that the activity progresses as expected, the defined process is followed and the right people are involved in the review team.

■ Selecting Review Team Members

The selection of the review team should be completed as early as possible. It is possible that the entire team might not be needed at the very early stages of the process or that some members may not be as actively involved as others. Team members should be identified early so they will be ready to participate when needed. Decisions about team membership should balance the importance of including the right people with the need to keep the size manageable.

The exact members will depend on what is being selected and should include representatives from clinical, organizational operations, IT and the business department to ensure all affected areas are involved. Below is a list of who might be involved in the selection team:

- Facilitator—Provides overall leadership and coordination of the system-selection process.

- Executive sponsors—Provide support, clarify mission, facilitate necessary resources and act as champions within the organization.

- Technical representatives—Provide technical expertise, such as IT, biomedical and/or telecommunications.

- Business representatives—Provide business or clinical end-user expertise. These individuals are highly knowledge about the current business and workflows and represent the end users.

- Program/project manager—Provides implementation and methodology expertise.

- Contracting representative—Provides contracting, negotiation and process expertise.

- Financial representative—Provides budgetary expertise.

- Organizational change leader—Provides expertise related to facilitating change within the organization.

- Governance committee—Provides oversight but is often not directly involved in the team. The selection team reports back to this group. Once implementation begins, this group will remain intact to monitor and ensure the project's success. In some organizations, this group is called a steering committee.

The role of team members is to represent their specific area within the organization. It is very difficult to include everyone who will be affected by the new system on the team. Members should be expected to gather information from their peers to bring back to the team. This process helps to ensure that the right information will be reviewed and included where needed throughout the selection process. All requirements should be reviewed and approved by the team.

■ Solution-Selection Activities

Once the requirements have been approved and the decision to buy has been made, it is time to look for vendors that are able to meet them. It is important to consult with your contracting representative to understand the organizational rules and regulations about contacting vendors prior to a signed contract. Some regulations are in place to avoid giving any one vendor an advantage. The contract representative will be able to guide you through the selection activities. The following elements may be involved in solution selection:

- **RFI.** The request for information provides a format for gathering information about which vendors are able to meet the high-level requirements. The responses are compared to the documented requirements, which may be modified prior to posting the RFP if it is clear some required items are not available or require more definition.

- **RFP.** The request for proposal provides the official request for vendors to submit how they will meet the requirements, which are more defined and include timelines and budget details.

- **Evaluation of RFP responses.** Responses should be reviewed and scored based on ability to meet required, preferred and optional requirements. This step is accomplished with the entire team doing independent scoring of each response followed by team discussion and consensus on a final score. This process helps identify which vendors can meet the organizational need and provides the first opportunity to eliminate any vendor that cannot.

- **Comparison to IT strategic plan.** When evaluating the responses, it is important to understand how a vendor's solution or planned implementation will fit with the organization's IT strategic plan. Is the IT road map leading in the direction of virtualization, to simplification of technologies, or to a decreased number of vendors? How does the offered solution fit with this road map? It might be OK if the solution does not fit, but that fact should be considered during selection.

- **Compliance with regulatory requirements.** Pertinent regulations should be part of your requirements and listed as essential. All vendors should be evaluated against any government, regulatory or security requirements.

- **Background checks.** Once the list of possible vendors is decreased, some research should be done. This would include evaluation of their financial stability, market share and customer satisfaction. How long a product has been on the market and how many other customers are using it should be matched your organization's risk-tolerance level. Are you an early adopter who can tolerate some issues with the application if you are able to work with the vendor on new features and functionality? Or would you prefer a solid, reliable application that the vendor has had time to refine? The outcome of this activity should be included in the scoring of each vendor.

- **Demonstrations.** Requesting a demonstration allows vendors to show how they can meet the request. This provides a visual that is very beneficial, but it is often done with a generic version of the product. This does not reflect how it can be customized to fit the organization's workflows or processes. Prior to the demonstration, it is suggested that a list of scenarios be provided to the vendors so they will show how their product can meet your needs rather than highlight only the features that they choose. All vendors should be guided to demonstrate the same scenarios to ensure they can be compared to each other. Whenever possible, the same people should be invited to all scheduled demonstrations. Having each vendor demonstrating how their product fits within the same scenarios and having the same people attending each meeting makes it easier to properly compare and score each option prior to final selection. It is important to control the agenda very tightly, making sure all scenarios are covered and, if you choose, allowing vendors to demonstrate additional functionality at the end. Demonstrations should be scheduled closely together, if possible, so the information is fresh when they are scored.

- **Site visits.** Visiting a site that has already worked with a vendor and implemented their solution provides an opportunity to speak with people directly, ask specific questions and see how the solution works within their workflows and processes. This helps to demonstrate how the system can be customized during the implementation to fit defined workflows and processes. Questions to ask during site visits would range from what it is like to work with the vendor, how they respond to requests for support during the implementation or after live, and how easy it is to customize the application or to integrate it with other systems. The number of site visits is often dependent on the number of vendors remaining at this point in the process. The decision on who should participate often depends on who will be affected by the implementation and the distance to be traveled for the visit. It is optimal if the organization, and not the vendor, chooses what sites to visit, but this is not always an option.

- **Client references.** If a site visit is not possible, a call with the reference site would still provide the ability to ask questions. While the selection team will not be able to actually view the system live, the same questions can be asked. Through use of remote Web-meeting technologies, it is possible to have a demonstration of how a client is using the system without the travel. This provides the ability to understand the implementation process, so remember to ask about any lessons learned from their experience. Just like a demo, there should be predefined questions to be asked for each reference site. Simple Web searches and informal contacts with peers can also provide some good reference information.

- **Selection meetings.** Throughout this process, the team is meeting regularly to continuously evaluate and score the remaining vendors against the new information obtained through the research, demonstrations, site visits and original proposal scores. Through this process the number of vendors should be decreased to one or a few. The team's comments and final evaluations of each of the remaining options are provided to the contracting representative for negotiations.

- **Negotiation.** The contract representative negotiates with the remaining vendors to obtain the best solution for the organization. This would include cost, software, hardware, implementation services, support and maintenance. The selection committee as well as a legal representative should carefully review all documents sent to the organization from the vendors because once the papers are signed, they are a binding contract. During negotiation, there may be multiple requested modifications to the documents that require back and forth communication. This process can take a while since each modification needs to be properly reviewed by the other party before they come back with their modifications, and so on. The cost tables should include costs for items such as software licenses, integration, data conversions, training, implementation services, hardware and third-party software licenses.

- ■ **Selection.** Based on the negotiations and the final offer from each of the remaining vendors, the team makes a selection. Each step of this process, along with the justification of the selection, should be documented in case any vendor chooses to contest the award. The final agreements often include items such as payment schedule, vendor and client responsibilities, delivery schedule, system installation and configuration documentation, specific deliverables, standard project plan, penalties for not meeting deadlines, termination process, assignment of licenses and process for upgrade or updates.

- ■ **Budget development.** During the negotiations, the budget is developed based on the costs defined during negotiation and selection. The budget often needs to include costs beyond the system vendor. Other items that might be included in the project budget are contractors to supplement the organization's staff; business change management requirements; hardware not purchased through the software vendor, such as new workstations or printers; costs from other vendors for integration services; training; travel; and standard fixed or variable costs, such as space and staffing. The budget is typically finalized within 30 days after the final contract is awarded.

The formality, steps included and length of this process can vary greatly. There are various reasons for this beyond the organizational contracting process. The contract size, a time constraint or the desire to stay with a single vendor might shorten this process. With each step, a document or process that is cut brings some level of risk. The organization needs to balance the risk versus the benefit of shortening the process.

■ Implementation Process

Now that a system has been selected, it is important to define how it will be implemented. While the phases of an implementation are fairly standard, there are a variety of defined methodologies that differ only in the terminology they use or the number of phases. The basic phases implementation projects go through include plan, design, build, test, train, go-live and closeout. It is important to remember that they all start with gathering information and planning what work is required along with when and how it will be done. Most projects fail due to lack of planning, poor planning or not following the plan. If the organization does not have a defined project management strategy, it would be important to take the time to decide what processes will be followed throughout the project. This includes defining the project team's roles, the project manager's authority, the documentation and deliverables expected throughout the project, and the role of the governance or steering committee.

The initial activity is to plan how the project will be accomplished. This includes defining what is within and outside the scope of the project. The project sponsors will approve the scope prior to any other plans being finalized. Also to be prepared are the risk management plan, the change management plan, the training plan, the testing plan, the issue management plan, the work breakdown structure and the communication plan. All of these documents make up the project management plan and define the tasks scheduled to successfully complete the project. When preparations begin for the activation (go-live), the activation plan is developed and approved.

At the end of the planning phase, after the sponsors approve the project management plan, a kick-off meeting is conducted to communicate the project to all stakeholders. The agenda often includes the following:

- The project scope

- The project management methodology, or the how the project will be managed

- The change management process, or how changes are requested, analyzed and approved

- Identified risks and their mitigation strategies

- Introduction of the project team and their roles

- High-level milestones and schedule

- The communication plan

■ Organizational Change Management

Any new system will have an impact on the organization and some change will need to occur. It is not good enough to just automate a process; the process should be improved through automation. Changes affect everyone from top management to end users. Planning for these changes and evaluating the different options for managing them should begin during the procurement process. It is important to have top-level support as well as a member of senior leadership on the change management team to show commitment and provide strong leadership. The team should also include members from all affected areas so they have a sense of ownership and commitment to the project's success.

The team should define a strategic plan similar to the project plan used for implementing the software. The strategic plan should take into consideration the organizational culture and politics related to how staff handles change. The types of resistance that might occur should be identified along with the strategy to break down the resistance and move on to acceptance. A clear communication plan will ensure the information is properly disseminated throughout the organization.

Adoption often is affected by users' perceptions of how the system fits with their workflow. Does it provide efficiencies or appear to be extra work? Does the system functionality cause a perceived negative change in processes, or can the system be made to fit within the processes and even improve them? Often the adoption is based on perceived benefit by the end users. The staff has to be ready for the change, which is why stakeholder involvement in the workflow redesign is critical. Having end users involved in hardware selection, such as workstations on wheels or mobile devices, provides feedback to the project team about the usability of the devices being evaluated.

■ Implementation Strategies

There are multiple strategies for implementing a new system. Early in the project, they should be evaluated to determine which one is the right fit for the organization.

- Big bang—Going live with all functionality to be implemented in all locations at the same time. If there is a legacy system being replaced, this might be the only option. This strategy requires a considerable amount of coordination to ensure that all areas are ready, with hardware in place, training completed and enough support staff available.

- Phased by location—Going live with all functionality to be implemented in one location at a time. This strategy extends the duration of the activation activity, but provides some benefits. The staff from the areas already live can assist with providing support to the ones that follow. Holding a meeting after each phase to discuss lessons learned could provide continuous improvement for later phases.

- Phased by functionality—Going live in all locations with one feature at a time. An example would be to bring the admissions process live first for admission, discharge and transfer and patient demographic information, followed by computerized practitioner order entry (CPOE) and then clinical documentation. This strategy also extends the duration of the activation and allows users to gradually get accustomed to the system before utilizing it fully. As above, meeting after each phase to discuss lessons learned could provide continuous improvement for future phases.

- Pilot—Going live initially with one location as a pilot test, then following with everyone else in a phased big-bang process. This allows the team to learn from a small group before going live with the entire user community.

- Like for like—going live with the same functionality that was in place prior to the project. Extra functionality is often added later through configuration management (discussed later in this chapter) or a later project. This strategy is often used when replacing a legacy system or during an upgrade. It helps to decrease the complexity of the activation and decreases the impact on the end users. There will always be some users who perceive this approach to be useless since they do not see an improvement.

■ Implementing Solutions

You have taken enough time to properly plan how the system will be implemented. You have selected a project team with the right skills, chosen the right implementation strategy, identified what features will be implemented and developed an outstanding communication plan. Now all you have to do is follow your plans.

This is when the project team takes the basic vanilla application the vendor provides and customizes it to meet the organization's needs. The vendor should provide training to the project team on how to make these changes. This includes configuring the clinical documentation data entry into notes and/or flow sheets as well as the output as reports. Each order that can be placed for a patient, such as medications, diagnostic tests, diets and consults, has to be configured in the system. Other items range from drop-down lists for a patient's religion during admission to how surgery will be scheduled. If there is a legacy system, the data conversion or loading of data also happens during this time. Even if data is immigrated early, some data migration will have to occur during activation to ensure that all data is in the new system when it goes live. Care should also be taken to avoid duplication of data during the migration. Data validation after each migration is an important step that should be combined with an action plan to resolve duplicate records if they occur.

Part of the methodology should include how changes are handled during the project. There will be some requests to change the scope of the project or some requirements during the execution phase. Having a defined process for evaluating each request to determine its impact on the project helps prevent scope creep. The change management plan should identify who can submit changes, how changes are evaluated, what documentation is required and who makes the final decision. A request may be approved, denied or deferred to a later time. The project sponsors usually make the decision with the project manager facilitating the impact analysis.

Testing activities occur throughout the execution. A test plan, which should have at least been started during the planning phase, describes all the different testing activities to be completed during the project. Often the first testing activity is verifying that the hardware and application were installed correctly. Each of the initial environments, such as development, testing and/or training, is required to ensure that the installations were successful. Testing will occur throughout the project based on the test plan and the different types of testing to be performed. The testing could include:

- Unit testing—Testing typically done by the person doing the configuration to verify the change that was made.

- Functional testing—Testing of a complete function, such as clinical documentation.

- Integration testing—Testing the data flow between systems or components, or from a device to the system.

- System testing—Testing of the entire system's functionality and performance and the fit of the whole application. This includes verifying all requirements and security controls, multisite testing, and the validation of the disaster recovery plan.

- User acceptance testing—Testing done by the users of the system to verify the fit within the new workflows and processes.

■ System Integration to Support Business Requirements

It is rare in healthcare today to have a stand-alone system that does not share data with another in some way. The electronic health record (EHR) should include data from the lab and radiology systems so those who need to make medical decisions can view the results. Patient demographic information should be shared between the outpatient clinic, or office system, and the inpatient EHR so the patient does not need to provide the same information over and over again. Integration allows data to be in multiple systems without manual data entry. Some types of integration to be considered include the following:

- Real-time data integration—Sharing of data nearly simultaneously when it is entered or modified, or when another defined trigger occurs. The standard for this type of integration is Health Level 7 (HL7), which defines the specifics surrounding the interface messages so what is sent from the source system is acceptable by the destination system.

- Scheduled data integration—Sharing of data in a batch according to a predetermined time frame, such as nightly at midnight or every so many hours. The data feed can be accomplished through formatted files or through HL7 messages.

- Integration of data from devices—Feeding of data from a specific device into an application. These devices can range from hemodynamic monitors, vital sign monitors and anesthesia machines to ventilators. This type of interface helps decrease manual data entry but may require the data to be verified before it becomes official within the system.

Integration utilizes an interface engine that receives information from the source system and either passes it directly to the destination system or makes some modification to the data before passing it along. For example, a modification would occur if the source system sent a patient's name as first name and last name, but the destination system could only accept a full name. The interface engine would accept the first and last names, combine them and send the full name on. Different systems have different requirements for how the data is structured and where in the interface message they expect the specific data to be located. The interface message has sections, and a mapping document describes where each piece of data is expected to be and if the interface engine needs to do any manipulation.

■ User and Operational Manuals and Training

As a project nears activation, it is necessary to educate the end users through documentation and training. If hands-on training is required, a training environment should be set up early in the project to allow the training team to develop materials and enter hypothetical patient data for any practice exercises that might be included. Training activities are tricky to schedule because they need to take place on the system that will actually be in use. As a result, the training environment cannot be fully set up until all the configuration is completed.

There are many factors that lead to the decision on what type of training should be provided. These include the organizational culture, extent of the change, number of users, users' work hours and even the staff's comfort level with computers. Training can be done through computer-based training modules, lectures, demonstrations, hands-on exercises or a combination of those.

Training should occur right before the activation so the users will retain what was taught. The timing depends on how many users need to be trained and how long the training classes will be. Experience shows that the best planning will not eliminate the need for just-in-time training. Someone will not make it to class or will not remember how to do something. End-user manuals and quick reference guides along with the presence of support staff during the initial week or so will help fill this gap.

■ Activation Planning and Immediate Post-activation Activities

Planning for the system go-live begins with the decision on implementation strategy discussed earlier in this chapter and continues through the remainder of the project. The organization should work with the vendor to define what activation activities can be completed in advance and which have to occur on the go-live day. The actual activities will depend on the specific project. If the organization is moving from a manual process to an automated one or is implementing a new system, the activation could be as simple as having users start using the system. When migrating from a legacy system or upgrading an existing system, the activation activities are more complex and include a period of time when the system is down, or unavailable. A detailed checklist of tasks that occur before and during the activation, whether a down is included or not, helps to ensure nothing will be missed or forgotten. A rehearsal of the activation provides an opportunity to test the process and fix any mistakes that occur. Evaluating the rehearsal helps to refine the process and the checklist to make the actual activation to go more smoothly. It also boosts the project team's level of confidence because they have already done the tasks at least once, depending on how many rehearsals are conducted.

The planning for activation goes beyond the actual tasks that will occur to bring the system up. Other considerations should include where everyone will sit; if a command center will be set up so the entire team will be in one location; if food and drink will be available, especially if the activity will go beyond a few hours; if there will be a place for the staff to rest; what forms of communication will be available for anyone not in the command center; and how status updates will be communicated to the end users. How will issues requiring escalation be handled, and will the vendor be on site or on the phone to provide assistance?

The type and duration of post-live support will depend on the impact of the change and the amount of just-in-time training expected. When implementing a new system in a clinic, the support staff might be available just before and during clinic hours for the first week. When implementing a new EHR in an acute setting, the support staff might be available around the clock for the first few weeks.

The users will almost immediately have suggestions for changing the system. Having a clear process for submitting requests for change will help users know their input is valuable. With that said, it is important not to make changes too early. Often the suggestions are just because the system, workflows or processes are new and different from the ways the users have always done things. Unless suggestions are critical to patient care, they should just be documented for now. Critical issues should be taken care of right away. The rest of the suggested changes should be evaluated after about a month to see if they are still needed.

■ Managing Healthcare Information Systems

Once the system is live, it moves into operations and maintenance mode. During this time, the IT department must ensure that it continues to support the mission and goals of the organization and remains reliable and stable. During the implementation project, various processes should be put into place in preparation for this phase. These processes include configuration management, release management, customer support through a service desk and resolution of any issues entered as trouble tickets. Documentation about how the system was configured feeds into good operations and maintenance documentation for resolving issues when they arise. Examples of operations and maintenance documentation include the following:

- Communication plan—Defines how end users communicate with the IT department about the new system. How will they request help for an issue? How will they request modifications to the system? How will they request help for general questions about how to use the system?

- Service-desk knowledge base—Explains how to identify and resolve issues when users contact the service desk. This includes questions to ask and decision trees to help identify the resolution or the escalation process if an issue cannot be resolved. The escalation process should include how to approach the vendor if an issue cannot be resolved internally as well as who has the authority to contact the vendor.

- Data flow documents—Identify where and how data flows from one system to another or from one location in the system to another, along with the dependencies between systems. This includes the triggers that prompt the data to flow, such as a change in the patient's location would trigger the information to be sent to update the lab system.

- Workflow documents—Explain end users' workflows and how the system fits into users' daily activities.

- Configuration management process—Defines how changes are made and what levels of approval and documentation are required for each change.

- Downtime procedures—Identify both what procedures end users will follow when the system is unavailable and what procedures the technical staff will follow to identify and resolve an issue causing downtime.

- Manuals—A group of documents ranging from end-user manuals to training guides and the configuration manual that provides step-by-step directions on how to make changes in the system.

Configuration management and release management are processes to control changes to the system, including software and hardware. They are involved in how changes are requested, the process for review and approval of changes, how changes are made and tested, and the process for releasing changes to the different environments to ensure that they are kept in sync and that each migration is verified. It is important that changes are made in a development environment, tested in a test environment and verified in production. Conducting regression testing after the changes are made ensures the new modifications do not break something else. Controlling how and when changes are made in each environment is critical in avoiding unexpected negative results.

Working with the vendor on scheduling updates for small fixes, sometimes called hot-fixes, to major upgrade releases will keep the system current while minimizing unexpected downtimes. Each new update should be evaluated prior to moving it through the configuration management process. If the update is large enough, it should be managed as a separate project.

Customer support is often provided through a help desk or a single phone number that goes to someone who can listen and help to resolve the issues the end users have. The calls may pertain to a bug, or issue with the system; a problem with the usability of the system; or a training or how-to question. Having a good knowledge base that allows the help-desk staff to ask the right questions and provide enough information to resolve the issue during the first call can keep customer satisfaction high. For times when the service desk cannot resolve an issue, it is important to have a process for providing second-tier support. Often this is done through a help desk or ticket management system, but a custom database with workflows and notifications could work also. Timely feedback to the customer is important until the problem is resolved.

■ Analyzing Data for Problems and Trends

Throughout the lifecycle of any application, it is good practice to look for trends in usage as well as problems. Within the first year after an application goes live, analysis should occur to see if it actually met the need that was identified prior to its purchase. This is an evaluation of how well the goals leading to the investment were met and if the expected return on investment was realized. The results should be brought back to the governance committee for possible action, especially if the need was not met.

There are many reasons to collect data and look for trends. A researcher may want to look for levels of new-system adoption over the months or years, evaluate user satisfaction with a system, or understand trends in system performance. The ways to collect data can be through surveys, user groups or visits to the users. On the technical side, looking for trends in error reports, help-desk logs, monitor logs or unexpected downtimes will help the technical staff plan for improvements in system performance.

■ Ensuring That Critical Functions Are Repaired, Maintained or Enhanced

The technical staff receives many different kinds of requests for change. These include feedback from users through help-desk calls, rounds, user groups and direct change requests. Some of these requests raise issues that must be fixed by the vendor or seek enhanced functionality not currently available. Vendors often provide updates, as mentioned earlier. Each change, or group of changes, should be evaluated and, if approved, prioritized. The smaller changes move through the configuration management process and are assigned and migrated according to the release management schedule. Larger requests or groups of requests should be managed as separate projects and follow the project management process.

■ Business Continuity and Disaster Recovery Plans

The criticality of the system within the organization will define the disaster recovery and business continuity plans. The business continuity plan defines how an organization prepares for and maintains the business functions related to the defined system. This includes the operations and maintenance of the system to ensure stability, the process of resolving issues that could or do cause the system to be unavailable, how the business will continue without the system and how to recover from an actual disaster.

The disaster recovery plan focuses on the technical aspects, such as data backup and recovery after the system goes down. Tape backups of the data are often done nightly and stored off site for a predetermined amount of time. There are hardware configurations that provide some level of continuity, such as automatic failover between clustered servers. Vendors can provide some options for how their systems can be configured. For critical systems, some organizations have off-site facilities where they can recover the system from backup tapes if needed. Part of the disaster recovery plan, or a separate technical downtime plan, should include the steps to follow when the system goes down from causes other than a disaster. How the issue is identified and resolved, who is involved, and the process for a root-cause analysis should all be included in this plan. These processes should be tested on a regular basis and updates should be made as needed.

The downtime plan focuses on business aspects, such as how to continue to operate without the electronic system. It includes procedures for communication, hard-copy forms for documentation and plans for how data will be entered into the system once it becomes available again. Once users become dependent on the system for their work processes, they are reluctant to use manual processes. Regular reviews of the downtime plan and communication before any scheduled down will help with adoption, but support staff should be available to provide assistance whenever the downtime plan is required.

■ Bibliography

Healthcare Information and Management Systems Society. *HIMSS Dictionary of Healthcare Information Technology Terms, Acronyms and Organizations.* 2nd ed. Chicago: Healthcare Information and Management Systems Society, 2010.

Schwalbe K. *Information Technology Project Management.* 4th ed. Cambridge, MA: Course Technology, 2006.

Houston S, Bove L. *Project Management for Healthcare Informatics.* New York: Springer, 2007.

Houston S. *The Project Manager's Guide to Health Information Technology Implementation.* Chicago: HIMSS, 2011.

Green M, Bowie M. *Essentials of Health Information Management Principles and Practices.* 2nd ed. Clifton Park, NY: Delmar Cengage Learning, 2011.

Project Management Institute. *The Guide to the Project Management Body of Knowledge.* 4th ed. Newtown Square, PA: Project Management Institute, 2008.

Morris P, Pinto J. *The Wiley Guide to Project, Program, and Portfolio Management.* Hoboken, NJ: John Wiley and Sons, 2007.

CHAPTER 6

Systems Testing and Evaluation

Chris Arricale, MS, PMP, CPHIMS

LEARNING OBJECTIVES

At the conclusion of this chapter, the reader will be able to:

☑ Define the purpose of information systems testing.

☑ Identify five key components of a testing methodology.

☑ Understand the major levels of testing and their intended use.

☑ List three testing controls used to maintain the integrity of a testing process.

☑ Identify three specific areas that are addressed in test reports.

☑ Understand the importance of post-implementation evaluations.

■ Purpose of Systems Testing

Healthcare organizations rely on information systems to manage clinical, administrative, financial and legal aspects of daily operations. As technology advances and new healthcare systems are developed and marketed, stakeholders must weigh the risks of implementing or modifying systems and mitigate those risks as much as possible. A critical component of that risk-mitigation strategy is testing and evaluating any new or modified system.

The fundamental purpose of system testing is to provide knowledge to assist in managing the risks involved in developing, producing, operating and sustaining systems and their capabilities.[1] Specifically, system testing provides knowledge of capabilities and limitations to the stakeholders for use in improving the system performance, and to the user community for optimizing system use and sustaining operations. Furthermore, system testing enables the stakeholders to identify the technical and operational limitations of the system under development so that they can be resolved prior to production and deployment.[1] Information systems have become an integral part of healthcare operations and, as such, often have a direct impact on patient safety. With this in mind, identifying and testing for areas that are likely to be major patient safety risks is very important.

System testing and evaluation are performed on both hardware and software. Hardware testing includes evaluation of the physical components of the system (circuits, drives, internal components, etc.). Software testing is an investigation of the quality of a software product or service with the goal of finding any "bugs" and fixing them before the product is released. Software testing can also provide an objective, independent view of the software that enables the business to appreciate and understand the risks of software implementation. Test techniques include, but are not limited to, executing a program or application with the intent of finding software errors or other defects. Comprehensive testing is a process of validating and verifying that a system:

■ Meets the requirements that guided its design and development.

■ Works as expected.

■ Can be implemented with the same functional characteristics across the entire organization.

■ Satisfies the needs of stakeholders.[2]

Appropriate testing is critical for the success of any new or upgraded system. A study conducted by the National Institute of Standards and Technology reported that software bugs (coding issues as well as integration challenges) cost the United States economy $59.5 billion annually.[3] More than a third of this cost could be avoided if better testing was performed; the earlier a defect is found, the cheaper it is to fix.

The first step in executing a successful test is creating a test methodology.

TEST METHODOLOGY

Different types of methodologies are used in the field of systems testing and quality assurance for today's complex healthcare IT systems. Whether testing an enterprise-level system or a specific piece of code, the methodology is equally important. Because of the complexity of healthcare systems, many healthcare organizations adopt a buy-not-build strategy, outsourcing development to companies that specialize in that area. As a result, their IT staff often has only a partial picture of their system's development history. In such cases, a well-defined testing methodology is critical to ensure that the delivered system meets the needs of the healthcare organization. In formulating a testing methodology, different sets of test cases and testing strategies are prepared in order to verify that the system is as close to error-free as possible and capable of providing accurate and optimum outputs.[4] Testing scenarios vary widely among healthcare systems and are tailored for each organization by the test teams and stakeholders. Nonetheless, there is consensus among testing and standards professionals that any sound testing methodology should include the following key steps:

- Defining the test strategy;

- Developing testing tools;

- Test execution;

- Employing test controls;

- Test reporting; and

- Final evaluation.[4]

Test Strategy

The test strategy is a formal description of how a system will be tested and is developed to address all levels of the testing process. The test team analyzes the requirements, writes the test strategy and reviews the plan with the project team and various end users and stakeholders. The test plan may include test cases, conditions, test environment, pass/fail criteria and risk assessment. It will also define the testing scope and objectives, current business issues to consider during the test, testing roles and responsibilities, status reporting methods, test execution methods, industry standards to follow, test automation and tools, measurements and metrics, risks and mitigation, defect reporting and tracking, and change/configuration management.[5]

Test Tools

Testing tools are widely available in the commercial market; the specific tools required will depend on the testing method(s) employed. Generally, system testing is performed either manually or through automation. Manual testing is simply direct human interaction with a system, testing for apparent defects. A member of the test team plays the role of an end user and tests most features of the application to ensure correct behavior. To ensure completeness of testing, the test team often follows a written test plan that leads them through a set of important test cases. Tools required for manual testing include a written test plan, test script or scenarios to follow, and a method of recording and reporting the results. Although manual testing may find many defects in a system, it is a laborious and time-consuming process. In addition, it may not be effective in finding certain classes of defects not immediately apparent to the end user.

Automated testing may be performed through the use of special software (separate from the software being tested) that controls the execution of tests, compares actual outcomes to predicted outcomes, sets up test preconditions, and performs other test-control and test-reporting functions. The use of automated testing tools in healthcare is expanding, and there are many automated tools available that can be tailored specifically to an individual system's testing needs. One of the most significant benefits of test automation is the ability to duplicate the testing process. Once tests have been automated, they can be run quickly and repeatedly. This is often the most cost-effective method for systems that have a long maintenance life; even minor patches over the lifetime of a system can cause features to break that were working at an earlier point in time, so repeated testing is required for each patch or upgrade.[2]

Test Execution

Performing and documenting the test activities is the primary focus of the testing methodology. Test professionals can use any number of methods to execute test events, and most fall into one of two categories: white-box testing or black-box testing.[2] These two approaches are based on the point of view that a test engineer takes when executing test cases. White-box testing (also known as clear-box testing, glass-box testing, transparent-box testing and structural testing) is a method of testing the *internal structures*, or workings, of a system as opposed to its functionality; the tester is not concerned with what the system is supposed to do but rather with how the system is supposed to operate on an internal level. Black-box testing is a method of software testing that tests the *functionality* of an application as opposed to its internal structures or workings; the tester is only aware of what the system is supposed to do and has no knowledge of the internal operations of the system. A hybrid of the two approaches is known as gray-box testing, which is a combination of white-box and black-box testing approaches; the tester has some knowledge of internal structures and also understands the expected functionalities. Gray-box testing is most useful when performing tests on existing systems that have been upgraded, patched or modified.

Test methods are classified and executed based on the level of the test or the specific objective of the test. During system development, tests are performed at specific levels of development: unit-level testing, integration testing and system testing. Test methods that are not associated with a specific level of development are classified by the testing objective, such as stress, acceptance and regression testing.[2] Recently, healthcare organizations began adopting operational testing as well. Operational testing is focused on ensuring that the solution delivers the return on investment (ROI) and benefits that are expected. Users perform operational testing in a production environment while being observed by independent testers. Operational testing is often repeated 90 to 180 days after deployment to ensure that the system is being properly used and is delivering the intended results.

■ *Unit testing* is performed by checking individual units of source code and sets of one or more computer program modules together with associated control data, usage procedures and operating procedures to determine if they are fit for use. Intuitively, one can view a unit as the smallest testable part of an application. Unit tests are created by programmers and white-box testers during the development process.

■ *Integration testing* involves combining individual software modules, or units, and testing them as a group. Integration testing takes as its input modules that have been unit tested, groups them into larger aggregates, applies tests defined in an integration test plan to those aggregates, and delivers as its output the integrated system ready for system testing. Integration testing can be done using any of the box methods (white, black or gray) but is best suited for gray-box testing, when the tester has some knowledge of the internal code of the individual units as well as the expected system functionality.

■ *System testing* is conducted on a complete, integrated system to evaluate the system's compliance with its specified requirements. System testing is one of the most common black-box testing methods and, as such, does not require knowledge of the inner design of the code or logic. System testing combines all of the integrated components that have successfully passed integration testing with software that has been integrated with hardware and tests them as a single system. The purpose of integration testing is to detect any inconsistencies between the software units that have been integrated (called assemblages) or between any of the assemblages and the hardware, as well as the exchange of data to external applications and systems.

■ *Stress testing* is a form of testing that is used to determine the stability of a given system. It involves testing beyond normal operational capacity, often to a breaking point, in order to observe the results. The stress test puts a greater emphasis on robustness, availability and error handling under a heavy load, rather than on what would be considered correct operation under normal circumstances. The goals of such tests may be to ensure the software does not crash in conditions of insufficient computational resources (such as memory or disk space), unusually high concurrency or denial of service attacks.

■ *Acceptance testing* is conducted to determine if the requirements of a specification or contract are met and to validate successful system implementation. Acceptance testing is usually created by business customers (the users or clients) and executed prior to accepting transfer of system ownership from the developer. Acceptance testing provides confidence that the delivered system meets the business requirements of sponsors and users. The acceptance test may also act as the final quality gateway, through which any quality defects not previously detected may be uncovered. Provided certain additional acceptance criteria are met (e.g., security testing, supportability and maintenance standards, usability standards, Section 508 compliance and standards compliance), system sponsors will normally sign off on a system as satisfying contractual requirements and deliver final payment upon successful completion of acceptance testing. Acceptance testing is also done internally when major upgrades, patches, and the like are involved. The terms *acceptance testing, system testing* and *integration testing* may be synonymous in some organizations and in some testing situations.

■ *Regression testing* is any type of system testing that seeks to uncover new bugs or errors in an existing, functional system that has been changed (by implementation of patches, enhancements or configuration changes). It is common for new issues to be uncovered through the introduction of new systems. The intent of regression testing is to ensure that a planned change in software or hardware did not introduce new faults into the system. A common method of regression testing includes rerunning previously successful tests, checking to see if program behavior has changed or previously fixed faults have re-emerged after a system change.

Test Controls

System controls are implemented to protect the confidentiality, integrity and availability of data and the overall management of a system during design, development, testing and deployment. Some of the most common types of test controls include version controls (also called revision controls), security audits and change controls.[2]

■ *Version control* (or revision control) tracks and provides control over changes to source code. Software developers and testers sometimes use version-control software to maintain documentation and configuration files as well as source code. As teams design, develop and test software, it is common for multiple versions of the same software to be running in different sites and for the software's developers to be working simultaneously on updates. Often bugs or features of the software will be present in only certain versions due to the fixing of some problems and the introduction of new ones as the program develops. Therefore, for the purposes of locating and fixing bugs, it is vitally important to be able to retrieve and run different versions of the software to determine in which version(s) a problem occurs.

■ *Security audits* are manual or automatic systematic, measurable technical assessments of a system or application. Manual assessments include interviewing staff, performing security-vulnerability scans, reviewing application and operating system access controls, and analyzing physical access to the systems. Automated assessments include system-generated audit reports and software that monitors and reports changes to files and settings on a system. Systems that require security audits can include personal computers, servers, network routers and switches.

■ *Change control* is a formal process used to ensure that changes to a product or system are introduced in a controlled and coordinated manner. It reduces the possibility that unnecessary changes will be made to a system without forethought, introducing faults or undoing changes made by other users. Typical activities that would call for change control are patches to software products, installation of new operating systems, upgrades to network-routing systems and changes to the electrical power systems supporting the infrastructure. Change control is also a means by which the number of changes in an environment at any one time is controlled.

Test Reporting

Test reporting occurs throughout the testing process—not just at the conclusion of a test event. Stakeholders and sponsors may expect monthly, weekly, or even daily updates on current testing status, activities, schedules and more. Test reporting can be challenging and should be planned out early in the testing process. Common challenges include tailoring test reports to your audience, clarifying confusion about the intent of testing, explaining how testing is actually done, and understanding which testing metrics are meaningful and why. At a minimum, test reports should address the mission of the test, system(s) covered, organizational risk of deploying the system, testing techniques, test environment, updated testing status and obstacles to texting.[6]

Final Evaluation

For most testing projects, the most important deliverable is the final evaluation report, which contains the findings, conclusions and recommendations of the system test. For successful system tests, the final evaluation should confirm to stakeholders that the system has achieved expected results and should specifically address how conducting the test will affect the customer's ROI. For example, if the results of a system test show that implementation of the system will significantly increase the organization's third-party insurance collections, the cost of conducting the test would be considered a sound investment and the benefits of the test would be clear. In addition to discussing ROI, the final evaluation report should address the most common stakeholder questions at the conclusion of a test event, including (but not limited to):

■ Does the system meet our quality and performance expectations?

■ Is the system ready for users?

■ What can we expect when x people simultaneously use the system?

■ What are we risking if we go live with the system now?

Final evaluations may reveal the need for specific end-user training prior to the go-live event and may be instructional for the testing teams themselves. Lessons learned from each test event should be leveraged by the team to improve the planning, execution and evaluation of future tests. Beyond the go-live date, evaluation continues to play a critical role in a system's life cycle. Post-implementation evaluations are critical for measuring initial and long-term user satisfaction, system usability, business and patient care impacts and benefits, and the system's potential for expansion or integration with other organizational systems.

■ References

1. Defense Acquisition University. *Defense Acquisition Guidebook*. Washington, DC: DAU, 2012.

2. Wikipedia, Software Testing. July 2012. http://en.wikipedia.org/wiki/Software_testing. Accessed July 21, 2012.

3. National Institute of Standards and Technology. Software Errors Cost U.S. Economy $59.5 Billion Annually. June 2002. http://www.abeacha.com/NIST_press_release_bugs_cost.htm. Accessed July 25, 2012.

4. Buzzle. Software Testing Methodologies. November 2011. http://www.buzzle.com/articles/software-testing-methodologies.html. Accessed July 25, 2012.

5. Testing Excellence. Test Strategy and Test Plan. November 2008. http://www.testingexcellence.com/test-strategy-and-test-plan/. Accessed July 28, 2012.

6. Kelly M. Dimensions of a Good Test Report. *InformIT*. March 24, 2006. http://www.informit.com/articles/article.aspx?p=457506. Accessed July 28, 2012.

Systems Privacy and Security

John B. Salmon, CPHIMS

LEARNING OBJECTIVES

At the conclusion of this chapter, the reader will be able to:

☑ Describe the tools that can be used to perform an organizational risk assessment.

☑ Identify the three main categories of data management security safeguards.

☑ Describe the components that should be included in an organization's disaster recovery and business continuity plans.

■ Introduction

Concerns about privacy and security of health records are not new to the age of electronic health records (EHRs). In the days of paper records, patients had valid concerns about the privacy of their health information; they expected that access to those records would be limited and that their contents would remain confidential. What has changed in the era of EHRs is the ease with which health records could potentially be lost or breached, even from great distances, and the potential scale of the incidents.

One can imagine the loss or theft of a single patient's chart from a doctor's office or hospital 50 years ago. What is much harder to imagine, in that era, is the theft of thousands of patients' financial information in a matter of mere seconds, or the felonious intrusion into a celebrity's health records by a malicious person located thousands of miles from the locked office of the celebrity's psychiatrist. In today's world, absent organizational understanding and adoption of appropriate privacy policies and security safeguards, the threat of events like those is all too real.

■ Defining Requirements, Policies and Procedures

Today, numerous laws and regulations exist on international, national and regional levels regulating the privacy and security of EHRs. As the use of technologies such as EHRs, personal health records (PHRs), health information exchanges (HIEs), and e-prescribing expands, the need for organizations to implement and maintain strong security will continue to be of high importance.

A primary area of focus for many laws and regulations is patient-sensitive health information that is transmitted or maintained in any form or medium. Those rules may impose restrictions on how organizations (including governments in some cases) may use or disclose health information.

In some cases, an individual organization may elect to put in place policies that further restrict access for a variety of reasons, especially when dealing with research that is on the front lines of medical science. For example, the presence in an individual's DNA of a certain genetic marker may not indicate anything today, but as science develops, that same marker could predict a condition that might have negative consequences for the person.

Based on an understanding of requirements, top management will develop policies and procedures in support of organizational aims. Policies describe an organization's rules and regulations. Procedures provide a stepwise accounting of how tasks are to be performed in order to ensure compliance with policies. Together, policies and procedures can be thought of as an organization's endeavor to put down in writing the rules and processes that its employees and business partners should follow. Before we explore the development of these plans at greater length, it is worth taking a moment to clearly define our terms. *Privacy* laws and rules deal with limits on the use and disclosure of health information. *Security* policies and procedures provide controls on electronic and physical access to health data.

■ Risk Assessment

Once an organization has developed an awareness and understanding of privacy and security laws and requirements, it should undertake an assessment of the organization's readiness with regard to those elements. That assessment should focus on identifying gaps that exist between what is required and what actually exists within the organization's operations. A number of tools may be used in such an assessment. Some examples include:

■ Review of current policies, procedures, contracts and other documents relevant to privacy and security;

■ Organizational surveys or questionnaires that gauge knowledge of, and compliance with, privacy and security requirements;

■ Facility walk-throughs to identify areas where physical security limitations need to be addressed;

■ Technical penetration attempts or other tests to assess security vulnerabilities;

■ Updated legislation, regulations or international agreements that may drive new approaches; and

■ Root-cause analysis of any security breach that may have occurred since the last assessment.

This information should serve to give the organization a realistic assessment of its risk. We can think of risk as the likelihood of a given incident occurring and the adverse impact of such an incident. We often think of such risks in terms of threats—potential scenarios that would have a negative impact on security or privacy—and threat sources—persons or events with the ability to actualize a threat. Examples of threat sources include humans (e.g., malicious hackers, employee saboteurs), natural disasters (e.g., floods, earthquakes) and environmental events (e.g., power grid failure, nuclear or chemical accident). Threats and threat sources are dangerous to any organization that has not made itself entirely immune to them. We use the term *vulnerabilities* to describe flaws or weaknesses that allow exploits or events to result in a security breach or other violation of an organization's security policies.

■ Vulnerability Remediation

The analysis resulting from a risk assessment should go a long way toward identifying the most significant vulnerabilities an organization faces. Additionally, audit reports, reports of anomalous system behavior, vendor advisories, and system security analysis can be used to identify system vulnerabilities. Once those issues have been identified, the organization should embark on a remediation process to eliminate or mitigate the related risks. During the process of remediation, existing policies and procedures will be reviewed, new policies and procedures will be developed, education and training will take place, and controls will be put into place to safeguard critical systems and data. The controls include physical safeguards, administrative safeguards and technical safeguards, which will be discussed below. With these tools at its disposal, an organization can decide to take one of two approaches to reduce risk to an acceptable level:

- No action. The current risk level is deemed acceptable by the organization.

- Mitigate. Implement safeguards to reduce risk to an acceptable level, along with policies and procedures in support of those safeguards.

■ User-Access Controls

To maintain data confidentiality, integrity and availability, an organization must control access to systems and data. User-access controls prevent access by unauthorized users. User-access controls can be broken down into the following categories, sometimes termed the AAA, or triple-A, approach[1]:

- Authentication

- Access

- Accounting

Authentication is the process of attempting to prove that users are who they say they are before allowing them to access a system. Three primary ways exist to authenticate users:

- Something a user knows (e.g., PIN, password);

- Something a user has (e.g., smart card, token); and

- Something a user is (e.g., fingerprint, retina scan).

Once a user has been authorized, an appropriate level of access must be set. Access privileges are ideally set to allow the minimum access necessary in order to perform a job. Role-based access is often defined by a user's role within the organization. For example, physicians generally have the ability to place orders and create and sign documents to which a nurse may not have access. A mid-level provider and medical student may each have subsets of the rights granted to a physician, while a pharmacist may have yet another set of privileges in the system.

Accounting is the final piece of the user-access puzzle. Audit reports and other controls will provide assurance that users are not overstepping their bounds by accessing information that is not required for care delivery and may be forbidden by many privacy laws (for example, looking up co-workers or neighbors in the system). Audit reports should be generated on both a scheduled and a random basis to ensure ongoing compliance.

■ Confidentiality, Integrity and Availability

A primary focus of healthcare IT security is the area of confidentiality. Confidentiality is the process of limiting disclosure of a patient's personal information to comply with policies and regulations, and to maintain the trust that patients have placed in healthcare organizations.[2]

Two other areas that concern healthcare security professionals are integrity and availability of data. Integrity refers to the accuracy and completeness of data. To preserve the integrity of its health information, an organization must successfully implement policies and procedures to protect the data from unauthorized modification, deletion or destruction and to keep it consistent with its source. Additionally, the organization must provide auditing mechanisms to ensure that data has not been altered, deleted or destroyed in an unauthorized manner. Availability calls for information to be protected from any unplanned destruction, whether by accident, vandalism, natural disasters, and so on. Availability also makes certain that information is available to patients when they need it. Care must be taken to ensure that records will be available and survive the organization in the event of closure, merger or similar events. This could also apply to other countries and their internal and external ties through treaties and the like.

■ Organizational Roles

An expert who understands which privacy laws apply to an organization and how they should be properly interpreted plays a crucial role in most healthcare organizations. Laws in many jurisdictions require that each organization appoint an individual, sometimes with the title of chief information security officer, who is tasked with these responsibilities. Among this individual's tasks will be:

- Assessing and maintaining knowledge of rules and regulations;

- Developing policies and procedures;

- Cultivating organizational and cultural awareness and developing educational plans in support of policies;

- Managing appropriate access for external business partners and ensuring documentation exists in support of such access;

- Monitoring compliance with policies;

- Responding to complaints and other issues that arise;

- Conducting or directing others to conduct scheduled and random access audits; and

- Investigating known security breaches and reporting information to appropriate regulatory and/or governmental agencies as required by law.

As with privacy rules, it is important for an organization to identify a person or persons who will be responsible for development of and compliance with security policies and procedures. Often, the first step in these activities is documentation of the organization's baseline state with regard to privacy and security. In many healthcare organizations, the compliance or risk management department serves this function. It is not unreasonable to expect that similar practices and procedures may also be present in other countries but may be worded differently to reflect local laws, culture, regulations and agreements.

■ Data Management Controls

To ensure the security of protected data, a number of safeguards may be deployed. These safeguards seek to meet certain goals, including controlling electronic access to systems containing sensitive patient information or other private data; controlling physical access to locations or devices that may have ready access to secure data; managing data in transit, including e-mail and file transfer; and encryption of data on laptop computers, flash memory drives, or other devices that might be easily lost or stolen.

Safeguards can be categorized into three main groupings: administrative, technical and physical. Administrative safeguards are administrative actions, policies and procedures that an organization deploys in support of its security aims. Administrative safeguards include such actions as the ongoing education of employees on security requirements and scenarios in which data may or may not be used or disclosed, and developing policies and procedures that provide safeguards within the physical and technical realms.

Technical safeguards are electronic means of ensuring that data is not accessible, or that it is encrypted in a way that makes it useless to a third party. Examples of technical safeguards would include the use of network firewalls, secure protocols on any public networks carrying patient data, and encryption of storage media on laptop computers and mobile devices.

The last type of measure, physical safeguards, consists of physical measures, policies and procedures that protect electronic information systems from natural and environmental hazards and unauthorized intrusion. Examples would include data centers that are located outside a flood plain and have redundant sources of power, and limited access to server rooms or areas where data may be accessed or damaged.

■ Disaster Recovery and Business Continuity Plans

Though not solely the province of healthcare IT security professionals, these individuals must be involved in the development of an organization's disaster recovery and business continuity plans. Contingency plans in this area should include the following:

- Analysis of applications and data criticality. Applications and data should be prioritized in order of importance to the organization so that a logical sequence of data recovery can be planned.

- Data backup plan. Detailed plans must be developed to ensure the existence of a retrievable backup copy of the organization's critical data.

- Disaster recovery plan. Procedures must be documented that define how to restore data after any loss, for any reason.

- Emergency-mode operation plan. Downtime plans should be spelled out that will enable the organization to continue to operate in emergency mode while access to electronic data is not possible.

- Testing and revision. All contingency plans must be routinely tested and revised to fill gaps that are discovered and to address changing organizational needs and infrastructure.

■ Auditing

An essential component of an organization's security plans is the ability to audit all access to protected data. No matter how good an organization's policies and procedures are or how strenuously it works to limit access, individuals may still be able to access records that they may not need to access to perform their daily duties. Audit reports enable an organization to identify any breaches or other policy violations, from employee snooping to a large criminal attack.

■ Ongoing System Evaluation

Of course, ensuring security is an ongoing process. Crucial to maintaining compliance is continual evaluation of the security features of existing and new hardware and software. Network diagrams that include the location and configuration of firewalls, servers and routers must be maintained. Documentation of software and hardware as well as vendor contact information must be kept up-to-date. As new applications are introduced, technical and user interfaces and other data access points must be evaluated, and care must be taken to assess whether an application or interface might introduce new security vulnerabilities. Additionally, existing applications must be reevaluated continuously in the face of organizational changes and evolving local, national and international attitudes, laws and regulations.

■ References

1. Newman RC. *Computer Security: Protecting Digital Resources*. Sudbury, MA: Jones and Bartlett, 2010.

2. Cooper T. CPRI Guidelines-Information Security Policies: Guidelines for Establishing Information Security Policies at Organizations with Computer-based Patient Record Systems. HIMSS Privacy & Security Toolkit. January 2007. http://www.himss.org/content/files/CPRIToolkit/version6/v7/D38_CPRI_ Guidelines-Information_Security_Policies.pdf. Accessed October 9, 2012.

Section III.
Administration

CHAPTER 8

Administration Leadership

Raymond A. Gensinger, Jr., MD, CPHIMS, FHIMSS

LEARNING OBJECTIVES

At the conclusion of this chapter, the reader will be able to:

☑ Understand the series of skills needed to guide and facilitate the development of information technology organizations.

☑ Effectively communicate in both written and oral presentations to other leaders and the organization, as well as effectively organize complex meeting structures.

☑ Assess the current systems status by personally interacting with the user community, understanding their perceptions of system and departmental effectiveness, and effectively monitoring performance indicators.

☑ Develop strategic analyses to better align the IT organization with the organization's mission, vision, goals and strategies while effectively managing conflicting interests and priorities through effective conflict resolution techniques.

☑ Learn to balance the necessary relationships with vendors while effectively maintaining a sound business ethic.

◼ Introduction

Leadership is a skill that every member of any organization is responsible for understanding and, when appropriate, undertaking. In the healthcare sector, teams or responsible parties will come together and disband in both well-established and very informal processes. Teams may be made up of two and three individuals or, in project teams, several hundred persons. Leadership skills are necessary in all aspects of the work we do.

◼ Participation in Organizational Strategic Planning

Leaders are responsible for setting the strategic goals for the company, division, department and projects. A strategy is a formal or informal plan of action to achieve a goal. Regardless of where an organization is today, its strategies focus on where it would like to be at some point in the future. To outline and explain its strategies, an organization typically will use one or a series of statements that will be published for the benefit of the employees and customers. These statements express the mission, vision, values and goals of the organization.

MISSION

The mission is a statement of why the organization exists—its purpose statement. Mission statements can vary from simple and concise to complex and hard to understand. The best mission statements are those that can be easily understood and remembered by any members of the organization or those that may be customers of your organization. An effective mission statement is "Do good, have fun, make money."[1] Once read, it is not easily forgotten.

At the organizational level, it is typically the CEO and board of directors who set the mission of the company. The mission does not change with any regularity unless the business of the company is changing as well. Nevertheless, each employee of that company has a responsibility to understand the mission to be sure that as they are evaluating their daily work, they can tie that work to the mission of the company.

VISION

A second expression that a company uses is the vision statement. A vision is the company statement that defines where it wants to go or what it wants to be. The vision is where the company is going and what the company is striving to achieve as it completes the daily work. The CEO and board also typically set the vision. Depending on how far the vision reaches into the future, it may be altered with more regularity than the mission.

VALUES

The addition of values to corporate ideologies has occurred recently. A list of values allows individuals to understand what the company supports and appreciates most. Values are often presented in a list that individuals can compare against in their own personal values as well as the values that are built into the activities they undertake at work. Examples of a healthcare organization's values might include compassion, service and respect. Use the values as guides. Assess whether the values align or conflict with your work assignments. If an initiative lacks alignment or is in conflict with at least one value, it should be called into question.

GOALS

Goals are the measures to support vision accomplishment. The list of goals needs to be SMART: (S) specific, (M) measurable, (A) attainable, (R) relevant and (T) time bound. Sample organizational goals include breaking even on Medicare reimbursement, leading America in clinical quality, and employing primary care providers of choice for the community. Clearly articulated goals that support the mission and vision serve as guides against which to measure the work.

■ The Organizational Environment

Every department of a large organization benefits from having a formalized plan that demonstrates how the work being performed aligns with the strategic goals and objectives of the organization. The complexity and detail of such a plan will vary by organization as well as by the size and complexity of a department. For very small information management and systems departments, the question that arises is whether a full-fledged strategic plan is appropriate. A plan with objectives is a good idea regardless of the organization's size.

In many organizations it will be satisfactory to create a table or spreadsheet that crosswalks the organizational vision and goals down through each of the individual projects or initiatives being worked on within a department or area. Companies often engage leaders in formal governance and leadership committees to promote understanding of the potential projects that may be coming in the next 12 to 18 months. A detailed plan is then created for that time period. Detailed planning much beyond 18 months out, other than for routine replacement, may be less valuable given the rapid changes in the IT industry.

Maintaining a project crosswalk provides a visual summary of the initiatives being handled by an area of service. This crosswalk can then be used within the department and at administrative review sessions to demonstrate the linkage between vision, goals and projects. Additionally, this same tool can serve as a link to the detailed work plans and

FIGURE 8-1. Project Rankings Based on Organizational Goals and Priorities

Index	Request	Weight	Exceptional Care	Effective & Efficient Use of Resources	Strategic Growth	Exceptional Experience	Nation Leading Research & Education	End User Experience	Innovation	Sites Impacted	Score	Relative Rank
			29.00%	24.00%	14.00%	9.00%	9.00%	5.00%	5.00%	5.00%		
Index	Request										0-9	
	Example: enhanced Privacy		**1**	**3**	**3**	**9**	**1**	**1**	**1**	**1**	**2.48**	**28**
1	Home Care/Hospice		9	3	1	3	1	3	1	9	4.48	15
2	Transplant		9	9	1	3	9	3	3	1	6.34	5
3	Mobile Devices		1	3	1	1	1	9	9	9	2.68	26
4	Nurse Triage		9	9	1	3	1	9	3	9	6.32	7
5	Surgical Clinic Outreach		9	3	1	3	1	9	1	1	4.38	16
6	Anesthesia IntraOp U/S/R		9	3	1	1	1	3	1	3	4	18
7	EKG upgrade		3	3	1	1	1	9	1	9	2.86	25
8	Remote Hospital Growth		9	9	1	9	1	3	1	1	6.06	8
9	Remote Clinic Growth		9	9	3	9	1	3	1	1	6.34	6
10	Hearth clinics		9	3	3	9	3	3	1	1	5.08	13
11	HR System		3	9	3	1	9	3	9	9	5.4	12
12	MFM ClinDoc Tools		9	9	1	3	1	3	1	1	5.52	11
13	Affiliate Epic Care Link		1	3	3	9	1	3	9	9	3.38	22
14	CPM Upgrade		9	9	1	1	1	9	1	9	6.04	9
15	Organizational Analytics		9	9	1	1	9	1	9	9	6.76	1

project updates that are maintained by staff. In Figure 8-1 you can see how a series of projects are weighed by scoring each against the organization's goals and priorities. The resulting score and relative rank of each project is calculated and can be shared.

■ Forecasting Technical and Information Needs of an Organization

Leaders in healthcare IT provide assistance and direction in support of the goals and initiatives of the company. This requires a careful balance of leadership and support. It is important that all organizational leaders understand that operational goals direct information technology and not the reverse. Unclear leadership responsibilities of those outside IT can put any organizational project at risk. Any project needs operational leadership and, as necessary, IT operational and management support.

Information management and system leaders need to be keenly aware of organizational goals and be ready to actively recommend appropriate systems and technologies in support of those goals. Organizations that stay focused on goals will not catch the IT leader off guard. When goal deviation does occur, the IT leader needs to be ready to challenge the request to deviate from organizational goals and be prepared to quickly gather appropriate supporting materials to attend to the updated goals. Remaining focused on goals will help the IT leader and the organization to avoid creating the service gap that occurs when requested services outstrip what the internal staff can provide.

New project requests are likely to come from a variety of sources. Some of the requests will be more fully developed than others. Requestors will need support in determining their project's scope, definition and objectives, and, at times, in forming a relationship with a vendor that can undertake the request at hand. The IT leader needs to have a program evaluation staff that can sit with requestors and help them work through a new project request. Lacking resources and structure, customers may suggest a solution to a problem that has not been well defined. They need to understand new technology and infrastructure opportunities, such as leveraging the existing application portfolio, network services, integrating devices, exploring new vendor offerings, and providing internal and external consulting services.

All leaders need to know how to access the tactical steps that are in place to support the organizational goals. Focused goals will bring clarity to the tactics that need to be implemented. Be wary if an organization does not have the discipline to understand what is within its scope to accomplish in any defined time period. Leaders have a responsibility to serve as the organization's conscience regarding IT requests and service overextension. Activities must be clearly prioritized so that all leaders are operating from an identical institutional strategic plan.

Goals, strategies and tactics will inevitably require both redirection and an occasional time-limited expansion of scope. Be aware of the personnel resources that are available in your scope of authority and their availability, and have a well-developed contingency plan for addressing resource needs when the unexpected occurs. This knowledge will help the organization remain nimble and make more efficient and well-thought-out decisions in matters requiring IT support.

Not only must IT leaders understand and support the organizational goals with their system-level knowledge and expertise, but they must also have a methodology that supports the organization's ability to measure activities against their stated goals and objectives. They must facilitate a process in which all leaders work together to define the organization's measures of progress and, ultimately, success. If agreement cannot be reached on a measure, it will be difficult to know when the related goal has been reached.

The measures that are put in place can be used in internal benchmarking, in which the organization defines its current place, defines the objective and then measures activity against both the starting point and the objective at regular reporting intervals. Local and national benchmarks may be available, but a contract may be required to use them. It can often be an expensive proposition to have access to such benchmark data.

Benchmarking data are available in many, but not all, aspects of IT management. Be sure that any benchmarks used are comparable to the data your organization is capable of supplying. Careful clarification on the front end may decrease the challenges of apples-to-oranges comparisons, but a few similar yet unlike data sets may well remain.

■ Developing the IT Strategic Plan

Among the many responsibilities of IT leaders is developing the IT strategic plan. In a very large organization the IT strategic plan may serve as a reference tool for prioritizing the work being done throughout the organization. In small or less complex organizations, the IT plan may be more appropriate as a section or addendum to the organizational strategic plan. When developing an IT strategic plan, it is important to include the input of organizational leaders and the staff responsible for the actionable components.

Begin the process of developing an IT strategic plan with copies of both the current IT plan and the organizational strategic plan. If the organizational plan has not been developed or refreshed in the last 12 months, then you must start the process by validating the strategies and tactics of the organizational plan first. The IT strategic plan must be perfectly aligned with all of the organizational priorities. If there is no previous IT plan to work from, myriad free templates and resources can be found on the web[2] and used as models of formatting and organization.

Consider taking the following steps to develop your IT plan:

- Initiate the document by including the mission, vision, goals and strategies of the organization. IT supports the business and therefore must be grounded in that business and its strategies.

- Identify the current state of the systems and processes that support the business, and assess their effectiveness in meeting their stated functions.

- Define the gap that exists between the functions that are or can be provided and those that need to be developed or procured.

- Compare the timeline for staff to manage development and the costs associated with external development or purchase.

- Identify who will take responsibility for the initiatives to be addressed.

The initial stages of the plan need to reinforce the idea that there is no such thing as an IT project. All projects are organizational and strategic in nature, and IT is only one component within the bigger initiative. Once top managers understand and agree to that, they will recognize why every major initiative will need to be sponsored by an operational leader or leaders. A well-developed plan will map the organizational strategies and the supporting applications and processes for each strategy. Once fully developed, the map will be a visual representation of the current systems' status, an indicator of the expected useful lifeline of the systems or the gap that exists between the strategy and the needed technology.

The remainder of the plan can focus on the gaps—the gap analysis. The plan can outline the current state and desired future state. An approach to consider would be to evaluate the (S) strengths, (W) weaknesses, (O) opportunities and (T) threats (SWOTs) of the current organization. In cases where it is not likely that the gap can be bridged with a single process or system change, the plan needs to outline the stepping stones that can be laid out to achieve the desired outcome. As many of the steps may each take several years to complete, the plan's details need only focus on the first step or two and then be more high level for the remaining steps. This is practical as the technologies and organizational priorities may change during the interval.

Finally, the plan needs to outline some of the more pure IT initiatives and personnel needs. Examples of this might include advanced Internet protocol (IP) technologies like voice over Internet protocol (VoIP), data center growth and capacity planning, network growth and development, and general systems-refresh strategies. Elements considering the current and future resourcing needs as well as the transition and succession plans for staff and leaders help to ensure consistent leadership.

At some point staff will be leaving the company. Is there someone who has the appropriate education and skill to step into an interim role? Does that person have the qualities to take on the role permanently? How about for any key managers and supervisors? Each leader should have a mentee within the organization who is being groomed and educated to move up when the time is appropriate. A well-prepared organization has the bench strength to maintain leadership continuity in the same way it has system redundancy to maintain continuity.

IMPLEMENTING THE IT STRATEGIC PLAN

Once developed, the IT strategic plan needs to remain a living object and therefore must be regularly maintained. To achieve this, the document needs to be part of the organizational strategic plan and updated according to any changes to its companion. The key IT objectives are visible to the entire department, so they have an opportunity to see and commit to each objective on a daily basis. Individuals' performance objectives can be tied back to this plan, and regular reports can be used as measures against the overall IT strategic plan. Finally, treat the plan itself as a project. Maintain a color-coded scorecard of goal progress and achievement for all to see.

■ Evaluating Performance

Measures that monitor the ongoing effectiveness and progress of a department's activities are necessary for leaders to judge the performance of a department or work area. In an operational unit that has both projects and services, two types of measures will be necessary.

The development of a Gantt chart may be the most effective way of tracking a project. A Gantt chart includes a series of rows detailing each of the steps and sub-steps to be completed within the project. Each row has multiple columns identifying start dates, projected end dates, dependencies, responsible parties, completion percentage and the like. The Gantt chart provides an excellent way of visualizing an entire project in both highly summarized and detailed ways. Commercial project-tracking software products are available, but many organizations effectively manage projects using a simple spreadsheet. An example of measuring a project against goals is included later in this chapter.

In departments where service is a component of the work done, it will be important to have a service level agreement (SLA) with indicators that are tracked at regular intervals. The expected service level can be internally derived, negotiated with the customers or driven by externally agreed-upon benchmarks. Service-level parameters can best be measured using a dashboard visualization tool. A dashboard is a series of graphs or tables that indicate the current performance, the historic performance for an appropriate time interval, the expected quality of services and, if appropriate, the acceptable level of variation below and above the stated goal. In addition to the quality-of-service goal, there may be a stretch goal, though it is not usually on a control chart. The stretch goal is typically an internally desired target that exceeds any quality-of-service parameters that have been agreed to.

A typical dashboard includes a series of control charts. Control charts are statistical representations of the graphs discussed above. They add lines representing the upper and lower control limits. This takes into account that there will be natural variation in the results represented around a mean. To the extent that a series of points begins to move in one direction or the other, it will become necessary to review the process looking for special-cause variation. In any business, variation will often increase costs. In healthcare, variation may also signal changes in the quality of patient care and therefore warrants immediate attention and understanding. A sample quality-of-service control chart is presented in Figure 8-2.

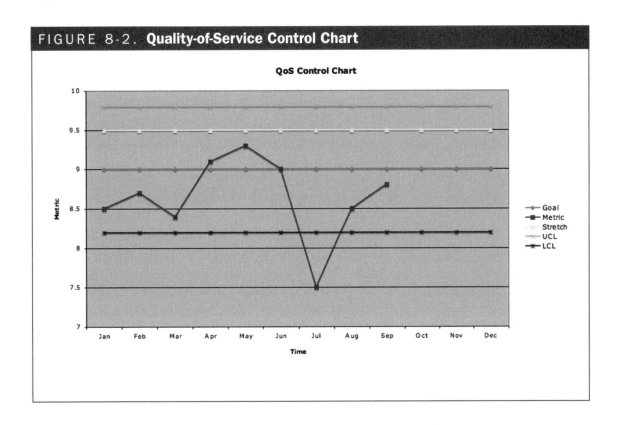

FIGURE 8-2. **Quality-of-Service Control Chart**

■ Evaluating Effectiveness and User Satisfaction

At times organizational leaders may find that they have become too insulated from the organization and the stakeholders they are serving. IT leaders may be especially prone to this because they often work in a separate location from where care services are provided or because the complexity of their work slowly removes them from the day-to-day environment of care.

Regular departmental and systems assessment will prevent isolation and enhance communication with stakeholder communities throughout the organization. The assessments need to include the effectiveness of both the systems supported and the services provided.

Measuring systems effectiveness needs to start with a baseline analysis. This ties in very nicely with the earlier discussion of understanding service-level benchmarks. It is important to have both an objective and a subjective assessment of the quality metrics. A simple example of this can be seen in an assessment of system availability. Ninety-nine percent uptime for a computer system sounds highly efficient and tracks very nicely along a control chart. Customers, however, report that they struggle with the average of 1.75 hours of system downtime each week, even though that falls within the 1% deemed acceptable. A customer assessment helps the leader understand the customer's point of view. The 24×7 healthcare environment has expectations of 99.999% system availability.

A baseline assessment can be accomplished in several ways. Face-to-face interviews have value for systems that affect only a small number of stakeholders, especially when they work in disparate parts of the company. Unit rounding will be effective when actual observation of the system in use is needed. What better way to demonstrate an interest in stakeholders' work than to be present in their environment? Typically, it is most efficient to meet with a group of users together. This can be done by going to departmental or unit meetings that are already scheduled. Alternatively, you may choose to call a townhall meeting to look at a general situation or a focus group to examine specific situations. Both can be organized as either physical or virtual meetings.

The baseline assessment is designed to gather data regarding the systems that the stakeholders are using and the way they are being used. Take the time to understand the stakeholders' expectations of system availability and performance. Listen to their past internal and external experiences, and pay special attention if they note adverse changes in systems performance. Use the assessment time to accept feedback regarding opportunities for system operating improvements. Be clear that not all requests can be accommodated, but be open minded to what will result if some meaningful feedback is directly addressed.

Once the baseline is determined, commit to a regular process of follow-up analyses. Identify the interval that is most appropriate. If the organization concurs with an initial assessment that the performance of IT systems and services is satisfactory, then an annual follow-up assessment will be sufficient. A lower than desirable assessment warrants a prompter turnaround and more frequent follow-up. Regular communication or monthly reports should address commitments to improvement. Effectiveness should be reassessed at regular intervals agreed to with customers.

The process of follow-up assessment can be accomplished by telephone or web-based surveys. Providing easily accessible feedback tools within the applications themselves will prompt regular responses. Customers will appreciate the availability of immediately accessible feedback because it will enable them to avoid making calls to the help desk.

Departmental effectiveness needs to be differentiated from systems effectiveness as you do your assessment. The distinction is necessary because customers and stakeholders have a multitude of different needs. The methodology for retrieving feedback about the two can be essentially the same, but the objectives will be different. In the departmental assessment, the value is in understanding how the personnel respond and relate to others within the organization.

Departmental effectiveness is measured using interpersonal metrics reported by customers. Leaders have an advantage because they have also had the opportunity to receive customer service. A typical first impression of customer service is formed by the response time to inquiries. Keep in mind that customers are providing clinical services and therefore are not typically in one physical location for more than a few moments at a time. Any response time greater than just a couple of minutes is likely to cause dissatisfaction. A popular service management framework to consider is ITIL, the Information Technology Infrastructure Library.[3]

Additional factors to consider evaluating include:

- Does staff empathize with the concerns and frustrations of customers?

- Does staff communicate regularly with customers when they are working on a problem that takes more than a short time to resolve?

■ Promoting Stakeholder Understanding of IT Opportunities and Constraints

Health information and management systems leaders have a responsibility to discuss the opportunities and systematic limitations of using information systems to address organizational goals and objectives. Leaders must assist stakeholders in understanding where there are opportunities to be gained through the use of automation tools. Equally important is the leaders' ability to temper enthusiasm by explaining any limitations that must be understood as well.

The initiation of a project charter is a critical juncture in IT's support of the organization. Success can be achieved using a well-articulated and accepted process that facilitates understanding and communication between the leader and the stakeholders. A method for initiating a project is via the utilization of an SBARC. SBARC is an acronym for situation, background, assessment, recommendation and communication. This is an extension of the SBAR (minus the communication step) developed at Kaiser Permanente by Michael Leonard.[4] The one- to two-page SBARC proposal helps to frame a situation or request and a method of addressing it. It is an easy way to document a situation and proposed approach to a very wide audience. The simplicity of the tool makes it easy for a knowledgeable team member to complete and provides a concise summary for leaders to assess prior to committing to a full project proposal or a pro forma financial plan.

The SBARC process begins a discussion of the key goals and objectives of an initiative and frames some of the potential strategies for resolution. As appropriate, the SBARC may be followed up with a more formal business planning process and pro forma financial plan. A disciplined approach to framing and initiating projects ensures that the stakeholder and the project team members are operating from an identical framework. Ways of assessing the process-improvement needs might include the utilization of either a Lean (production practice looking at resource consumption) or Kaizen methodology (continuous improvement processes) as a tool for optimizing the performance of a system. Once developed, the framework includes the deliverables of the project along with the cost and timing, together defined as the scope of the project.

A well-written plan that has been signed off on by all stakeholders will help to eliminate the opportunity for scope creep to infiltrate the project. Scope creep is a common event in the life of a project. New opportunities or events will warrant that new analyses occur. A disciplined analysis following the project planning approach outlined above will weigh the merits of new opportunities in the context of the project as a whole. This is referred to as scope or project change control management. If a value-added suggestion is made and approved, then the plan is amended and communication undertaken. Scope creep is the undisciplined addition of new goals, objectives and milestones that may have a negative effect on the cost or timeline of a project. This occurs when inadequate analyses of suggestions are allowed to work their way into the process. An effective way of eliminating scope creep is to anticipate it and have a method of reviewing recommended changes in scope with the project's leadership team on a regular basis.

At times a more appropriate method of project planning is the agile methodology. Using this approach, initial objectives are expressed and a series of sprints are defined. At the end of each sprint, the team members review the product and suggest enhancements to be included in the next sprint interval. This method allows for more flexible development cycles.

■ Developing Policies and Procedures for Information and Systems Management

The implementation of policies and procedures within an organization facilitates the standardization of actions and operations for employees, patients and guests. Often, policies and procedures can be implemented in any portion of the organizational structure, from the entire company to the very smallest operation. Leaders face two questions: Is the policy really needed? If so, at what level of the organization must that policy be implemented? To maintain accreditation in the United States, a healthcare organization is required to have a defined set of policies on information management and security and privacy policies. IT leaders in other countries will need to understand the accreditation standards that apply to their operations.

Prior to policy implementation, consider for what purpose are you developing a policy, and whether it is necessary to have a policy and procedure to govern that activity or process. If so, do not begin from scratch. Peers, both locally and nationally, have addressed many of the issues you face, and those same peers will have advice and examples to share. Start with a local survey of your peers. This has the advantage of helping you establish local networking connections and begin to create a community standard for the policy in discussion.

If local support is not available, then move to national peer groups, but ask yourself why you may be in front of the curve for your particular community. You can always look to organizations like HIMSS,[5] IFHIMA,[6] and IMIA[7] or other national professional associations. These organizations will all have examples of a variety of policies.

A reason for *not* adopting a particular policy or procedure is your inability to audit and report on the effectiveness of the policy in question. If you do not have the ability to audit, then you run the risk of a challenge by local health system accreditors. Do what is measurable, measure what you do, review what you have measured, and act on the results of what you have reviewed.

Be prepared to act on the results of your audit measurements, and make sure that the implications of failing to adhere to a policy are built into the policy itself. The consequences of noncompliance, when embedded within the policies and procedures, will help close the loop for employees. If there needs to be room for exceptions, those exceptions must be outlined as part of the policy as well. Once again, if there are no consequences for deviation from policy, then you must ask yourself whether there is a need for the policy in the first place.

On some occasions, policies and procedures are used as much for education as for any other purpose. A good example of this is a password policy. It is inevitable that a challenge will be brought forward regarding the implementation of a password policy. As most, if not all, systems allow the definition of the policy to be incorporated directly into the software, it really is unnecessary to have a separate policy because the system will not allow staff to create a password that does not meet the standard. In this case, a policy explaining the risks of weak password construction in addition to meaningful education on how to create a strong password that is easy to remember might be a better overall strategy.

■ Complying with Legal and Regulatory Standards

The discipline of information and management systems includes a complex web of legal, regulatory, accreditation and other compliance issues. Each country is going to have its own sources of oversight. IT leaders have a responsibility for knowing the sources of those standards in their own country. In the United States, navigation of Meaningful Use, e-prescribing, Conditions of Participation and HIPAA is just the beginning of this complex responsibility. Effective leaders need to either understand the many nuances of these standards or have easy access to individuals who can assist in their understanding.

Those individuals include the corporate compliance officer or equivalent, legal counsel and the lead Joint Commission liaison, among others.

Depending on the size of the organization, all of the responsibilities may fall on the shoulders of one individual. Most likely, though, the responsibilities will be distributed around the organization, with those individuals coming together under the auspices of a corporate compliance committee, a Joint Commission International[8] steering committee, or perhaps an audit and education committee. The information that these individuals are responsible for is ever changing. Their knowledge comes from several key documents, most of which are available directly or by purchase over the Internet. In the United States, the information can be obtained from the Centers for Medicare & Medicaid Services (CMS),[9] and internationally, from Joint Commission International.[10]

The two most influential sources of standards for healthcare organizations in the United States are CMS and The Joint Commission, formerly known as the Joint Commission on Accreditation of Healthcare Organizations.

CMS can be found at http://www.cms.hhs.gov/. CMS is within the Department of Health and Human Services (HHS). The key operating document for a hospital that receives any funding from CMS is "Conditions for Coverage and Conditions of Participation." The details of this framework are detailed at http://www.cms.hhs.gov/CFCsAndCoPs/. A healthcare organization is held to these conditions in order to receive funds for services. On a day-to-day basis the Federal Register serves as the "the official daily publication for rules, proposed rules, and notices of Federal agencies and organizations, as well as executive orders and other presidential documents," and the first and last indications of proposed rules changes.

Joint Commission International (JCI) is located online at http://www.jointcommissioninternational.org/. It serves as the voluntary accreditation body for more than 400 healthcare organizations throughout the world. Accreditation is accomplished by complying with a comprehensive list of standards published by JCI. Organizations meet the standards through preparation followed by a scheduled site review by a team of JCI surveyors.

■ Adhering to Ethical Business Principles

Corporate financial implosions and evidence of legal and ethical impropriety bring the need for organizational and leadership ethics to the forefront. As an organizational leader, it is important to the practice of your profession and your position as a role model to your staff that you adhere to an identifiable code of business or corporate ethics.

In the context of your role you must know and adhere to the corporate code of ethics as established by the administration or board of directors of the organization where you work. On one end of the spectrum, business ethics are meant to ensure that all members of the organization are complying with local, state and federal laws in the work that they do and that they as individuals feel both compelled and safe to report any activities that are not within the scope of the law. Both large and small organizations will have a person or department charged with corporate compliance.

Corporate compliance programs are made up of a set of basic elements. Senior management must be aware of and involved in the process of compliance. Policies and procedures must reflect the organization's procedures for achieving compliance. Education about compliance must be given to both management and employees. And there must be both monitoring programs and disciplinary procedures to act upon those not adhering to the compliance approaches. Actions need to be in the best interest of the company and absent any financial gain for individuals or for any of their immediate family.

At the other end of the spectrum, business ethics extend the concepts of fairness and equity both within and outside the organization. The organization is a member of the business and local communities, and there is an implied duty to be a contributor to those communities.

■ Employing Comparative Analysis Strategies

Organizational leaders need to understand more than their own departmental measures and metrics. Information technology leaders are often part of the operational leadership of the entire organization. They need to understand the organization's overall financial and budgetary reports, its comparative benchmarks and its overall performance.

BUDGETS

To understand how the organization is doing financially, it is necessary to be able to read and understand a budget spreadsheet. Typically such reports will be summarized and reviewed by the financial leaders of the company. These reports include the annual budgets by line item and the projected budget and expenditures to date. Variances between budgeted and actual expenditures to date will be reported, and there may also be a column that enables comparison with actual expenses for the most recent historic comparable period of time. This often consists of last year's expenses for the same time period. Many expenses are spread evenly over the year and are easy to predict, measure and compare. Other expenditures have unique timing considerations that, if not understood, can lead to a false understanding of the reports. Revenues and expenses that are recognized on a semi-annual or quarterly basis can make year-to-date results appear far from expected, especially if the budget is constructed with an even distribution of those same expenses and revenues. A well-constructed budget report will include notation explaining the timing of events.

An organization will classify many of its expenses as either capital or operating expenses. Capital expenses are treated as assets and have enduring value to the organization. Each asset is then depreciated over a period of time that depends on the expected useful life of the asset. An asset with a useful life of five years will then have a depreciation expense of one-fifth of its original value that then shows up as an operating expense in the annual budget. This depreciation expense may show up in either IT or the operating depart-ment to which the asset was attributed. Expenses that would typically be classified as operating include salaries, benefits, maintenance, travel, utilities and supplies.

OTHER FINANCIAL AND NON-FINANCIAL INDICATORS

Financial and non-financial indicators are measured to compare one organization to the next or to national benchmarks. Days in accounts receivable, or AR days, is an expres-sion of the average amount of time it takes for the organization to receive payment from payers after the bills have been submitted to the guarantor. The discharged not final billed (DNFB) is an indicator of the expected amount of money to be billed to the guar-antor but not yet submitted because of outstanding documentation or procedural issues. Both of these indicators are important, as they represent money due to the organization but not yet received. Cash available to the organization is referred to as the days cash on hand and represents the number of days the organization could continue to operate if no further new funds were received by the organization. The larger the number, to a point, the better it is for the organization.

BENCHMARKS

In addition to the previously discussed benchmarks specifically for information and management systems, there are benchmarks for organizational operations. These too are made up of both internal and external comparisons. The internal benchmarks are usually set by operations or the board of directors and often are reflections of the finan-cial indicators listed above. Typically the organization will set its goals for the number of days in AR and days cash on hand. External benchmarks may include additional financial indicators but are likely to reflect quality, safety, regulatory or accreditation measures.

QUALITY INDICATORS

Quality indicators set by the state's department of health or payers to the organization are fixed measures that cannot be controlled by the organization. They may serve as goals to be met. Each country may have its own voluntary or required quality bench-marking processes. In the United States, other indicators are available from external services like the University HealthSystem Consortium or Premier®. These entities will take extracts of your organization's data and aggregate them with comparable data from other organizations. This information is then distributed back to the data contributors so that each organization can compare its own results with different slices of the health-care continuum. The advantage of these external comparison groups is that they enable an organization to compare itself to other organizations of like size, educational service, payer mix, geographic location, and so forth. The downside is that these are subscription services that provide comparisons only to paid subscribers.

■ Preparing and Delivering Business Communications

Leadership skills are going to be assessed on a regular basis from both written and verbal communication, as well as the ability to organize and manage a typical business meeting. Organized meeting preparation assists the attendees in understanding the goals and objectives of the time invested. Well-prepared documents outline the topics and time to be spent on each issue. An example of a comprehensive meeting agenda is presented in Figure 8-3.

A departmental template for all meeting agendas and minutes will facilitate communication. This creates a uniform method of communication that allows the staff to learn how to identify issues, actions and decisions in a consistent way. Each variation in formatting adds a level of complexity for the customer.

The agenda template in Figure 8-3 starts with the organization name and committee name clearly evident. Each header defines the section to follow. "Meeting Information" states the date, time and location of the meeting, while the subsequent section, "Attendees," lays out the expected participants and the roles they will play. The agenda itself lists each of the discussion points, the expected outcomes, the parties responsible to lead the discussion and the time limit for the presentation, discussion and decision, if necessary.

The "Committee Action Items" and "Committee Action Register" sections list the pending actions from the most recent meeting and other prior meetings, respectively. These sections enable all parties to have a comprehensive understanding of the status of all action items that remain open. Lacking those sections, it would be easy for a busy committee to lose track of items that have lower levels of priority than others. It is acceptable to push back the date of some deliverables, but those changes should be made in a transparent way with the support of the committee as a whole.

The remaining sections of the agenda keep a record of actions and issues that are yet to be resolved. "Open Issues" lists items that were not completed by the desired action during the previous scheduled meeting. Any item that has been tabled will be left in the "Open Issues" section. "New Issues" serves as a tracking section for the meeting record

FIGURE 8-3. **Meeting Agenda Template**

Organization Name	NAME OF YOUR Committee

Meeting Information

Meeting Name:	November ITSC	Meeting Date:	11/28/2007
Time:	7:00 am to 9:00 am	Location:	Room 106

Attendees

Names:	□ → Chairperson	□ → Attendee 2	□ → Attendee 3
	□ → Attendee 1	□ →	□ →

November Guests:
□ → Guest 1 and reason for attendance
□ → Guest 2 and reason for attendance

Agenda

Discussion Point	Expected Outcome	Responsible Party	Time (Min)
Agenda Review	Agree to meeting goals		5
Prior Meeting Review	Approve prior meeting minutes. Review/Update Action Items Review/Update Issues Status		5
Item 1	Discussion v. Decision		10
Item 2	Discussion v. Decision		10
Item n	Discussion v. Decision		30

Committee Action Items

Action Item	Comments/Progress Made	Responsible Party	Completion Date Original	Revised	Status
2008 IS Budget	• → Send 2008 IS budget communication to ITSC committee members		10/31/07		
Data Center Approval Request — November Board	• → Send Data Center summary information to ITSC committee members		11/2/07		
Tactical plan for all IS Initiatives	• → Listing of all current and requested service requests for IS • → Tool will become a part of decision making process • → Draft to be presented at October ITSC for approval		12/20/07 Awaiting System Capital Project Approval Process		

Committee Action Register – Pending Items

Action Item	Comments/Progress Made	Responsible Party	Completion Date Original	Revised	Status

FIGURE 8-3. *Continued*

Organization Name	NAME OF YOUR Committee	

Complete IS 5 year assessment / estimate of infrastructural requirements and associated cost	• → Expand 5 year incremental costing grid to include expense / capital impacts related to replacement equipment / upgrades etc. (known costs of doing business)		TBD			
Develop ITSC Dashboard	• → Define metrics – situational / operational	Team	TBD			

Open Issues (from previous meetings)

Issue	Action Taken or Required	Assigned to		Status

New Issues Raised

Issue	Action Taken or Required	Assigned to

Tentative Future Meeting Agendas

Discussion Point	Planned Outcome	Responsible Party	Time (Min)
Simple Sign on / CCOW / Biometric Access technology	Establish strategy for technology access • → Educate committee on capabilities, pros/cons, complexity, and implementation impacts • → Decide how to perform exploration – funding • → Potential to neutral / external party with industry expertise define scope	Team	

Key Decisions Made:

Meeting Minutes

Discussion Point	Discussion Notes	Time (Min)
Agenda Review	Meeting began at 7:00am.	
Prior Meeting Review		
Item 1		
Item 2		
Item n		
Adjourn	Meeting adjourned at 9:00 AM	

keeper and the chair. This location is used to add issues that will need attention or completion in the time between meetings.

Presentation skills help define a leader. Leaders speak clearly and with authority. Let the audience know the purpose and the desired outcome of your presentation. Is the purpose to inform or to have an action result from the materials presented? During the presentation, include all the information that attendees need to understand, but highlight the key points rather than every detail. At the close, restate both the purpose and the desired outcome. Address questions and concerns at the close as this prevents disruption and loss of continuity during the presentation.

Project communication plans and status reports are important materials for everyone from project and organizational leaders through line staff. Figure 8-4 shows an example of a project status report for an organization's EHR implementation. Specific issues and sub-issues are identified with both a color-coded and a numeric indication of their status. Each issue also includes the specific current completion date. This report does not reflect the project budget. The budget status needs to be reported on a regular basis and clearly demonstrate the status overall and year-to-date. All variances greater than a predetermined amount need to be explained.

FIGURE 8-4. Status Report for an EHR Implementation

STATUS HISTORY

Legend symbols: ⊙ ⊙ ◎ ⬆ ⬇ ◯ ⬤

Area	Topic	Apr-05	May-05	Jun-05	Jul-05	Aug-05	Sep-05	Oct-05
Project Assessment	Overall Status	◎	⊖⬆	⊖	⊖	⊖	⊖	⊖

Area	Topic	Apr-05	May-05	Jun-05	Jul-05	Aug-05	Sep-05	Oct-05
Project Management	Staffing	◎	◎	◎	⊖⬆	⊖	⊖	⊖
	Detailed Project Plan	◎	◎	◎	◎	◎	◎	◎
	Implementation Progress	◎	⊖⬆	⊖	⊖	⊖	⊖	⊖
	Communication	◎	⊖⬆	⊖	⊖	⊖	⊖	⊖
	Change Management	◎	⊖⬆	⊖	⊖	⊖	⊖	⊖
Go Live	On Schedule	◎	◎	◎	◎	◎	◎	◎

Area	Topic	Apr-05	May-05	Jun-05	Jul-05	Aug-05	Sep-05	Oct-05
Cadence	Staffing and			◎	⊖⬆	⊖⬆	⊖	⊖
	Workflows			◎	⊖⬆	⊖	⊖	⊖
	Reporting Needs			◎	◎	◎	◎	◎
	System Build				◎	◎	◎	◎
	Testing							
	End User Training							
	Post Live Activities							
HIM	Staffing and			⊖	⊖	⊖	⊖	⊖
	Workflows			◎	⊖⬆	⊖	⊖	⊖
	Reporting Needs			◎	◎	◎	◎	◎
	System Build				◎	◎	◎	⊖⬆
	Testing							
	End User Training							
	Post Live Activities							

Like other communications, status documents need to provide an initial brief summary and follow with the necessary supporting documentation. For project communications, the timeline and the completion status are the best first materials for review. In a project status report, a color-coded summary of tasks and status provides valuable visual clues. Use of arrows also provides quick indicators of the general direction of the elements compared to their immediately preceding status. Keep the reports simple by using red, yellow and green to identify tasks that are out of compliance, at risk or on track, respectively. Status reports need only be a single page with a table of color-coded tasks, a summary of the issues related to the tasks' color codes, the responsible parties for each task, and the estimated date of resolution or completion.

■ Facilitating Group Discussions and Meetings

As important as it may be for a leader to direct a conversation, it is equally important to know how to facilitate a group through a difficult discussion. This differs somewhat from a typical business meeting. Knowing the issues, controversies and positions of meeting participants helps to manage the discussion. Construct meeting agendas with consideration for the time it will take to resolve issues, and keep controversial decisions at the top of the agenda or as the sole item so there will be adequate time for discussion and resolution. If able, meet with and begin a process of negotiation and education with key committee members in advance of the meeting.

Complex decisions and controversial topics can make meeting management a challenge. Become familiar with *Robert's Rules of Order*[11] and define the expected rules of participation with committee members at the formation of the committee or at the beginning of any particularly challenging meeting. Keep a record of all motions and seconds. Record the essence of key discussions, including the names of participants when there is dissension. Ideally, decisions will be arrived at by consensus, but when necessary keep a detailed record of the vote. As the discussion leader, do not let any committee members dominate the conversation, especially if they do not wait their turn in the queue. Ask speakers to clarify whether they are speaking in favor of or against the particular motion. Do not hesitate to clarify whether a member is contributing new insights to the discussion or just echoing another's thoughts. In the interest of time, the focus needs to be on contributions.

The committee chairperson must not dominate the conversation. The chair carefully guides the conversation through the selection of speakers, asks probing and clarifying questions, and contributes or highlights commentary as necessary. Use the straw poll as a tool. Identify those in favor of a motion and those who can live with the motion. If some attendees cannot live with the motion as stated, they should be asked to offer an alternative motion that serves the goals of all parties at the table. This keeps attendees accountable for problem solving.

■ Providing In-house Consulting Services

Consulting services are frequently purchased when personnel resources are in short supply or when a specified skill mix is lacking within the organization. Most frequently an organization goes to the outside to facilitate a large initiative when internal resources cannot be spared. It is possible to retain professional services on an issue-by-issue basis or to keep a firm on retainer. Additionally, an organization could supply in-house consultation as a means of managing, staffing or advising on any manner of need.

In-house consultation can be provided by individuals on an as-needed basis, but larger organizations are beginning to develop a project management office (PMO).[12] The information technology and facility/plant management departments and staff often have the greatest depth of experience in managing large and complex projects at any organization, and the PMO may grow out of one or both of those areas. The PMO has personnel who are trained and/or certified in project management methodology as sponsored by the globally recognized Project Management Institute.[13]

Staff of the PMO are skilled at meeting with operational personnel to understand the detailed requirements of the project at hand and translate those requirements into a plan for execution. They understand the processes of resource gathering, project planning and project scope management and the tools for visualizing the life of the project. They have the skills to manage development of the project's pro forma financial statements and the ongoing project budget. As the organization moves from IT projects to strategic operational projects with IT components, the IT project leaders can begin to alter their focus from operational leadership to true project management.

Information technology leaders may also serve as the voice of internal expertise. As departments throughout the healthcare organization begin to automate, they may need guidance or advice as to how to incorporate technologies into their workflow. The IT leaders or the IT PMO can provide innovation support to explore existing technologies to implement or watch for these departments. Partnership between the operational and technology experts creates an opportunity for innovation.

■ Developing Educational Strategies for IT Staff

Leaders are hired due to a combination of their experiences and skills. They will likely select individuals to work for them based on similar criteria. The staff will continue to gain experience as they do their jobs, but there is very little opportunity for them to continue their education and expand their knowledge unless someone creates opportunities for them. Education can be provided in many ways and at relatively little overall cost.

At the very least, education needs to be valued. Commit to the time it will take for staff to complete further education, and commit to supporting the cost of the education as well. Encourage staff to broaden their skills by taking opportunities to stretch their current skills or cross train to areas that are beyond their current experiences. When it becomes tempting to reduce costs by eliminating educational support, also consider how much it will cost to recruit new staff and whether the skills sought are those that the current staff may be lacking.

Initiate your educational support by creating low-cost educational opportunities for the staff. Ensure that staff members are signed up as members of all the vendor user groups, both locally and nationally. Take advantage of professional societies, interest groups and other local educational opportunities as well. Many of these sponsor local presentations and educational dinner meetings as conveniences to their members. Societies like HIMSS offer both local and national membership. Education provided by the society is free in many cases and is often available in multiple media formats so that individuals can attend in person or via webcasting, webinars and other telecasting options. Many vendors will also make free educational opportunities available to the staff.

When funds are available consider having staff take turns attending vendors' user conferences or professional society conferences. That way staff members are able to go to conferences every couple of years. Ask those staff who go to take time to explore specific educational sessions of interest to the whole organization. Upon the conference attendee's return, arrange for a team luncheon at which that person can report on information learned and share any gathered materials. Most societies and large user groups make their conference presentations available online, so it is very easy to share the content with staff.

As noted earlier, succession planning is an important part of the overall IT planning process. An investment in education and the thoughtful application of the new skills expands the capabilities of the IT staff and helps to ensure a well-balanced and mature department.

■ Staying Current on IT Technologies and Trends

The overall education of the IT team members extends beyond the applications they service and the immediate issues and objectives that are at hand. Team members need to stay connected to a variety of disciplines related to their specific sphere of expertise. The greatest opportunity for this added education comes from within the organization itself. Listen to the expertise of colleagues and peers. Be engaged and ask questions to become more knowledgeable. So much of the work we do overlaps with the work of others. Knowledge will expand your effectiveness in the work you do.

Outside of your own colleagues, a valuable educational resource is the media and printed press. *The Guardian, Healthcare IT News, People's Daily* and *The Wall Street Journal* are often the first to pick up on and report trends or activities that have national or international significance in many disciplines. Take the time to review the headlines and articles. Organizational leaders will be regularly asked to comment on materials in those publications.

Many publications now offer really simple syndication (RSS) or other services that will e-mail the headlines or article titles that align with subjects you are interested in. With so many potential sources of new information, having the option to push material of selected interest is a time-saver. Given the option of being proactive or reactive, a successful leader will choose the former path.

■ Managing Risk

A key piece of the IT planning process integrates with the organizational efforts to manage risk. Issues of risk can be addressed along two dimensions. The first is magnitude of risk: If the event does occur, how big an impact will it have on the organization, process or project? The second dimension is the likelihood of the risk: What is the best estimate of the likelihood that the risk event will in fact occur? Within each dimension the risk is low, medium or high and assigned a point value of 1 to 3, respectively.

The tool shown in Figure 8-5 depicts these two dimensions in a matrix. The values of each pair of dimensions are multiplied to generate a numeric score. A score of 1 is the lowest risk, while a score of 9 indicates the greatest risk. Color-coding the scores highlights the degree of risk being borne.

Organizations' risk management strategies will vary depending on their tolerance for risk. Typically scores of 6 or higher will warrant the creation of a contingency plan. A contingency plan is an alternative path, project or process that would be considered in the event that the primary path is disrupted. A simple example would be a backup plan

FIGURE 8-5. Risk Matrix

		Magnitude of Risk		
		Low 1	Medium 2	High 3
Likelihood of Risk Occurring	Low 1	**1**	**2**	**3**
	Medium 2	**2**	**4**	**6**
	High 3	**3**	**6**	**9**

to print and distribute paper reports in the event that the electronic distribution process is disrupted for longer than a preset amount of time. Within any one very large project there are likely to be multiple smaller contingency plans to account for any individual event that may occur.

Risk management and business continuity planning are taking on great prominence in healthcare. Leaders have the responsibility to bring to light the full effects of system loss and the costs associated with mitigating those risks. The solutions are often expensive and will create considerable conversation, especially around the likelihood of any particular event happening.

■ Quality Standards and Practices

Oversight for an information technology department, especially one that has responsibilities for software development, requires careful attention to quality control standards. Recently in the United States, the Institute of Medicine published *Health IT and Patient Safety: Building Safer Systems for Better Care.*[14] While a U.S. publication, the principles and recommendations set forth have international relevance.

Software as delivered and its subsequent configuration by IT staff require comprehensive and regular review to ensure safe and high-quality performance. Quality assurance begins with the staff that implement and configure the software technically. Performance can be measured against testing results provided by the software vendors themselves and internally developed quality assurance scripts. External quality and patient-safety organizations such as The Leapfrog Group[15] can provide testing to ensure appropriate decision support and alerts for computerized practitioner order entry (CPOE) programs.

Leaders must set clear expectations, or a plan, for the quality standards to be delivered and then measure, report and modify the plan to continually improve on the products delivered. Publishing current performance as well as the goal and stretch objectives will remind the entire department of the expectations and aspirations for which the group is striving.

■ References

1. Mission Statement, Epic Corporation.

2. http://www.healthcareitnews.com/news/5-tips-creating-strategic-plan-it. Accessed September 16, 2012.

3. http://www.itil-officialsite.com/home/home.aspx. Accessed September 8, 2012.

4. Institute for Healthcare Improvement. SBAR Technique for Communication: A Situational Briefing Model. 2012. http://www.ihi.org/knowledge/Pages/Tools/SBARTechniqueforCommunicationASituationalBriefingModel.aspx. Accessed August 27, 2012.

5. http://www.himss.org/ASP/topics_pstoolkitsDirectory.asp?faid=569&tid=4. Accessed September 8, 2012.

6. http://www.ifhima.org/. Accessed October 13, 2012.

7. http://www.imia-medinfo.org/new2/. Accessed October 13, 2012.

8. http://www.jointcommissioninternational.org/. Accessed October 13, 2012.

9. http://www.cms.gov/Regulations-and-Guidance/Legislation/CFCsAndCoPs/index.html?redirect=/CFCsAndCoPs. Accessed September 16, 2012.

10. http://www.jointcommissioninternational.org/. Accessed October 13, 2012.

11. http://www.robertsrules.org/. Accessed September 16, 2012.

12. Price MP. *Business Driven PMO Setup*. J. Ross Publishing, Inc., 2009.

13. https://www.pmi.org/. Accessed October 13, 2012.

14. Institute of Medicine. *Health IT and Patient Safety: Building Safer Systems for Better Care*. Washington, DC: National Academies Press, 2011.

15. http://www.leapfroggroup.org/. Accessed October 13, 2012.

CHAPTER 9

Administration Management

James W. Brady, PhD, M.Ed, CISM, CISSP, PMP, CPHIMS, FHIMSS

LEARNING OBJECTIVES

At the conclusion of this chapter, the reader will be able to:

☑ Define roles and responsibilities for IT-related functions.

☑ Assure staff competency in information and management system skills.

☑ Manage projects and portfolios of projects (e.g., initiate, plan, execute, control, close).

☑ Manage relationships with vendors (e.g., contract cost, schedule, support, maintenance, performance).

☑ Facilitate steering committee meetings and/or topics.

☑ Assure adherence to industry best practices (e.g., change control, project management).

☑ Maintain system, operational and department documentation.

☑ Provide customer service (e.g., service-level management, request tracking, problem resolution).

☑ Manage budget and financial risks.

☑ Manage customer relationships with business leaders.

■ Introduction

As you move from the previous chapter on Administration Leadership to this chapter on Administration Management, it is important to understand that today's healthcare IT professionals must possess both leadership and management skills to be effective. Understanding management concepts is vital to being an effective member of the leadership team. Management principles address matters such as resource allocation, staffing, and initiating and directing ongoing department management. This chapter will cover principles related to department management; project, portfolio and program management; vendor management; contract management; financial management; IT service management and documentation; and customer service and customer relationships.

■ Roles and Responsibilities for IT-Related Functions

The increased adoption of technology in healthcare has expanded the role of IT. In addition to traditional or general IT functions, the field of healthcare IT has created new roles and responsibilities. Healthcare IT is the area of IT involving the design, development, creation, use and maintenance of information systems for the healthcare industry. Healthcare IT includes electronic coding, accounting and billing systems; electronic medical records (EMRs) or electronic health records (EHRs); and clinical or departmental applications such as lab, radiology, pharmacy and nutrition. Health informatics, a discipline that is closely aligned with healthcare IT, is the study of resources and methods for the management of healthcare information. Health informatics includes medical informatics, nursing informatics, clinical informatics and biomedical informatics.

IT-related careers in healthcare can be found in many different types of organizations. These include hospitals and healthcare-provider systems, healthcare-payer organizations, health information exchanges, community health centers and long-term care facilities, ambulatory centers and small physician practices, education institutions and academic medical centers, government agencies and the military, vendor organizations, and consulting companies. Both general IT and healthcare IT roles exist in these organizations. Individuals with a clinical background who are interested in a career in healthcare IT will find excellent opportunities in most of the aforementioned organization types. Those from general IT making a transition to healthcare IT without prior medical or clinical experience may find job opportunities difficult to attain, largely due to the intense competition and high number of applicants.[1]

SENIOR MANAGEMENT ROLES AND RESPONSIBILITIES

Board of director, executive management and medical executive committee support are essential for the success of IT in a healthcare organization. The chief information officer (CIO) is generally the most senior-level IT executive. In many health systems, this role also carries the vice president or senior vice president designation. Additional IT-related leadership roles can include the chief medical information officer (CMIO), the chief nursing information officer (CNIO), the chief technology officer (CTO), the chief information security officer (CISO), IT department directors and chairs, and physician and nurse champions. Recently, health systems have developed new roles, such as the chief innovation officer, chief applications officer and chief privacy officer positions to meet the evolving technology environment.

GENERAL IT ROLES AND RESPONSIBILITIES

Healthcare organization IT departments are staffed with internal full-time employees (FTEs) or outsourced staff that support traditional IT-related roles. Job descriptions for these roles are categorized as senior-level, mid-level and junior-level, and typically include titles such as director, manager, architect, analyst, engineer, technician, administrator, programmer and developer. Common fields that these roles cover are applications, business intelligence, data warehouse, database, data center, directory services, help desk, IT security, mobile applications, server, network, telecommunications, storage, systems integration, backup, messaging, collaboration, technical documentation, virtualization, and website.

HEALTHCARE IT ROLES AND RESPONSIBILITIES

To meet the evolving technology demands of healthcare organizations, particularly in light of the increased usage of EHRs, many clinical, business and project-related roles now require healthcare IT knowledge and a blend of clinical, management and technical experience. Some of the more in-demand clinical and business positions are analyst roles. These include specialty roles covering systems, administrative support, applications, clinical systems, reports, finance, supply chain, human resources and payroll, revenue cycle, decision support, interfaces and business intelligence. Other important healthcare IT roles have positions in informatics, clinical engineering, go-live events, implementation consulting, integration, project management, quality assurance and usability.

CAREERS IN HEALTHCARE IT

The U.S. Office of the National Coordinator for Health Information Technology identified six healthcare IT workforce roles that healthcare organizations will need to fill as they deploy EHRs.[2,3] These include the following:

- **Practice workflow/information management redesign specialist.** Workers in this role assist in reorganizing the work of a provider to take full advantage of the features of healthcare IT to improve health and care.

- **Implementation manager.** Workers in this role provide on-site management of mobile adoption support teams for the period of time before and during implementation of healthcare IT systems in clinical and public health settings.

- **Implementation support specialist.** Workers in this role provide on-site user support for the period of time before and during implementation of healthcare IT systems in clinical and public health settings. These individuals will provide support services above and beyond what is provided by the vendor to be sure the technology functions properly and is configured to meet the needs of the redesigned practice workflow.

- **Clinician/practitioner consultant.** This role is similar to the practice workflow and information management redesign specialist but brings to bear the background and experience of a licensed clinician or public health professional.

- **Software support technician.** Workers in this role maintain systems in clinical and public health settings, including patching and upgrading of software. They also provide one-on-one support in a traditional help-desk model to individual users with questions or problems.

- **Trainer.** Workers in this role use adult learning principles to design and deliver training programs to employees in clinical and public health settings.

Achieving Staff Competency in Information and Management System Skills

EMPLOYEE DEVELOPMENT

Employee development is a key component in ensuring that healthcare IT staff attain competency in information and management system tools and skills. Mastering those skills, along with developing the soft skills needed to collaborate and work together as a team, is essential in ensuring the success of the organization. Staff improvement programs provide employees with the proficiencies and qualifications needed for advancement within the organization, and help staff form attitudes and interpersonal skills to work effectively. Employee development can be provided through training and in-service programs, certification classes, community college or university educational courses, conferences and workshops, professional association involvement and self-study through books, industry magazines, videos and online resources.

Organizational Training and In-Service Programs

Training and in-service programs may originate from several sources. Human resources typically has responsibility for organization-wide training requirements (e.g., security and safety regulations, discriminatory practices and quality improvements). Supervisory, management and leadership development may be designed and offered by a leadership department within the organization or through human resources. The department or group in which an employee works provides programs such as in-service or line training. In addition, IT projects for information and management system deployments usually include a training budget for system developers, administrators and end users who will be supporting and using the product.

Job-Related IT Certifications

IT-based certifications have long been a mainstay of IT education and professional credentials. Certifications have two main advantages. First, they provide a framework by which technical staff can learn and gain a level of proficiently in a specific IT-related topic. Second, a certification provides the recipients with a credential showing they have a defined body of knowledge in a specific area. Although a certification by itself will not qualify a person for a new job or promotion, it does demonstrate that the individual has mastered the basic level of a specific knowledge area, and is often viewed as a positive contributing factor in the decision of whom to hire. It is recommended that clinicians keep their clinical licensure and certifications active and up-to-date, even if they are no longer in a clinical role. IT professionals should also consider keeping their IT certifications active, particularly those certifications that are in high demand in healthcare IT.

The CPHIMS (Certified Professional in Healthcare Information and Management Systems) certification is an essential credential for all healthcare IT management, management engineering and process improvement professionals, U.S. military personnel and consultants. It is the only credential sponsored by a healthcare IT professional association (HIMSS), and eligible candidates become certified by passing the challenging CPHIMS exam. The CPHIMS certification verifies that individuals have the knowledge necessary to be successful in healthcare IT. CPHIMS are members of an elite group of healthcare professionals with demonstrated expertise in the important categories of healthcare and technology environments, IT systems, leadership and management.

Many of today's highly sought-after healthcare IT certifications can be obtained only by employees of organizations that are engaged in a specific vendor product deployment, such as an EHR or healthcare information systems project. However, healthcare systems also value generally available certifications, particularly if they are in the process of deploying related methodologies throughout their organization. These include certifications such as Project Management Professional (PMP), Information Technology Infrastructure Library (ITIL) and Lean Six Sigma.

Miscellaneous Professional Development

Healthcare IT professionals should consider other professional development and education opportunities. These are particularly useful in helping individuals become well-rounded and remain current in the rapidly evolving healthcare environment. Employees are typically responsible for the costs of their professional development, but many companies pay for such education as a benefit of employment. Several of the more common sources of professional development are healthcare IT conferences and workshops; programs sponsored by national and local professional associations such as HIMSS; university certificate and bachelor's, master's and doctoral degree programs in healthcare IT, informatics, information management and information systems; and self- or group-study using books, industry magazines, videos and such online resources as vendor white papers, webinars, conferences and training.

PERFORMANCE EVALUATION

Performance evaluation is an important tool healthcare administrators can utilize to monitor and improve employee competency. Performance evaluation is the ongoing process in which employees' work, outcomes, attitudes and interpersonal skills, professional growth, and adherence to organizational values are assessed and feedback is provided. In the evaluation process, the employee's actual performance is compared against the expected performance. In order to be effective, the performance evaluation process must start with clearly measurable performance goals. The performance goals should be defined and communicated to the employee at the start of the year.

A variety of methods can be used in the performance evaluation process, the most common being the rating scale. The scales will specify personal traits and behaviors expected, such as teamwork, communication skills, adherence to values, dependability, and initiative. Also specified will be job attributes such as quality and quantity of work.[4] Each trait or behavior is accompanied by a range of numbers or words that the evaluator marks to indicate an employee's level of performance.

Some organizations use the 360-degree method of performance appraisal. In this method, other individuals are asked to rate the employee on specific criteria. Raters may include individuals who work with the employee on teams, subordinates, peers in the same department, employees in other departments, and oftentimes outside customers and vendors. The employee is also given the opportunity to perform a self-assessment. The results of all of these assessments are taken into consideration in the final evaluation that is completed for the employee. In this process, it is important to provide confidentiality to the raters for the evaluations they provide.

In the performance appraisal process, it is important for the manager to provide feedback to employees at regular intervals during the year. In this way, employees will not be surprised when, during the appraisal, they are found to be performing at a less-than-adequate level. In addition, it gives them the opportunity to improve performance. Alternatively, if an employee is performing at an excellent or exceptional level, the interim positive feedback will help to preserve that positive behavior. Although interim reviews can be done formally or informally, it is advisable to complete a formal interim review if an employee's performance requires improvement.

When disciplinary action is needed, it must be taken based on clear facts and with documented justification. If disciplinary action is needed, it should be done progressively over time—starting with verbal discussions, then utilizing written and verbal communication, and possibly ending with termination. This approach provides consistent communication to the employee about what needs to be done to resolve the problem. Communication may be oral at first. If the problem persists, documentation should be completed in the form of notes to the employee's record and written warnings with substantive examples of the inadequate performance. At all steps in the process, it is advisable to communicate with and seek the advice of human resources.

■ Managing Projects, Portfolios of Projects and Programs

Another major role of the IT professional is project management. Project management methodology is used by healthcare organizations to successfully implement new and complex IT systems. Project management is the discipline of planning, organizing, securing, managing, leading and controlling resources to achieve specific goals. A project is a temporary endeavor with a defined beginning and end. The temporary nature of projects stands in contrast with organizational operational initiatives, which consist of repetitive, permanent or semi-permanent functional activities. Hospitals that support both project and functional initiatives are called matrixed organizations. In cases where multiple interdependent projects exist, program management is used to manage all the projects as a group.

Health systems with multiple independent projects and resources that require a formalized framework for tracking, allocating, and managing them effectively often adopt project portfolio management (PPM). PPM is the centralized management of processes, methods and technologies used by project managers and project management offices (PMOs) to analyze and collectively manage a group of current or proposed projects based on numerous key characteristics. As the PPM landscape has been evolving rapidly, healthcare organizations are looking to manage their project initiatives through a single, enterprise-wide system called enterprise project portfolio management (EPPM).

In contrast to the traditional approach of combining manual processes, desktop project tools and best-of-breed PPM applications for each project portfolio environment, EPPM takes a more integrated and top-down approach to managing all project-intensive work and resources across the enterprise.

Project management has the following five phases:

1. **Initiating phase.** In this phase, project stakeholders are identified, the project charter and the preliminary scope statement are developed and the project charter is approved.

2. **Planning phase.** This phase involves planning the project scope, quality and risk management, and schedule. The project scope is defined through creating the project management plan, developing the scope management plan, and creating the work breakdown structure (WBS). Quality and risk management planning involves identifying and analyzing risks and planning the risk responses. The project schedule is developed by defining and sequencing activities, estimating activity resources and duration, determining the project schedule, and planning human resources.

3. **Executing phase.** This phase involves directing and managing project execution; acquiring, developing and managing the project team; performing quality assurance; and procuring project resources.

4. **Monitoring and controlling phase.** This phase involves managing the integrated change-control process; controlling quality; controlling changes in cost, schedule and scope; measuring performance; and monitoring and controlling risks. An effective change-control methodology will address both reactive and requested changes, and will include processes for categorizing changes and determining how changes will be requested, reviewed and implemented.

5. **Closing phase.** This phase involves releasing the final deliverables to the customer, handing over project documentation to the organization, terminating supplier contracts, releasing project resources and communicating project closure to all stakeholders. The final step is to undertake a post-implementation review to identify the level of project success and note any lessons learned for future projects.

According to the Project Management Body of Knowledge (PMBOK) Guide, project management consists of nine knowledge management areas.[5] These include:

1. **Project scope management**—Involves ensuring that all the required work is performed to complete the project successfully. Scope creep is a key reason why many projects fail. Project scope management is accomplished by defining and controlling what is included in the project and what is not. Project scope management activities include the scope plan, scope definition, WBS, scope control and scope verification.

2. **Project time management**—Involves developing and controlling the project schedule. Project time management components include activity definition, activity

sequencing, activity resource scheduling, activity duration, schedule development and schedule control.

3. **Project cost management**—Involves estimating the project cost and ensuring that the project is completed within the approved budget. Accordingly, cost management includes the cost estimate, cost budgeting and cost control.

4. **Project human resource management**—Includes obtaining, developing and managing the team that will perform the project work. Project human resource management includes planning human resources, acquiring the project team, developing the project team and managing the project team.

5. **Project procurement management**—Encompasses managing the acquisition of products and services from external sources in order to complete the project. Project procurement management includes planning acquisitions, negotiating contracts with sellers, selecting sellers, administering contracts with sellers and closing contracts.

6. **Project risk management**—Focuses on the identification of project risks and appropriate responses. Project risk management includes identifying risks, performing a risk analysis, developing a risk response plan, and monitoring and controlling risks.

7. **Project quality management**—Involves ensuring that the project satisfies its objectives and requirements. Project quality management includes performing quality planning, performing quality assurance, and performing quality control.

8. **Project integration management**—Manages the integration of the various project activities. Project integration management includes developing the project management plan, directing and managing project execution, monitoring and controlling the project work, and closing the project.

9. **Project communications management**—Ensures that project information is generated and distributed promptly. Project communication management includes planning communication, distributing needed information to project stakeholders in a timely fashion, reporting the project performance and the project status, and communicating to resolve issues among the stakeholders.

The project manager (PM) is an important stakeholder in bringing projects to successful completion. The PM is responsible for working with project sponsors, the project team and others involved in the project to meet project goals and deliver the project within budget and on schedule. The PM should also control the assigned project resources to best meet project objectives; manage project scope, schedule and cost; report on project progress; and facilitate and resolve issues, conflicts, risks and other obstacles to project success.[5]

MANAGING VENDOR RELATIONSHIPS

Healthcare CIOs are increasingly turning to vendors for the expertise and support they need to meet the technology requirements of their organizations. This reliance on vendor partnerships has enabled vendors to play a key role in the success of many healthcare organizations. A well-managed vendor relationship will result in increased customer satisfaction, reduced costs, better quality and better service from the vendor. If problems arise, a well-managed vendor will be quick to remedy the situation. Vendor management is not simply negotiating the lowest price possible. It involves working with vendors on contract performance, schedules and costs, product functionality, and support and maintenance agreements in order to mutually benefit both organizations.

The vendor management process begins with selecting the right vendor for the right reasons. This involves analyzing business requirements, performing a vendor search, selecting the winning candidate and successfully negotiating the contract. The contract should be carefully considered to ascertain that restrictions or exclusions, penalties and terms are beneficial to both parties. Once the relationship with the vendor has begun, vendor performance must be monitored at all times, with particular attention to the requirements that are most critical to the healthcare organization. Regular communication between the vendor and the healthcare organization will help to avoid misunderstandings and address issues before they become problems.

Three common pitfalls should be avoided in order to achieve successful vendor management.[6] First, it is important not to confuse vendor selection with vendor management. Equal importance needs to be given to managing the vendor relationship during and after the selection and contracting phases. Second, do not select a vendor based on price alone. Instead, give priority to a vendor that understands the value of developing a relationship that is mutually beneficial. Third, do not forget to evaluate how your vendor relationships affect your business. In addition to examining service-level agreements (SLAs) and contract fulfillment, IT leadership determines whether an engagement has brought value to the organization and whether both parties have received a return on their relationship.

The following ten vendor management principles will enable healthcare organizations to build effective relationships with their suppliers and service providers[7]:

1. **Use project management methodology.** Due to the high visibility and accountability of today's complex healthcare projects, attention should be given to the basics of project management, such as creating a well-defined and properly planned project, recruiting effective project sponsorship, clarifying roles and responsibilities, establishing formal change control management and ensuring effective issue management.

2. **Understand that vendor management is multifaceted.** Effective vendor management involves evaluation and selection, contract development, relationship management and delivery management.

3. **Be aware of the contract details.** This includes understanding what the vendor is responsible for, managing the project and vendor according to the contract, and understanding what incentives motivate the vendor.

4. **Formal documentation is key.** All changes to the project and communications must be in writing and formally controlled.

5. **Contract complexity should be consistent with project risk.** The procurement process and the contract's level of detail should correspond to the level of project risk.

6. **Include all important deliverables in the contract.** Important deliverable specifications; the methodology used to create the deliverable; specific resources, roles and responsibilities; planned communications; deliverable acceptance criteria; and project success criteria should be included in the contract.

7. **Management commitment is key.** Senior management's commitment and flexibility are important to making the vendor-customer partnership work.

8. **Focus on benefiting both the customer and the vendor.** Both parties to the contract should give high priority to develop mutually beneficial resolutions should issues and tensions arise.

9. **Clarify contractual terms and expectations.** All terms and processes in the contract should be reviewed, explained and clarified to avoid conflicts and misunderstandings.

10. **Ensure that vendor and customer roles and responsibilities are clear.** All parties' roles and responsibilities should be precisely defined in the contract. Particular attention should be paid to interactions between the procurement department and the project team, the contract administrator and the project manager, and the vendor's project manager and the vendor's sales, accounting, and legal departments.

▪ Facilitating Steering Committee Meetings

In today's complex healthcare environment, steering committees are essential in providing guidance and practical direction for IT project and operational initiatives. According to the Computer Economics IT Management Best Practices 2011/2012 study, nearly 80% of all IT organizations have steering committees and 69% of those organizations make full use of their committees.[8] The use of IT steering committees ranks first as the most mature IT management practice out of 15 practices covered in the study.

A steering committee is defined as an advisory committee, usually made up of high-level stakeholders and/or experts, that provides guidance on key issues such as company policy and objectives, budgetary control, marketing strategy, resource allocation and decisions involving large expenditures.[9] IT steering committees are a best-practice approach in healthcare organizations for aligning strategic business and IT priorities. Steering committees, which usually include executives and departmental heads, focus on three main tasks: IT strategic planning, project prioritization and project approval. Clear mandates and a real ability to influence decision making through executive participation increase the value of IT steering committees.

To ensure success in this important area of IT governance, healthcare CIOs should consider adopting four strategies[10]:

1. Create a charter that includes the desired outcomes. This should help everyone understand the role and purpose of the group, which includes promoting improved communication and recognizing the partnership required for a successful IT deployment.

2. Establish a scope that reflects a corporate-wide perspective. The broader focus will be helpful when mediating conflicts in priorities and/or departmental perspectives that may not be in the best interest of the entire organization.

3. Consider specifically indicating the authority level of this group and its role in decision making. For example, the committee may be identified as a coordinating body that will resolve priorities, endorse proposals prior to approvals and monitor progress of major IT initiatives, but will have no role in budget approval or other departmental expenditure decisions.

4. Designate someone other than the CIO to chair the IT steering committee. Assigning a non-IT person, such as the chief operating officer (COO), CMIO or chief finance officer (CFO), to chair the group communicates the message that IT is accepted as a critical resource and recognized as such by the entire organization.

To form an effective IT steering committee and keep it on track, three important steps should be considered[11]:

1. It is important to develop a case by aligning IT priorities with strategic business priorities. Focus on core IT steering objectives and not IT resource allocation. In addition, stress shared decision making and fostering a culture of communications between business units.

2. Develop a steering committee charter. It should outline the key tasks and responsibilities of the committee.

3. Keep the IT steering committee small and schedule regular meetings. Ensuring that the membership is consistently informed, that it is engaged as often as needed based

on the project scope and timelines, and that it includes executive decision-making authority is critical to the success of the IT steering committee.

The use of IT steering committees is a proven method of driving better IT–business alignment, particularly in the area of IT governance, strategic planning, and project prioritization and approval. By developing IT steering committees with clear objectives, strong executive participation and a commitment to meeting regularly, IT leaders can significantly improve the value of IT to the business units.

■ Adhering to Industry Best Practices

IT management has matured as an organizational function over the years. As a result, certain policies and standards have been adopted by many of the top-performing IT organizations. Some of these are well-established disciplines and are commonly accepted as industry best practices or benchmarks. Industry best practices are methods or techniques that have consistently shown results superior to those achieved by other means. In addition, industry best practices can evolve as improvements are discovered.

A recent survey of over 200 IT organizations identified the following 15 IT management best practices[12]:

1. Regular meeting of the executive IT steering committee;

2. Regular meeting of the IT change control board;

3. Periodic testing of the disaster recovery plan;

4. Auditing of IT security-policy compliance;

5. Multi-year IT strategic planning;

6. User-satisfaction surveying;

7. Use of project management office;

8. Benchmarking IT spending levels;

9. Publishing IT performance metrics;

10. IT project portfolio management;

11. Use of IT asset management system;

12. Conducting post-implementation audits;

13. IT infrastructure library (ITIL) adoption, which encompasses service strategy, service design, service transition, service operation and continual service improvement;

14. Use of IT balanced scorecard; and

15. Active contribution to open-source projects.

■ Developing System, Operational and Department Documentation

SYSTEM DOCUMENTATION

System documentation includes the documents that support analysis, decision making, acquisition and implementation processes; it also addresses system features, functionalities and technical requirements. Systems analysis documentation includes the information gathered in the process of "collecting, organizing, and evaluating data about IS requirements and the environment in which the system will operate."[13] It also includes documents such as functional requirements, design specifications, requests for information and proposals, and related vendor responses. Also considered part of system documentation are procedure manuals, computer programs and machine operating manuals; details of standards compliance; and records of the initial system testing process and results (e.g., data collection and input procedures).

OPERATIONAL DOCUMENTATION

Operational documents relate to ongoing systems operations and maintenance. They include information about ongoing testing of systems and results, audit processes and database management, as well as training manuals. Operational documents also encompass implementation time frames, flow charts and progress reports; data backup and recovery procedures; and system retirement, tuning and logistic support requirements.

DEPARTMENT DOCUMENTATION

Department policies and procedures (P&Ps) help to guide the processes and actions that employees use to perform their work, and are essential for healthcare organizations to achieve various accreditations. A department or organizational policy formalizes what is expected or required of employees, among other things. A procedure document describes how an outcome is to be accomplished. Therefore, policies and procedures serve two purposes—they set performance requirements that can be used to motivate or discipline employees, and they serve as ongoing references for employees and orientation documents for new hires.[13] In developing P&Ps, the following steps are useful: (1) identify a need; (2) draft a policy or procedure that addresses the need; (3) get management approval; (4) distribute the approved document to employees and educate them on its contents; (5) revise, replace or withdraw the policy or procedure as needed;

and (6) coordinate with human resources, corporate compliance or other areas when applicable.

Department P&Ps will address elements such as security (e.g., access control, entity authentication, audit trails, data encryption, firewall protection and virus checking); privacy protection (definitions of access rights and instructions for handling specific information and patients); and information retention and availability of medical information. In addition, communication of medical information, management of licensed software, handling of service requests, the IT strategic plan and the IT budget should be addressed. It is also important to consider change management, project management and process improvement; development methods and standards; and copyrights and ownership in department P&Ps.

■ Providing Customer Service

Healthcare is primarily a people business—it calls for the organization to be particularly customer focused, or customer-centric. HIMSS defines *customer-centric* as "placing the customer as the center or focus of design or service."[14] It is excellence in service that distinguishes the IT department as responsive and knowledgeable, or as customer-centric. There are several specific factors and approaches to consider in organizing the customer service functions in the IT department.

SERVICE LEVEL MANAGEMENT

Because IT departments undertake many tasks, service level agreements are needed to define the service levels to be met. It is desirable to cover each incoming service request with an SLA that documents the specific levels of service expected and the metrics that will be used to evaluate them. The SLA should also address what resources will be provided, including the level of assistance that can be supplied and who will supply it. Also, the SLA should detail the reporting mechanisms. Specifically, how will performance be monitored and communicated, can trouble-ticket performance be tracked, and how much time is allowed to elapse between the reporting of an issue and its resolution?

REQUEST TRACKING

In managing an SLA, the IT department will need to implement request-tracking processes that include help-desk triage, issue tracking and user-satisfaction surveys. As part of help-desk triage, each reported problem should be assigned a priority level and worked on accordingly. Issue tracking, which is the ongoing monitoring of open, new and closed service requests, helps identify problems. It also warns of the need to focus additional resources on requests that are approaching the time limit specified in the SLA statement. Upon completion of a service, users will respond to a user satisfaction survey that will be used to assess how well the provider met the service objectives. The survey can be a short question, such as "Are you satisfied with the service you received?" The surveys reflect users' perceptions, which drive the overall IT perception and, if necessary, give IT management a chance for service recovery—an attempt to correct any dissatisfaction users may have. User feedback usually generates excellent opportunities for employees involved in providing service.

The most-measured IT area is usually the help desk. A key measure of effectiveness is the first-call resolution rate—the number of service requests that are resolved during the initial call to the service technician. A first-call resolution rate of 70% means that most problems are being diagnosed and resolved on the phone with the customer and are not being transferred to someone else for resolution. That rate is good for customers, who get their problems fixed immediately; it is also good for the other members of the IT department, who will not have to take time away from other assignments to help resolve a customer's problem. First-call resolution is high if service technicians are well trained and materials for reference and troubleshooting are readily available.

Another help-desk measure is the call-abandonment rate, the percentage of times callers hang up without speaking to a technician. If average wait times are high, the call-abandonment rate will probably be high as well. The longer callers wait, the more likely they are to give up. This is a serious problem for the help desk, even if superb services are provided to callers who finally get through to speak to someone.

Other metrics include system performance rates related to uptime and response time. High availability and fast response times are important, particularly with widely used systems or those used in direct patient care.

PROBLEM RESOLUTION

Theoretically, the customer should be pleased anytime the service-level goals are met. If a customer is disappointed, other customers probably feel the same—even if they are not saying so and SLA goals are being met. In resolving inconsistencies such as these, consider that if a customer's expectation was that something should have been done but was not, an explanation is in order. For example, if a customer's survey response indicates that the technician should have simply gone to the local office-supply store and purchased a replacement drive, explain why policy prohibits that practice. In resolving these issues, it is also important to take the customer's perspective and ask, "Does the policy make sense or is the customer possibly right?"

■ Managing Budget and Financial Risks

FINANCIAL RISK MANAGEMENT

It is important that healthcare systems make sound decisions in order to manage financial and budget risks. Without a solid understanding of financial risks and their impact, hospitals cannot be expected to make the right decisions about their capital and operating structure. The fundamental idea behind managing financial risk in healthcare is to reduce and protect against the inherent unpredictability of future costs.

Enterprise risk management (ERM) is a proven methodology that organizations use to manage overall risk. While ERM has been used to address clinical, human resource and legal risks in hospital settings, it has not been frequently applied to financial risk management.[15] This could be due to the complex and highly specialized nature of the tax-exempt capital markets, which can be intimidating to many risk-management professionals. In spite of its complexity, financial risk can be handled in the same four steps as other forms of risk[15]:

- **Identification**—Listing financial risks that can occur as a result of either negative factors or favorable events (e.g., when unexpected success leads to exponentially increased demand for services).

- **Quantification**—Assessing the likelihood or probability that a risk-related event will occur and the magnitude of its impact.

- **Risk response**—Determination and implementation of a response to the risk, such as acceptance, transference, mitigation or avoidance.

- **Monitoring**—Continuous review of existing and future risks.

Core financial skills are needed to reduce the risks associated with IT investments. Today's IT professionals should be knowledgeable about budgeting and planning; financial purchasing options, such as capitalized and depreciated assets; operating expenses; basic accounting principles and standards; financial models and methods; and compliance regulations. In addition, the IT professional should use a broad range of methods and tools, such as return on investment (ROI) calculations, budget-tracking tools, revenue-creation reports, monthly financial reports and variances, technology pilots where available, SLAs to improve vendor performance, and soliciting buy-in for IT initiatives from business and clinical unit executives to minimize and reduce IT procurement risks.

BUDGET RISK MANAGEMENT

Managing budgets is one of the basic disciplines that all managers must master. An organized approach to developing and maintaining the budget will go a long way in helping reduce budget risk. In addition, to prepare for the possibility that some risks will not be managed successfully, a risk contingency budget should be created. Funds from the risk contingency budget can then be used to prevent a project from going over budget.

For today's IT managers, having solid budgeting and forecasting skills is critical in reducing budget risk. Understanding the annual budget cycle is important, particularly in avoiding the fiscal year-end crises that often occur as organizations attempt to balance their budgets. The business requirements for expenses should be accurately assessed. The budget should be developed in detail. At the line-item level, capital and operating expenditures should be differentiated, and long-range capital planning should be identified. Capital expenditures are payments by the organization for fixed assets, such as buildings and equipment. Capital expenses are incurred when a company buys assets that have a useful life of more than one year; they are typically depreciated. The long-range capital plan, which covers five years or more, should be the result of an executive review process that determines the proper mix of existing assets and new investments needed to fulfill the healthcare organization's mission, goals and objectives, and should reflect decision makers' priorities for the future. Operating expenditures are incurred in the course of ordinary, day-to-day business activities and include payments for rent, utilities, insurance and the like. Operating expenses relate to items that have a useful life of one year or less and are not depreciated.

It is important that a consistent model or software system be used to manage the budget. Budget risk can be addressed by paying attention to contracts and maintenance fee increases, and by adjusting and re-forecasting the expenditures. Because healthcare organizations may be required to make budget reductions, maintaining multiple budget scenarios is important. These can be reserved for times when revenue is low, when critical enhancements are made, or when revenue-generating projects are planned.

The following important steps should be considered when managing budgets[16]:

- **Negotiate an effective budget to start with.** Spending the necessary time at the beginning of a project will eliminate budget challenges later in the project schedule.

- **Plan for unexpected expenses.** This will allow for flexibility should unforeseen expenses arise.

- **Prepare early for year-end budget activities.** Finalizing budgets at the end of the fiscal year is an important activity. It is best to start planning for this early.

- **Stay close to budget.** Attempt to finish as close to budget expectations as possible and avoid being significantly over or under budget, as this will affect the following year's budget allocations.

- **Account for cost allocations.** Identify charges or transfers that may occur to or from other departments to your department.

- **Understand the key budget numbers.** Know all the critical numbers for your department, and be aware if any of the numbers are wrong.

■ Managing Customer Relationships with Business Leaders

Customer relationship management (CRM), a widely accepted practice in healthcare, is an organization's approach to interactions with customers, patients, vendors and other business associates.[17] CRM involves using proven methods to attract new customers, retain current customers and re-establish relationships with past customers. It also involves leveraging technology, such as the Internet and social media, and traditional marketing techniques to organize, automate and synchronize business processes. Using CRM, healthcare organizations can achieve increased quality and efficiency, reduced overall costs and greater profitability.

Unlike many industries that are product-driven, healthcare organizations are uniquely service driven, ultimately aimed at developing relationships to improve patient loyalty. By getting the right information to the right individuals at the right time, healthcare organizations can communicate that they care about what is important to patients, employees, physicians, nurses and others involved in the continuum of care. By customizing service offerings to better meet customer expectations, and by continuously training and rewarding employees for delivering exceptional customer service, healthcare organizations can achieve profitable customer relations not only with patients, but also with payers, regulators, vendors and all stakeholders.

To improve customer-satisfaction levels, a comprehensive systems approach is recommended.[18] It is critical to set a clear customer experience strategy. Customer service involves more than creating an organizational slogan. To establish a good strategy, it is important to understand the organization's vision and mission; determine the organization's customer-service direction, slogan and values; share the customer-service strategy by using a comprehensive communications program; emphasize that customer service is a key responsibility for each department; and ensure that the customer-service strategy aligns with the other organizational strategies.

Selecting the right team and developing, motivating and managing staff members are two important areas of consideration. Interpersonal skills and the right attitude are two qualities that are critical for employees to possess when providing customer service. Emphasizing functional expertise, technical competence and knowledge is less important, and many of these can be taught. Employees working directly with the customer need to understand the organization's culture and learn key communication skills. Four steps needed to build a culture of excellent customer relations are as follows (1) provide training in key skills needed to deliver excellent personal service; (2) use ongoing coaching and feedback to reinforce improved customer relations; (3) regularly measure and monitor performance levels; and (4) reward performance with both monetary and non-monetary awards.

Effective service delivery creates efficient customer interaction, eliminating the need for third-party intervention to keep customers satisfied. To help ensure a positive customer experience, it is important to identify preferred service-delivery processes, review critical success points in those processes, and determine service standards and objectives. In addition, it is vital to establish service-delivery procedures to maximize material service and create service level agreements to improve customer satisfaction.

Regardless of how well trained the staff is or how effective the organization's current service-delivery processes are, opportunities for improvement can always be identified. It is important that problems and issues be resolved quickly by building continuous improvement into the service-delivery procedures. To properly manage the customer experience, it is important to identify where opportunities for improvement are by actively soliciting customer feedback; teach staff how to handle customer complaints effectively by using the correct blend of empathy, apology and resolution; focus on the root problem and not just the symptoms; and be proactive in seeking to prevent issues instead of reacting to events that have already occurred.

Although senior management support is vital for creating and maintaining a successful CRM program, involving mid-level management in the change process and empowering them to be key change agents is essential. To do this, it is important to engage the management team early and often, to involve management members in formulating the customer-service strategy, and to develop managers' coaching skills so that they are able to understand and reinforce key personal-service skills. In addition, management should include managers as facilitators during training sessions; reward managers for establishing, monitoring and updating service-delivery processes; and motivate managers to be examples to their teams.

Delivering outstanding service requires the building of a culture that focuses on customer relations. This can involve changing all aspects of an organization's service delivery. The investment of time and effort can be significant, but the pay-off can be enormous, building long-term patient and customer loyalty and helping to ensure business profitability.

■ Summary

With the increased adoption of healthcare IT, new roles and responsibilities in general IT, healthcare IT and IT management are being developed. Managers are looking to ensure that their staff members are properly trained and educated. Today's leaders require a blend of clinical awareness; experience in operational, financial and project management; and technical knowledge to be successful. Healthcare organizations are increasingly turning to vendors and consultants for the expertise and support they need to meet their IT requirements. Stakeholder management using effective steering committees, implementation of industry best practices and experience with well-defined customer service processes are important requirements for healthcare administrators. By maintaining appropriate documentation, giving careful attention to financial and budget risks, and managing customer relationships, healthcare organizations will continue to experience success.

■ References

1. Santiago A. How to break into a career in healthcare IT. http://healthcareers.about.com/od/administrativeandsupport/p/HealthITjobs.htm. Accessed August 27, 2012.

2. Preparing skilled professionals for a career in health IT. http://healthit.hhs.gov/portal/server.pt/community/healthit_hhs_gov__community_college_program/1804. Accessed August 27, 2012.

3. Get the facts about Health IT Workforce Development Program. http://healthit.hhs.gov/portal/server.pt?open=512&objID=1432&mode=2. Accessed August 27, 2012.

4. Longest B, Rakich S, Darr K. *Managing Health Services Organizations*. 4th ed. Baltimore, MD: Health Professions Press, 2000: 536-550.

5. PMBOK. PMBOK® *Guide* (or) *A Guide to the Project Management Body of Knowledge*. 4th ed. Newton Square, PA: Project Management Institute, 2008: 12.

6. Perelman D. Six steps to successful vendor management. http://www.eweek.com/c/a/IT-Infrastructure/Six-Steps-to-Successful-Vendor-Management/. Accessed August 27, 2012.

7. Horine G. *Absolute Beginner's Guide to Project Management*. 2nd ed. USA: Que Publishing, 2009.

8. Trembly A. IT steering committees: do they have any power? http://www.insurancenetworking.com/blogs/it_steering_committee_ce_it_management_best_practices-28649-1.html. Accessed August 27, 2012.

9. Steering committee. http://www.businessdictionary.com/definition/steering-committee.html. Accessed August 27, 2012.

10. IT steering committee: advocate or adversary? http://www.ctg.com/industries/healthcare-providers/insights-columns/april-2005-it-steering-committee. Accessed August 27, 2012.

11. Establishing an effective IT steering committee. http://www.slideshare.net/Info-Tech/establish-an-effective-it-steering-committee. Accessed August 27, 2012.

12. IT management best practices: adoption and growth of 15 IT disciplines. http://www.computereconomics.com/page.cfm?name=IT_Management_Best_ Practices. Accessed August 27, 2012.

13. Austin CJ, Boxerman SB. *Information Systems for Healthcare Management.* Chicago: AUPHA/Health Administration Press, 2005: 283.

14. *HIMSS Dictionary of Healthcare Information Technology Terms, Acronyms and Organizations.* Chicago: HIMSS, 2010: 21.

15. Bogacz P. *A four-step process for identifying and managing financial risk.* http://www.hfma.org/Templates/Print.aspx?id=24400. Accessed August 27, 2012.

16. Owen J. *The Leadership Skills Handbook.* 2nd ed. San Francisco: Jossey-Bass, 2012.

17. Shaw R. *Computer Aided Marketing & Selling.* Butterworth Heinemann, 1991.

18. Nash D, Nash S. Customer relationship management: 6 steps from customer service. http://www.teamtechnology.co.uk/customerservice.html. Accessed August 27, 2012.

Questions

For answers to the questions in this section, see the Answer Key beginning on page 203.

■ Chapter 1. The Healthcare Environment

■ Question 1

Among the multiple types of hospital ownership, which is not a common model?

A. Public (government) owned and managed.

B. Private, not-for-profit (non-profit).

C. Physician owned.

D. Private, for profit.

■ Question 2

Hospitals may be classified many different ways. Which of the following statements is true regarding hospital classification?

A. Private hospitals are always for-profit organizations.

B. Urban, rural and children's hospitals are classified by their geographic locations.

C. Rural hospitals are most frequently classified as teaching hospitals.

D. Hospitals may be classified in more than one way, such as an urban hospital might also be classified as a government-owned hospital or as a general hospital.

■ Question 3

An ambulatory surgery center would be best classified as:

A. A teaching hospital.

B. An outpatient care setting.

C. A general hospital.

D. A rehabilitation hospital.

■ Question 4

From the perspective of the healthcare delivery organization, payments generally come from three types of entities:

A. Employers, employees and government entities.

B. Government-financed and managed programs, insurance programs managed by private entities and patients' personal funds.

C. National health systems, national insurance systems and multi-payer systems.

D. Uninsured, underinsured and insured.

■ Question 5

In considering the purpose for interrelationships among healthcare organizations, identify the purpose below that is correct:

A. Enable access to comprehensive care services from only one healthcare organization.

B. Ensure effective transfers of care facilitated by the provision of essential health information.

C. Facilitate obtaining appropriate rewards for care referrals.

D. Facilitate marketing of healthcare services regardless of patients' consent.

■ Question 6

Ensuring the general portability of healthcare is facilitated by:

A. Health information exchanges (HIEs) such as Canada's Health Infoway and the U.S. HIE programs, including the Nationwide Health Information Network (NwHIN).

B. The Organisation for Economic Co-operation and Development (OECD).

C. Insurance programs administered by private entities.

D. The secondary use of healthcare information.

■ Question 7

An example of the secondary use of a patient's health information would be when the information is shared:

A. To support transfer of the patient's care between two providers.

B. Through an authorized health information exchange to support the portability of care.

C. In support of a diagnostic test required to further the treatment of a patient.

D. With public health officials for statistical reporting or in support of clinical research.

■ Question 8

In the financial reimbursement area, the interrelationships between healthcare organizations:

A. Are unrelated to the efficiency of healthcare claims processing.

B. May assure government payers that quality healthcare services have been delivered.

C. Does not support private insurance organizations in their assessment of the quality of delivered healthcare services.

D. Are designed to maximize reimbursement for covered healthcare services.

■ Question 9

Key information technology and information management professionals in healthcare organizations include the:

A. Chief information officer (CIO), chief executive officer (CEO) and chief medical information officer (CMIO).

B. Chief information officer (CIO), chief security officer (CSO) and chief medical information officer (CMIO).

C. Chief information officer (CIO), chief financial officer (CFO) and chief technology officer (CTO).

D. Chief information officer (CIO), chief executive officer (CEO) and chief nursing informatics officer (CNIO).

■ Question 10

Non-government professional associations may perform regulatory roles for their profession. Which of the following is NOT a typical role for a professional association?

A. Determining qualifications for a profession by defining professional examination criteria.

B. Making laws and regulations regarding reimbursements for their profession.

C. Issuing a code of conduct to guide professional behavior.

D. Implementing disciplinary procedures for those in their profession.

■ Chapter 2. The Technology Environment

■ Question 1

Patients have an expectation that healthcare providers will keep health information entrusted to them:

A. Private and secure.

B. Available Monday through Friday.

C. On paper.

D. Available for research.

■ Question 2

Data warehouses include:

A. Data from one hospital only.

B. Information from the patient.

C. Data from many different applications.

D. Financial data only.

■ Question 3

Interface engines support:

A. Interoperability and data integration.

B. Manual connections to financial systems.

C. Cloud storage of patient information.

D. Encryption of patient identifiable data.

■ Question 4

Telehealth can be used to:

A. Constrain patients to specific providers.

B. Provide specialist care to patients in rural areas.

C. Prohibit transfers of patients.

D. Mandate admissions to academic medical centers.

■ Question 5

mHealth applications can address:

A. Medical records.

B. Global health initiatives.

C. Issues concerning supply-chain inventory.

D. Only cell phones.

■ Chapter 3. Systems Analysis

■ Question 1

What system will give informative guidelines to practitioners regarding medication and procedures, including warning systems relating to high-risk medications and processes?

A. Clinical decision support system (CDSS).

B. Computerized practitioner order entry (CPOE).

C. Picture archiving and communications system (PACS).

D. Electronic health record (EHR).

■ Question 2

When defining problems and opportunities, major areas of change can occur in the following areas:

A. Analytical, supervisory, financial, administrative.

B. Clinical, administrative, financial, application.

C. Supervisory, administrative, financial, clinical.

D. Application, analytical, administrative, financial.

■ Question 3

When defining requirements, what is the key to implementing safe, sustainable and cost-effective IT practices?

A. Quality tools.

B. Sustainment plan.

C. Control plan.

D. Project plan.

■ Question 4

Sustainable controls for IT implementation can result in:

A. Uncontrolled security.

B. Serving minimum purpose possible.

C. Determining what is practical for local area implementation and testing.

D. Satisfying integration with policy regulations.

■ Question 5

When performing cost-benefit analysis, important variables to be considered include:

A. Sustainability versus total costs per month.

B. Time and cost of implementation.

C. Impact on internal parties.

D. Process mapping.

■ Question 6

The benefits of developing proposals in support of integrating healthcare practices can include:

A. Secure information sharing.

B. Minimal communication between various localized care providers.

C. Stand-alone architectures for various equipment and software applications.

D. Enhanced efficiency in the communication flow.

■ Question 7

When presenting your analysis to your executive leadership, key elements may include:

A. Possible changes in the project implementation that can be driven by changes in technology standards.

B. Requirements that may change, affecting the strategic capability of the proposal.

C. Sensitivity to challenges or changes in the internal environment that may rely on the establishment of a support team within the organization.

D. Expectations that the implementation of analysis and subsequent proposal will rely on the presence of standard operational processes in the internal environment.

■ Question 8

When managing projects and resources, it is important to have a work plan that:

A. Is aimed at establishing a generic implementation setup for a project.

B. Includes equipment costs.

C. Plans the intended workflow processes by managing personnel.

D. Analyzes processes and evaluates outcomes.

■ Question 9

Promotion and application of system analysis can include:

A. Evaluating past operational situations in an average healthcare facility.

B. Identifying the minor problems in processes with respect to optimization of IT use.

C. Identification of primary solutions to problems through the implementation of IT policies.

D. Evaluation of alternative solutions' alignment with the specific objectives set out in the plan.

■ Question 10

What are possible characteristics that you may encounter when analyzing future healthcare IT trends?

A. Integration of possible entities within an organization in preparation for standardization.

B. Alignment with emerging trends on the local IT platform.

C. Loss of a low volume of business due to nonalignment of health-sector players.

D. Importance of implementing an operational work plan to align the healthcare sector with current IT trends.

■ Chapter 4. Systems Design

■ Question 1

All of the following are parts of a request for information (RFI) except:

A. Background.

B. Submittal information.

C. Cost requirements.

D. Introduction.

■ Question 2

The following roles are typically represented in a system design team except:

A. Technical lead/architect.

B. Board member.

C. Information security officer.

D. Procurement.

■ Question 3

Which of the following must be considered during system design?

A. System monitoring.

B. Disaster recovery.

C. Availability.

D. All of the above.

■ Question 4

Detailed technical specifications address all of the following except:

A. System monitoring.

B. Programming language.

C. Security and data encryption.

D. Government regulations.

■ Question 5

If the design team decides that the system should be built rather than bought, the following more technical roles should be brought onto the design team except:

A. Data modeler.

B. Application developer.

C. Legal.

D. Technical architect.

■ Question 6

Unclear or poorly written technical requirements can lead to any of the following except:

A. Positive vendor relationships.

B. Vendors submitting high bids.

C. Inability of the vendor to deliver.

D. Litigation.

■ Chapter 5. Systems Selection, Implementation, Support and Maintenance

■ Question 1

Functional requirements could include the following:

A. Printers.

B. Workflow redesign.

C. Backup and recovery plans.

D. System documentation.

■ Question 2

Which is a characteristic of a request for proposal?

A. A collection of documents with high-level requirements.

B. A collection of documents with detailed requirements.

C. May or may not include costing information.

D. An informal request for information.

■ Question 3

Implementation execution includes the following:

A. Definition of the team's roles and responsibilities.

B. Decision on implementation strategy.

C. Planning for how to manage organizational changes.

D. System configuration or build.

■ Question 4

The implementation strategy in which all functionality is implemented in one location followed by everywhere else is called:

A. Phased by location.

B. Big bang.

C. Pilot.

D. Phased by functionality.

■ Question 5

End-user training should be completed at what point in the implementation?

A. During the activation.

B. Right before the activation.

C. As early as possible.

D. Right after planning.

■ Question 6

Planning for activation should include which of the following?

A. Completing a root-cause analysis.

B. Scheduling post-live support staff.

C. Defining the testing plan.

D. Configuration management.

■ Question 7

After the system is live, which of these should be measured and evaluated?

A. System usability.

B. Duration of the implementation.

C. Quantity of printers.

D. Number of vendors responding to the RFP.

■ Question 8

The business continuity plan includes:

A. The release management plan.

B. The disaster recovery plan.

C. The risk management plan.

D. The configuration management plan.

■ Chapter 6. Systems Testing and Evaluation

■ Question 1

The fundamental purpose of information systems testing is:

A. To give leadership the information necessary to perform a build-versus-buy analysis.

B. To give end users an opportunity to provide inputs regarding system development and functionality.

C. To manage risks of developing, producing, operating and sustaining systems.

D. To justify the expense of the proposed system to the board of directors.

■ Question 2

Test tools include manual and automated tools. Which of the following is a manual test tool?

A. Automation software.

B. Black-box test.

C. Anti-virus program.

D. Test script.

■ Question 3

Testing performed to validate successful system implementation is called:

A. Acceptance testing.

B. Integration testing.

C. System testing.

D. Stress testing.

■ Question 4

System controls are implemented to protect the confidentiality, integrity and _____ of data during testing.

A. Usability.

B. Availability.

C. Format.

D. Security.

■ Question 5

Test reporting occurs throughout the testing process and, at a minimum, should address:

A. The test team members and their experience levels.

B. The estimated cost of the test.

C. The expected outcomes of the test.

D. The mission of the test.

■ Chapter 7. Systems Privacy and Security

■ Question 1

Access privileges for each role should be set:

A. To provide the maximum access necessary.

B. To provide the minimum access necessary.

C. Based on the user's request.

D. Based on the user's physical location.

■ Question 2

Which of the following is typically among the responsibilities of a chief information security officer?

A. Assessing rules and regulations.

B. Validating integrity of backup tapes.

C. Developing encryption algorithms.

D. Approving all individual access requests.

■ Question 3

The AAA, or Triple A, approach deals with which area?

A. Financial auditing.

B. Physical safeguards.

C. User-access controls.

D. Security auditing.

■ Question 4

What should an IT analyst do if she suspects there may have been a loss of data that may contain multiple patients' sensitive health information?

A. Contact the organization's risk management or compliance department.

B. Inform all affected patients.

C. Notify the government regulatory department in charge of the relevant regulations.

D. Purge other database records that may be accessed using this health information.

■ Question 5

Locked doors, property-control tags on devices and employee identification badges are all examples of what?

A. Technical safeguards.

B. Physical safeguards.

C. Audit controls.

D. Access management.

■ Chapter 8. Administration Leadership

■ Question 1

The company's statement that defines where it wants to go or what it wants to be is known as the:

A. Mission statement.

B. Vision statement.

C. Statement of values.

D. Statement of goals.

■ Question 2

A control chart typically contains each of the following EXCEPT the:

A. Stretch goal.

B. Upper control limit.

C. Mean.

D. Lower control limit.

■ Question 3

An SBARC includes each of the following EXCEPT the:

A. Situation.

B. Background.

C. Assessment.

D. Constitution.

■ Question 4

Each of the following is a recommended initial assessment tool EXCEPT:

A. Face-to-face interviews.

B. Web surveys.

C. Unit or departmental meetings.

D. Focus group meetings.

■ Question 5

The international organization that serves as a voluntary accrediting, quality and safety organization is:

A. PMI.

B. CMS.

C. JCI.

D. IFHIMA.

■ Question 6

The actions of doing good, being honest and acting fairly are all components of a sound:

A. Business impact analysis.

B. Systems design.

C. Corporate mission.

D. Business ethics position.

■ Question 7

Successful conflict resolution is achieved through a mutual focus on:

A. Eliminating the differences of opinion or positions.

B. The common ground of the parties in conflict.

C. Understanding the personality types of the parties in conflict.

D. A proposed solution provided by the mediator.

■ Question 8

Which of the following items is NOT typically a part of the IT strategic plan?

A. Current systems state.

B. Desired future systems state.

C. A summary of IT initiatives supporting organizational goals.

D. The IT project sponsors for each initiative.

■ Chapter 9. Administration Management

■ Question 1

IT workforce roles that healthcare providers will need as they transition to EHRs include:

A. Revenue cycle manager, software support technician, trainer.

B. Clinician/practitioner consultant, implementation support specialist, payroll manager.

C. Materials management consultant, clinician/practitioner consultant, trainer.

D. Implementation support specialist, clinician/practitioner consultant, trainer.

■ Question 2

A project manager has been assigned to manage the implementation of a new clinical system. The project manager is responsible for:

A. Appointing the project steering committee from hospital management.

B. Delivering project objectives within budget and on schedule.

C. Delegating project scope decisions to the appropriate team members.

D. Reporting change requests to the CIO for approval or rejection.

■ Question 3

When undertaking a new project assignment, the BEST order of approach is:

A. Initiate, plan, control, execute and close.

B. Plan, initiate, execute, control and close.

C. Control, plan, initiate, execute, and close.

D. Initiate, plan, execute, control, and close.

■ Question 4

An advisory committee made up of high-level stakeholders and/or experts who provide guidance on key issues such as company policy and objectives, budgetary control, marketing strategy, resource allocation and decisions involving large expenditures is called:

A. An IT steering committee.

B. A system-development life-cycle committee.

C. A vendor-selection committee.

D. A policies and standards committee.

■ Question 5

An important step to AVOID when managing budgets is to:

A. Negotiate a good budget at the close of the budget cycle.

B. Stay close to budget.

C. Beware of cost allocations.

D. Use proven budget tools and techniques.

■ Question 6

The widely accepted practice in healthcare for managing an organization's interactions with customers, patients, vendors and other business associates is:

A. Enterprise risk management.

B. Project portfolio management.

C. Customer relationship management.

D. Project quality management.

Answer Key

■ Chapter 1. The Healthcare Environment

■ Question 1

Among the multiple types of hospital ownership, which is not a common model?

Correct answer: C. Physician owned.

■ Question 2

Hospitals may be classified many different ways. Which of the following statements is true regarding hospital classification?

Correct answer: D. Hospitals may be classified in more than one way, such as an urban hospital might also be classified as a government-owned hospital or as a general hospital.

■ Question 3

An ambulatory surgery center would be best classified as:

Correct answer: B. An outpatient care setting.

■ Question 4

From the perspective of the healthcare delivery organization, payments generally come from three types of entities:

Correct answer: B. Government-financed and managed programs, insurance programs managed by private entities and patients' personal funds.

■ Question 5

In considering the purpose for interrelationships among healthcare organizations, identify the purpose below that is correct:

Correct answer: B. Ensure effective transfers of care facilitated by the provision of essential health information.

■ Question 6

Ensuring the general portability of healthcare is facilitated by:

Correct answer: A. Health information exchanges (HIEs) such as Canada's Health Infoway and the U.S. HIE programs, including the Nationwide Health Information Network (NwHIN).

■ Question 7

An example of the secondary use of a patient's health information would be when the information is shared:

Correct answer: D. With public health officials for statistical reporting or in support of clinical research.

■ Question 8

In the financial reimbursement area, the interrelationships between healthcare organizations:

Correct answer: B. May assure government payers that quality healthcare services have been delivered.

■ Question 9

Key information technology and information management professionals in healthcare organizations include the:

Correct answer: B. Chief information officer (CIO), chief security officer (CSO) and chief medical information officer (CMIO).

■ Question 10

Non-government professional associations may perform regulatory roles for their profession. Which of the following is NOT a typical role for a professional association?

Correct answer: B. Making laws and regulations regarding reimbursements for their profession.

■ Chapter 2. The Technology Environment

■ Question 1

Patients have an expectation that healthcare providers will keep health information entrusted to them:

Correct answer: A. Private and secure.

■ Question 2

Data warehouses include:

Correct answer: C. Data from many different ERHs.

■ Question 3

Interface engines support:

Correct answer: A. Interoperability and data integration.

■ Question 4

Telehealth can be used to:

Correct answer: B. Provide specialist care to patients in rural areas.

■ Question 5

mHealth applications can address:

Correct answer: B. Global health initiatives.

■ Chapter 3. Systems Analysis

■ Question 1

What system will give informative guidelines to practitioners regarding medication and procedures, including warning systems relating to high-risk medications and processes?

Correct answer: A. Clinical decision support system (CDSS).

■ Question 2

When defining problems and opportunities, major areas of change can occur in the following areas:

Correct answer: B. Clinical, administrative, financial, application.

■ Question 3

When defining requirements, what is the key to implementing safe, sustainable and cost-effective IT practices?

Correct answer: D. Project plan.

■ Question 4

Sustainable controls for IT implementation can result in:

Correct answer: C. Determining what is practical for local area implementation and testing.

■ Question 5

When performing cost-benefit analysis, important variables to be considered include:

Correct answer: B. Time and cost of implementation.

■ Question 6

The benefits of developing proposals in support of integrating healthcare practices can include:

Correct answer: A. Secure information sharing.

■ Question 7

When presenting your analysis to your executive leadership, key elements may include:

Correct answer: A. Possible changes in the project implementation that can be driven by changes in technology standards.

■ Question 8

When managing projects and resources, it is important to have a work plan that:

Correct answer: D. Analyzes processes and evaluates outcomes.

■ Question 9

Promotion and application of system analysis can include:

Correct answer: D. Evaluation of alternative solutions' alignment with the specific objectives set out in the plan.

■ Question 10

What are possible characteristics that you may encounter when analyzing future healthcare IT trends?

Correct answer: A. Integration of possible entities within an organization in preparation for standardization.

■ Chapter 4. Systems Design

■ Question 1

All of the following are parts of a request for information (RFI) except:

Correct answer: C. Cost requirements.

■ Question 2

The following roles are typically represented in a system design team except:

Correct answer: B. Board member.

■ Question 3

Which of the following must be considered during system design?

Correct answer: D. All of the above.

■ Question 4

Detailed technical specifications address all of the following except:

Correct answer: B. Programming language.

■ Question 5

If the design team decides that the system should be built rather than bought, the following more technical roles should be brought onto the design team except:

Correct answer: C. Legal.

■ Question 6

Unclear or poorly written technical requirements can lead to any of the following except:

Correct answer: A. Positive vendor relationships.

■ Chapter 5. Systems Selection, Implementation, Support and Maintenance

■ Question 1

Functional requirements could include the following:

Correct answer: B. Workflow redesign. (All others are non-functional requirements.)

■ Question 2

Which is a characteristic of a request for proposal?

Correct answer: B. A collection of documents with detailed requirements. (All others are characteristics of a RFI.)

■ Question 3

Implementation execution includes the following:

Correct answer: D. System configuration or build. (All others are part of implementation planning.)

■ Question 4

The implementation strategy in which all functionality is implemented in one location followed by everywhere else is called:

Correct answer: C. Pilot.

■ Question 5

End-user training should be completed at what point in the implementation?

Correct answer: B. Right before the activation.

■ Question 6

Planning for activation should include which of the following?

Correct answer: B. Scheduling the post-live support staff.

■ Question 7

After the system is live, which of these should be measured and evaluated?

Correct answer: A. System usability.

■ Question 8

The business continuity plan includes:

Correct answer: B. The disaster recovery plan.

■ Chapter 6. Systems Testing and Evaluation

■ Question 1

The fundamental purpose of information systems testing is:

Correct answer: C. To manage risks of developing, producing, operating and sustaining systems.

■ Question 2

Test tools include manual and automated tools. Which of the following is a manual test tool?

Correct answer: D. Test script.

■ Question 3

Testing performed to validate successful system implementation is called:

Correct answer: A. Acceptance testing.

■ Question 4

System controls are implemented to protect the confidentiality, integrity and _____ of data during testing.

Correct answer: B. Availability.

■ Question 5

Test reporting occurs throughout the testing process and, at a minimum, should address:

Correct answer: D. The mission of the test.

■ Chapter 7. Systems Privacy and Security

■ Question 1

Access privileges for each role should be set:

Correct answer: B. To provide the minimum access necessary.

■ Question 2

Which of the following is typically among the responsibilities of a chief information security officer?

Correct answer: A. Assessing rules and regulations.

■ Question 3

The AAA, or Triple A, approach deals with which area?

Correct answer: C. User-access controls.

■ Question 4

What should an IT analyst do if she suspects there may have been a loss of data that may contain multiple patients' sensitive health information?

Correct answer: A. Contact the organization's risk management or compliance department.

■ Question 5

Locked doors, property-control tags on devices and employee identification badges are all examples of what?

Correct answer: B. Physical safeguards.

■ Chapter 8. Administration Leadership

■ Question 1

The company's statement that defines where it wants to go or what it wants to be is known as the:

Correct answer: B. Vision statement.

■ Question 2

A control chart typically contains each of the following EXCEPT the:

Correct answer: A. Stretch goal.

■ Question 3

An SBARC includes each of the following EXCEPT the:

Correct answer: D. Constitution.

■ Question 4

Each of the following is a recommended initial assessment tool EXCEPT:

Correct answer: B. Web surveys.

■ Question 5

The international organization that serves as a voluntary accrediting, quality and safety organization is:

Correct answer: C. JCI (Joint Commission International)

■ Question 6

The actions of doing good, being honest and acting fairly are all components of a sound:

Correct answer: D. Business ethics position.

■ Question 7

Successful conflict resolution is achieved through a mutual focus on:

Correct answer: B. The common ground of the parties in conflict.

■ Question 8

Which of the following items is NOT typically a part of the IT strategic plan?

Correct answer: D. The IT project sponsors for each initiative.

■ Chapter 9. Administration Management

■ Question 1

The U.S. Office of the National Coordinator for Health Information Technology (ONC) identified six healthcare IT workforce roles that healthcare providers will need as they transition to EHRs. These include:

Correct answer: D. Implementation support specialist, clinician/practitioner consultant, trainer.

■ Question 2

A project manager has been assigned to manage the implementation of a new clinical system. The project manager is responsible for:

Correct answer: B. Delivering project objectives within budget and on schedule.

■ Question 3

When undertaking a new project assignment, the BEST order of approach is:

Correct answer: D. Initiate, plan, execute, control, and close.

■ Question 4

An advisory committee made up of high-level stakeholders and/or experts who provide guidance on key issues such as company policy and objectives, budgetary control, marketing strategy, resource allocation and decisions involving large expenditures is called:

Correct answer: A. An IT steering committee.

■ Question 5

An important step to AVOID when managing budgets is to:

Correct answer: A. Negotiate a good budget at the close of the budget cycle.

■ Question 6

The widely accepted practice in healthcare for managing an organization's interactions with customers, patients, vendors and other business associates is:

Correct answer: C. Customer relationship management.

Acronyms Used in This Book

Acronym	Term
AAA	authentication, access, accounting (triple-A approach)
AAAASF	American Association for Accreditation of Ambulatory Surgery Facilities
AAAHC	Accreditation Association for Ambulatory Health Care
AADE	admission following adverse drug effect
AAPA	American Academy of Physician Assistants
ACHC	Accreditation Commission for Health Care, Inc.
ACO	accountable care organization
ACR	American College of Radiology
ADE	adverse drug effect
ADM	automated dispensing machine
AHIMA	American Health Information Management Association
AMIA	American Medical Informatics Association
AO	accreditation organization
AOA	American Osteopathic Association/Healthcare Facilities Accreditation Program
AR	accounts receivable
ARC-PA	Accreditation Review Commission on Education for the Physician Assistant
ASC	ambulatory surgery center
ATA	American Telemedicine Association
ATM	asynchronous transfer mode
BI	business intelligence
BPM	business process management
BPMN	Business Process Model Notation
BPR	business process reengineering
BYOD	bring your own device
CAH	critical access hospital
CAP	College of American Pathologists
CDA	clinical document architecture
CDC	Centers for Disease Control and Prevention
CDS	clinical decision support
CDSS	clinical decision support system
CHC	community health centre (in Canada)
CHCF	California HealthCare Foundation
CHIM	Certification in Health Information Management (in Canada)
CHIO	chief health information officer
CHAP	Community Health Accreditation Program
CHIP	Children's Health Insurance Program (in U.S.)
CHPS	Certified in Healthcare Privacy and Security

Acronym	Term
CIO	chief information officer
CISO	chief information security officer
CISSP	Certified Information Systems Security Professional
CLIA	Clinical Laboratory Improvement Amendments
CMIO	chief medical information officer
CMS	Centers for Medicare & Medicaid Services
CNIO	chief nursing information officer
CoP	Conditions of Participation
COTS	commercial off-the-shelf [solution]
CPHIMS	Certified Professional in Healthcare Information and Management Systems
CPOE	computerized practitioner order entry (or computerized provider order entry)
CPT	Current Procedural Terminology
CPU	central processing unit
CRM	customer relationship management
CSO	chief security officer
CT	computed tomography
CTO	chief technology officer
DAMA®	Data Management International
DICOM	Digital Imaging and Communications in Medicine
DMAIC	define, measure, analyze, improve, control
DMS	document management system
DNVHC	DNV Healthcare
DNFB	discharged not final billed
eHealth	healthcare practice supported by electronic processes and communication
EHR	electronic health record
eMAR	electronic medication administration record
EMM	electronic materials management
EMR	electronic medical record
EPPM	enterprise project portfolio management
ERM	enterprise risk management
FDA	Food and Drug Administration (in U.S.)
FTE	full-time employee
GB	gigabyte
GDP	gross domestic product
GP	general practitioner
GUI	graphical user interface

Acronym	Term
HCPC	Health and Care Professions Council
HHA	home health agency
HIE	health information exchange
HIM	health information management
HIMSS	Healthcare Information and Management Systems Society
HIPAA	Health Information Portability and Accountability Act
HITECH Act	Health Information Technology for Economic and Clinical Health Act
HITSP	Healthcare Information Technology Standards Panel
HL7	Health Level 7
HRSA	Health Resources and Services Administration
ICD	International Statistical Classification of Diseases and Related Health Problems
ICU	intensive care unit
IDS	integrated delivery system
IEEE	Institute of Electrical and Electronics Engineers
IFHIMA	International Federation of Health Information Management Associations
IHE	Integrating the Healthcare Enterprise
IM	information management
IMIA	International Medical Informatics Association
IP	Internet Protocol
IPv4	Internet Protocol version 4
IPv6	Internet Protocol version 6
ISC^2	Information Systems Security Certification Consortium, Inc.
ISPOR	International Society for Pharmacoeconomics and Outcomes Research
IT	information technology
ITIL	Information Technology Infrastructure Library
JCI	Joint Commission International
KPI	key performance indicator
LAN	local area network
mHealth	mobile health
MPLS	multiprotocol label switching
MRI	magnetic resonance imaging
NHS	National Health Service (in UK)
NPI	National Provider Identifier
NwHIN	Nationwide Health Information Network (in U.S.)
OECD	Organisation for Economic Co-operation and Development
OPT	outpatient physical therapy provider
P&Ps	policies and procedures
PA	physician assistant

Acronym	Term
PA-C	Physician Assistant-Certified
PACS	picture archiving and communication system
PANCE	Physician Assistant National Certifying Exam
PCP	primary care provider
PHI	personal health information
PHR	personal health record
PM	project manager
PMBOK	Project Management Body of Knowledge; PMBOK Guide
PMO	project management office
PMP	Project Management Professional
PPM	project portfolio management
PQRI	Physician Quality Reporting Initiative
PQRS	Physician Quality Reporting System
RDBMS	relational database management systems
RFI	request for information
RFID	radio frequency identification
RFP	request for proposal
RHC	rural health clinic
RHIA	Registered Health Information Administrator (in U.S.)
RHIO	regional health information organization
RHIT	Registered Health Information Technologist (in U.S.)
ROI	return on investment
RPO	recovery point objective
RSS	Really Simple Syndication
RTO	recovery time objective
SBARC	situation, background, assessment, recommendation and communication
SLA	service level agreement
SMART	specific, measurable, attainable, relevant, time bound
SNOMED	Systematic Nomenclature of Medicine
SUS	Secondary Use Services (in UK)
SWOTs	strengths, weaknesses, opportunities, threats
TCP	transmission control protocol
VoIP	voice over Internet protocol
VPN	virtual public network
WAN	wide area network
WBS	work breakdown structure
WHO	World Health Organization
XPDL XML	Process Definition Language

Index

"*f*" next to page number denotes a Figure
"*t*" next to page number denotes a Table

A

Acronyms used in this book, 217–221

Administration leadership, 133–158

  business communications, 149–153, 150*f*–151*f*, 152*f*

  business principles, ethical, 146–147

  comparative analysis strategies, 147–149

    benchmarks, 148

    budgets, 147–148

    financial and non-financial indicators, 148

    quality indicators, 148–149

  compliance with legal and regulatory standards, 145–146

  consulting services, in-house, 154

  educational strategies for IT staff, 155

  ethical business principles, 146–147

  evaluating effectiveness and user satisfaction, 141–143

  evaluating performance, 139–140, 141*f*

  facilitating discussions and meetings, 153–154

  forecasting technical and information needs, 136–137

  IT strategic plan development, 138–139

  managing risk, 156–157, 157*f*

  organizational environment, 135–136, 136*f*

  performance evaluation, 139–140, 141*f*

  policies and procedures, development of, 144–145

  quality standards and practices, 157–158

  review questions for, 197–199

  risk management, 156–157, 157*f*

  stakeholder understanding, promotion of, 143–144

  strategic planning, 134–135, 138–139

  technologies and trends, staying current on, 156

Administration management, 159–180

  budget risk management, 175–176

  customer relationship management (CRM), 177–178

  customer service, 173–175

    problem resolution, 174

    request tracking, 173–174

    service level management, 173

  documentation, development of, 172–173

    department, 172–173

    operational, 172

    system, 172

  financial risk management, 175

  industry best practices, adherence to, 171–172

  project management, 165–169

    knowledge management areas, 166–167

    phases of, 166

    vendor relationships, 168–169

  project portfolio management (PPM), 165–166

  review questions for, 200–201

  roles and responsibilities for IT-related functions, 160–162

    careers in healthcare IT, 161–162

    general IT, 161

    healthcare IT, 161

    senior management, 161

  staff competency, 162–165

    employee development, 162–164

    performance evaluation, 164–165

  steering committee, facilitation of meetings, 169–171

  vendor relationship management, 168–169

B

Benchmarks

  data for, 137

for organizational operations, 148
service-level, 141
Budget risk management, 175–176
Budgets, 59, 72*t*, 103, 147–148, 175–176
Business communications, 149–153, 150*f*–151*f*, 152*f*
Business continuity plan, 112–113, 129

C

Centers for Medicare & Medicaid Services (CMS), 13–14, 18, 20, 21*t*, 146
Comparative analysis strategies, 147–149
Compatibility of system components, 80
Contracts, vendor, 168–169
Cost-benefit analysis, 67–69, 68*t*–69*t*
Customer relationship management (CRM), 177–178
Customer service, 173–175
problem resolution, 174
request tracking, 173–174
service level management, 173

D

Data management, 85–86
Data management controls, 128–129
Data warehouses, 38
Disaster recovery plan, 112–113, 129
Downtime plan, 112–113

E

Education. *See* Training and education
Electronic health records (EHRs)
clinical applications, 30
and current clinical processes, 58
implementation of, sample report, 152*t*
privacy and security of, 38–39
standardization of, 48–50, 61–62
and system integration, 107
Environment of healthcare. *See* Healthcare environment

G

Goals of organization, 135, 136*f*
Government
as healthcare payer, 10–11
healthcare regulatory agencies, 18
HITECH Act, 49
role in healthcare delivery, 17–18

H

Health information exchanges (HIEs), 36–39
Health Information Technology for Economic and Clinical Health (HITECH) Act, 49
Health Insurance Portability and Accountability Act (HIPAA), 15, 58, 145
Health Level 7 (HL7) standards, 12, 32, 80, 107
Healthcare environment, 3–24
access to comprehensive care, 12
government and other regulatory agencies, 17–21, 20*f*
accrediting organizations, 20, 21*t*
healthcare regulators, 18
professional associations, 18–19, 19*f*
health expenditure per capita of various countries, 5*f*
healthcare organizations, 7–15
ambulatory care, 9
community health, 9–10
diagnostic and pharmaceutical, 10
hospitals, 8–9
interrelations within and across, 11–15
payers, 10–11
information and management system professionals, 15–17
organizational models of care, 14–15
portability of care, 12–13
public and population health information, 13
reimbursement for care, 13–14
review questions for, 182–185

roles and responsibilities of IT professionals, 15–17

transfers of care, 12

HIPAA (Health Insurance Portability and Accountability Act), 15, 58, 145

HITECH (Health Information Technology for Economic and Clinical Health) Act, 49

HL7 standards, 12, 32, 80, 107

I

Interoperability and standardization, 32, 63, 66t

J

Joint Commission, 20, 21t, 146

Joint Commission International (JCI), 20, 146

L

Leadership. *See* Administration leadership

M

Management. *See* Administration management

Mission of organization, 134

N

Networks, 27, 28, 80, 84–85

O

Organisation for Economic Co-operation and Development (OECD), 4, 5f, 6f, 7f

P

Picture archiving and communication system (PACS), 29, 31t, 49

Privacy and security of information. *See also* Systems privacy and security

and health information exchanges, 38–39

HIPAA (Health Insurance Portability and Accountability Act), 15, 58, 145

Project crosswalk, 136f

Project management

definition of, 165

and implementation process, 103–104

knowledge management areas for, 166–167

office, 154

phases of, 166

and vendor relationships, 168

Project Management Body of Knowledge (PMBOK), 166–167

Project management office (PMO), 154

Project portfolio management (PPM), 165–166

Q

Quality indicators, 148–149

Questions for review, 181–201

answer key for, 203–215

R

Regulatory, professional, and accreditation agencies, 17–21

Request for information (RFI), 86–87, 96, 101

Request for proposal (RFP), 89–91, 96, 101

Review questions, 181–201

answer key for, 203–215

Risk management, 156–157

budget risk management, 175–176

financial risk management, 175

matrix for, 157f

S

Security. *See* Privacy and security of information; Systems privacy and security

Software applications

administrative, 31

clinical, 30–31, 31t

compatibility of system components, 80

consumer-oriented, 33–35

financial, 33

industry standardization and, 63–64

prescription errors, reduction in, 64

systems testing of, 116–121. *See also* Systems testing and evaluation

Staff
change management and, 104–105
competency, 162–165
education and training, 108, 155, 163
employee development, 162–164
performance evaluation, 164–165
productivity and satisfaction, 52
roles and responsibilities for IT functions, 160–162
software applications for administrative use, 31
and system activation planning, 109

Stakeholders
communication with, 167
satisfaction with information system, 141–142
and system testing, 116, 117, 121
understanding of information system, 143–144

Strategic planning, organizational, 134–135

SWOT (strengths, weaknesses, opportunities, and threats) analysis, 79, 138–139

Systems acquisition. *See* Systems selection

Systems analysis, 47–76
administrative and financial services, 50
alternative approaches to current processes, 63–65
comparative analysis of, 65, 66t
clinical functions, 48–49
clinical processes, current, 57–61, 59f, 60f
cost-benefit analysis, 67–69, 68t–69t
current clinical processes, 57–61, 59f, 60f
current deficiencies in IT healthcare practices, 62–63
current healthcare IT integration status, 61–62
deficiencies in IT healthcare practices, current, 62–63
industry standardization, 63, 64–65, 66t
patient support and satisfaction, 62, 66t

prescription errors, 63, 64, 66t
reduction in revenue generation, 62–63, 64–65
healthcare IT integration status, current, 61–62
infrastructure, 50–51
needs analysis, 51–53
needs summary, 53
operational needs, 51–52
patient access to services, 53
patient safety, 52
quality of care, 52–53
revenue increases and cost optimization, 52
staff productivity and satisfaction, 52
needs prioritization, 53–54, 54f
problems and opportunities for IT, 48–51
project proposal, sample of, 70–74, 72t
proposal evaluation, 65, 67
proposal sensitivity analysis, 69
review questions for, 187–190
work plan development, 54–57

Systems design, 77–93
business process management, 79
buy-versus-build decision, 87–91
build decision, processes for, 88, 89t
buy decision, 88
factors influencing, 87–88
compatibility of system components, 80
definition of, 78
process to address industry trends, 81
request for information (RFI), 86–87
request for proposal (RFP), 89–91
review questions for, 190–191
standards compliance, 80
team, structure of, 81
technical specifications for, 82–86
business process reengineering, 84
data management, 85–86
key areas of, 82–83
information infrastructure, 84–85, 85f
usability, 83

Systems implementation, 103–113
  activation planning, 109
  analyzing data for problems and trends, 111
  business continuity plan, 112
  change management, 104–105
  disaster recovery plan, 112
  downtime recovery plan, 112–113
  integration to support business require-ments, 107–108
  management and maintenance, 110–111, 112
  organizational change management, 104–105
  post-activation activities, 109
  process of, 106–107
  review questions for, 192–194
  strategies for, 105–106
  testing, 106–107. *See also* Systems testing and evaluation
  user manuals and training, 108
Systems management and maintenance, 110–111
Systems privacy and security, 123–130
  applications for, 50–51
  auditing, 129
  confidentiality, integrity, and availability, 127
  data management controls, 128–129
  disaster recovery and business continuity plans, 129
  requirements, policies, and procedures, 124–125
  review questions for, 196–197
  risk assessment, 125
  roles related to, 127–128
  system evaluation, ongoing, 130
  user-access controls, 126–127
  vulnerability remediation, 126
Systems selection, 95–103. *See also* Vendors
  activities for, 100–103
  budget development, 103
  criteria for, 97–99

  demonstrations, 101–102
  implementation process, 103–104. *See also* Systems implementation
  review questions for, 192
  review team members, selection of, 99–100
  site visits, 102
Systems support, 110–111
Systems testing and evaluation, 106–107, 115–122
  controls for, 120–121
  execution of, 118–120
  final evaluation, 121–122
  methodology of, 117
  ongoing, 130
  purpose of, 116
  reporting, 121
  review questions for, 194–195
  strategy, 117
  tools, 117–118
  types of, 107, 119–120

T
Technology environment, 25–44
  business intelligence, 35–36
  communications, 37
  consumers and, 33–35
  data integration, 37
  data storage, 37–38
  data warehouses, 38
  hardware, 27–29
    medical devices, 28–29
    technology infrastructure, 27–28
  health information exchanges, 36–39
  interoperability and standards, 32
  privacy and security, 39–40
  review questions for, 185–186
  servers, 38
  software, 29–33
    administrative applications, 31–32
    clinical applications, 30–31, 31*t*
    financial applications, 33
  telehealth, 35–36

Telehealth, 35–36

Training and education

continuing, for IT staff, 156

employee development, 162–164

in-service programs, 163

IT-based certifications, 163–164

professional development, 164

requirement in request for information, 86, 90

requirement in request for proposal, 86, 90

strategies for IT staff, 155

of system users, 108

trends, staying current on, 156

for vulnerability remediation, 126

Trends

analyzing data for, 111

of IT industry, 81

staying current on, in IT, 156

V

Values of organization, 135

Vendors

relationships with, 168–169

request for information (RFI), 86–87, 96, 101

request for proposal (RFP), 89–91, 96, 101

Vision of organization, 134